Professional P

Continues

Part III: PHP Design Case Study

Professional
PHP Design Patterns

Professional
PHP Design Patterns

Aaron Saray

WILEY

Wiley Publishing, Inc.

Professional PHP Design Patterns

Published by
Wiley Publishing, Inc.
10475 Crosspoint Boulevard
Indianapolis, IN 46256
www.wiley.com

For general information on our other products and services please contact our Customer Care Department within the United States at (877) 762-2974, outside the United States at (317) 572-3993 or fax (317) 572-4002.

Library of Congress Control Number: 2009931463

To the big one for always being a
little bit better, and the little one for
reminding me that I can be.

About the Author

Aaron Saray was introduced to a second-hand Commodore 64, with no persistent storage, when he was 8 years old. This fueled his appetite for computer science which carried him through many different languages and computers. Aaron finally settled on PHP as his language of choice in 2001. From then on, he continued to pepper in various other web languages such as HTML, CSS and JavaScript while continually building on his PHP expertise. Along his career path, Aaron has designed and maintained web site tools for an Internet Service Provider, created web based account management tools for subscribers of a major dental insurance company and led the development efforts of back-office websites for Internet connected Point of Sales systems. After becoming a Zend Certified Engineer, Aaron started his own web development company based around open source software. He continues to release open source software and keeps an updated PHP centric blog at `aaronsaray.com`.

Credits

Acquisitions Editor
Jenny Watson

Project Editor
Maureen Spears

Technical Editor
Steve Suehring

Production Editor
Kathleen Wisor

Copy Editor
Foxxe Editorial Services

Editorial Director
Robyn Siesky

Editorial Manager
Mary Beth Wakefield

Production Manager
Tim Tate

Vice President and Executive Group Publisher
Richard Swadley

Vice President and Executive Publisher
Barry Pruett

Associate Publisher
Jim Minatel

Project Coordinator, Cover
Lynsey Stanford

Proofreader
Dr. Nate Pritts, Word One

Indexer
Robert Swanson

Acknowledgments

My technical people: Steve Suehring, James Rodenkirch, Billy Gilbert, Bruce Crevensten, Jason Keup and Jared Alfson

My friends and family: The Gorals/Cains/Sarays, The Cichons, The Delta Ladies, and Mikey's Crew

Contents

Contents

Part II: Reference Material

Contents

Contents

Introduction

PHP is mainstream. Wherever you look, you will see PHP meet-ups, job openings, and major companies using this open source language to support their business. An open source language with such humble beginnings is now heavily rooted in the enterprise world. PHP is brushing shoulders with the "the big kids" now—the enterprise-level languages with support from companies like IBM and Microsoft. This friendly confluence brings in new blood and new ideas. One of the most notable new pushes is to develop PHP applications in a more robust, scalable, businessworthy deployment. Programmers who have been around much longer than PHP have introduced great concepts to the PHP audience along these lines. In this book, the focus is on one major concept: Design Patterns.

Who This Book Is For

When determining a target audience for this book, I had to make some difficult decisions. Should I write for the beginning coder who is just learning PHP and its features and concepts, or should I focus more on the programmers with many years of experience? Should any assumptions be made about the level of expertise the reader has with PHP's object-oriented features? Do I need to continue to include support for PHP4? (It may be easy to answer that last question: "No, PHP4 is no longer supported." However, considering that it is still deployed in the wild, with developers still tasked to create new functionality, the answer isn't so easily decided.) In order for the book to reach the widest audience for implementing Design Patterns in PHP, while not becoming a PHP language reference, the following guidelines apply to the audience requirements of this book.

The reader:

- ❑ Must be thoroughly experienced in the PHP language or at least have `http://php.net` bookmarked. Some examples may use functions that a beginning programmer may not have run into before.

- ❑ Must have an intermediate to advanced understanding of Object Oriented Programming (OOP) techniques in PHP. Intermediate-level OOP programmers will find Chapter 2's investigation into the more advanced OO features of PHP very useful.

- ❑ Must be using PHP5 or above to both have the full set of object-oriented features available as well as execute the examples and case study code.

- ❑ Should be familiar with the Universal Modeling Language (UML).

Simply put, the examples and concepts used in this book are going to be most useful to programmers who have some experience building interactive applications at least as complex as a blog. If you've only used PHP for very simple things like templating or contact forms, you may find it harder to follow the pattern chapters.

How This Book Is Structured

There are three parts to this book: Introductory Chapters, Reference Chapters, and Case Study Chapters. Each follows a different cadence with its own emphasis.

Introduction Chapters

The first chapter is both an introduction to Design Patterns and a call to be dedicated to using them in PHP. Those talented PHP programmers out in the world are always hungry for new knowledge. This chapter aims to expand their realm of hunger from just PHP-based concepts to the more architecturally sound Design Patterns realm.

The second chapter focuses more on the tools that are available in PHP to build the roots of these Design Pattern concepts. Reviewing such things as the intermediate and advanced OOP features of PHP, the Standard PHP Library, and the existing open source PHP frameworks that are common will help make concrete the coupling of PHP and Design Patterns.

Reference Chapters

The reference chapters are the middle chapters or the actual Design Pattern meat-and-potato portion of the book. They will be broken down into four main parts: the name, the problem and solution, UML diagrams, and finally a quick object-oriented code example. These cover the main functional portions of Design Pattern, while not being overly verbose. (If you're familiar with other books on Design Patterns, you may recognize my approach as being more simplistic than the 8 to 10 sections included in most other documentation standards.)

The Case Study

The last portion of the book is an in-depth case study, where I cover the exact specifications of the project and proposal, the analysis of the patterns available, and then the step-by-step approach for applying these.

Feature Analysis

Generally, when you receive a set of specifications, they're not in final form. During your initial review, your mind should already be spinning with ideas about the architecture. You'll want to explore the requirements to determine if it is a singular instance only ever used once or an extensible project. What kinds of features are planned for the future? In cases where you're not a subject matter expert, you may need to obtain answers to specific questions that are assumed to be known by the business analysts.

In the case study, you'll receive the specifications from the client. I'm going to iterate through the thought process of reviewing the specifications, asking questions, and getting clarifications. This section will end with the updated specifications document.

Pattern Analysis

Any project that you do should start with an analysis phase. I've seen too many instances where programmers hit the ground running, either blaming it on such a short timetable or just being overly exuberant to get the project going. It's important to take a step back, look at the specifications, and start to determine a plan of attack.

In the case study pattern analysis, you're going to sketch your basic design and business flow, and then turn to the architecture. You'll compare different ways to solve the problem using the pattern arsenal and create UML diagrams of your patterns customized with specific business logic and rules.

Step-by-Step Code Creation

This is the section of the case study that goes a bit awry from the main expectations set for this book. This section contains extensive code examples based on UML diagrams. It steps you through the exact thought process behind building each portion of the application from the pattern level. The focus isn't the analysis of language specific features, however. Intermediate programmers may need to reference the PHP manual from time to time.

With the completion of the code, you'll take a run back over your application and review all your choices to make sure that no other pattern is a better fit now that you have the whole picture in place. Design Patterns are not meant to be strict rules that you must adhere to but building blocks and framing points for your application. It's not unheard of or "illegal" to swap out a Design Pattern farther along into the project to create a more architecturally sound code base.

What You Need to Use This Book

Because a good portion of this book is more conceptual than practical, the requirements are pretty simple:

- ❑ Windows or Linux operating system
- ❑ PHP 5.2 or above
- ❑ MySQL 5.0 or above

Chances are that most of the sample code will work even if you don't stick to these requirements. However, the last case study will require these specific versions.

Conventions

To help you get the most from the text and keep track of what's happening, we've used a number of conventions throughout the book.

> Boxes like this one hold important, not-to-be forgotten information that is directly relevant to the surrounding text.

Notes, tips, hints, tricks, and asides to the current discussion are offset and placed in italics like this.

As for styles in the text:

- ❑ We *highlight* new terms and important words when we introduce them.
- ❑ We show keyboard strokes like this: Ctrl+A.
- ❑ We show filenames, URLs, and code within the text like so: `persistence.properties`.
- ❑ We present code in two different ways:

```
We use a monofont type with no highlighting for most code examples.
We use gray highlighting to emphasize code that's particularly important in the
present context.
```

Source Code

As you work through the examples in this book, you may choose either to type in all the code manually or to use the source code files that accompany the book. All of the source code used in this book is available for download at `www.wrox.com`. Once at the site, simply locate the book's title (either by using the Search box or by using one of the title lists) and click the Download Code link on the book's detail page to obtain all the source code for the book.

> *Because many books have similar titles, you may find it easiest to search by ISBN; this book's ISBN is 978-0-470-49670-1.*

Once you download the code, just decompress it with your favorite compression tool. Alternately, you can go to the main Wrox code download page at `www.wrox.com/dynamic/books/download.aspx` to see the code available for this book and all other Wrox books.

Errata

We make every effort to ensure that there are no errors in the text or in the code. However, no one is perfect, and mistakes do occur. If you find an error in one of our books, such as a spelling mistake or faulty piece of code, we would be very grateful for your feedback. By sending in errata you may save another reader hours of frustration, and at the same time you will be helping us provide even higher-quality information.

To find the errata page for this book, go to `www.wrox.com` and locate the title using the Search box or one of the title lists. Then, on the book details page, click the Book Errata link. On this page, you can view all errata that has been submitted for this book and posted by Wrox editors. A complete book list, including links to each book's errata, is also available at `www.wrox.com/misc-pages/booklist.shtml`.

If you don't spot "your" error on the Book Errata page, go to www.wrox.com/contact/techsupport. shtml and complete the form there to send us the error you have found. We'll check the information and, if appropriate, post a message to the book's errata page and fix the problem in subsequent editions of the book.

p2p.wrox.com

For author and peer discussion, join the P2P forums at p2p.wrox.com. The forums are a Web-based system for you to post messages relating to Wrox books and related technologies and interact with other readers and technology users. The forums offer a subscription feature to e-mail you topics of interest of your choosing when new posts are made to the forums. Wrox authors, editors, other industry experts, and your fellow readers are present on these forums.

At http://p2p.wrox.com, you will find a number of different forums that will help you not only as you read this book but also as you develop your own applications. To join the forums, just follow these steps:

1. Go to p2p.wrox.com and click the Register link.

2. Read the terms of use and click Agree.

3. Complete the required information to join as well as any optional information you wish to provide, and click Submit.

4. You will receive an e-mail with information describing how to verify your account and complete the joining process.

> *You can read messages in the forums without joining P2P, but in order to post your own messages, you must join.*

Once you join, you can post new messages and respond to messages other users post. You can read messages at any time on the Web. If you would like to have new messages from a particular forum e-mailed to you, click the Subscribe to this Forum icon by the forum name in the forum listing.

For more information about how to use the Wrox P2P, be sure to read the P2P FAQs for answers to questions about how the forum software works as well as many common questions specific to P2P and Wrox books. To read the FAQs, click the FAQ link on any P2P page.

Professional
PHP Design Patterns

Part I

Getting Acquainted with Design Patterns and PHP

1

Understanding Design Patterns

Usually when I pick up a book and see a chapter longer than five pages about a topic that I'm not the most familiar with, I tend to get scared. More than five pages may see me dropping the book and running away, flailing my arms and shouting about how tough these computers are! While this chapter may be longer than five pages, don't be discouraged. The term *Design Pattern* is just a fancy name for something that is not all that complex. A good portion of this chapter is taking what you may already know and use regularly and refining it to a more concise definition. So, let's jump in and see what Design Patterns really are.

What Are They?

The story of Steve that follows helps describe Design Patterns in a real-world context. I'm hoping that you're not too familiar with this story!

An All Too Common Example

Steve works at a large insurance firm. His most recent task was developing a way to show customer information to the call center representatives over a web interface. He designed a complex system that would allow the reps to search for a customer, enter call logs, update customer coverage information, and process payments. The system went into place smoothly, minus the few bumps and hiccups that a new installation in a production environment always runs into. Steve is happy, relaxed, and ready to sit back in the break room sipping his free coffee.

Overnight, the insurance company triples in size from its most recent investment. Not only is Steve called back to work on providing new scalability and enhancements to the call center software but there has also been buzz about adding some new features to the corporate site to support the new acquisition's customers. Steve's department is also increased to include two new developers, Andy and Jason.

The news comes down from the vice president that the corporate site needs to allow customers to process their payments after they have completed a successful, secure user log in. Additionally, the system needs to show how many times the customer has called in to the call center. Finally, it needs to show an audit log of every change the call center has made to the customer's account.

Steve knows that he can easily update the call center software to provide the audit log and then copy over the code, tweak it, and make use of the payment processing. However, the new programmers need to be tasked without much time to get up to speed on the new system. Steve's boss has assigned them the portions of the project that Steve is most familiar with. Since Steve is the rock-star PHP programmer with the most experience, his boss needs him to work on the other portions of the corporate site as soon as possible after which he'll then come around and make use of the new programmers' changes to the auditing on the call center software. In the end, it will be his responsibility to provide hooks for the new payment-processing portion of the user login screen.

Steve's code isn't bad, but it seems to be taking Jason a bit longer to follow through and port the payment-processing portion into the corporate site. Instead, he determines he could finish faster by writing it in his own method. He mentions this to Steve and continues on his way. Andy is also struggling. Since his Master's in computer science is newly acquired, he hasn't had much time to gain experience with the jumbled code that sometimes supports existing enterprises.

Through much struggle and late nights, the team is successful and deploys the new code changes. Andy feels like everything could have been architected better. Steve thinks that if the other programmers would have just copied and pasted his code, things would have gone must faster; Jason and Andy just needed to make a few tweaks and it would have been solid. Jason mentioned that he was confused about why some functionality was implemented in one way in one section of the code and in a different way in a different piece. That is what threw him off.

As the website continues to gain more visitors, the performance begins to suffer. Steve's boss suggests that the team take a few days and look at the code for optimization.

Jason discovers that the method that he wrote for payment processing is nearly the same as Steve's. Jason combines and tweaks the methods into one class. Steve is starting to see similarities between the authentication code that he wrote for the call center site and the classes he authored for the corporate site's user login. Andy is realizing that every PHP page they create has the same set of function calls at the top of it. He creates a bootstrap type class to bring this all into one location to reduce code duplication.

From outside this example, you can objectively see many things. Steve's code could have benefited from commonality in its approach. Andy's formal education in software design made him sometimes question PHP's ability to accomplish the tasks and question the architecture. Jason couldn't easily understand Steve's payment system, so he opted to create his own, causing code duplication. Finally, after the software analysis, the team started discovering patterns in their seemingly jumbled code base. This is the beginning of this team's foray into Design Patterns.

Design Patterns Are Solving the Same Problem

In the previous example, Steve's team stumbled into the first important part of the Design Pattern concept. Patterns are not intentionally created in software development. They are more often discovered through practice and application in real-world situations. The payment application system and the bootstrap type calls being consolidated into classes are examples of identifying patterns in programming.

It was once said that every single piece of music that could be written already has been. Now, new music creation is just the rearranging of those particular sets of notes to different tempos and speeds. It's the same with general software development, barring a few major groundbreaking exceptions. The same problems come up repeatedly and require common solutions. This is exactly what Design Patterns are: reusable solutions for these common problems.

No book mentioning Design Patterns would be complete without the reference to the *Gang of Four*: Erich Gamma, Richard Helm, Ralph Johnson, and John Vlissides, authors of the original Design Patterns book. After a considerable amount of time in the field, they started noticing particular patterns of design emerging from various development projects. Collectively, they gathered these ideas together to form the initial Design Patterns concept. Recognizing these as templates for future development, they were able to put them into an easy-to-understand reference with digestible segments for large, complex programming concepts.

While Design Patterns can encompass many things — from interface design to architecture, and even marketing and metrics — this particular book will focus on development language construction using Object Oriented Programming.

A problem in software design consists of three parts:

❑ The "what" is considered the business and functionality requirements.

❑ The "how" is the particular design that you use to meet those requirements.

❑ The "work" is the actual implementation, or the "how" put into actual application and practice.

Design Patterns fit into the "how" of this process, and as a result, this book describes the "how" of solving these problems as well as portions of the "work" necessary to make these solutions successful. You can picture PHP as the vehicle behind the "why" of the problem solving. Once you know "what" the software needs to do, and you've designed "how" it can do it, the "work" becomes a lot easier with a lot less refactoring.

I can't stress this enough: the PHP language, your grasp of it and the way you understand its intricacies is not the focus of this book. Instead, I bring common, time tested methodologies into focus, describe them, and relate them to PHP.

Patterns naturally start to come out of software development, as you saw in the example. However, having a full playbook that references existing patterns can make the architecture planning faster and the choices better. As an added bonus, programmers coming from different software realms may recognize the pattern and just have to adapt to the specifics of the language. Having a clear set of patterns in your application may also help new members of your team grasp your project, lowering your ramp-up time.

Design Patterns Are Around You All the Time

You've seen how Steve's team was able to grasp basic patterns in their software and create reusable items. You may also be able to draw parallels to your own software development now. How many times have you created the same user login and authentication system using your user class? Do you have a db() function sitting around somewhere that you favor? These are examples of how you've already been using patterns.

Even more detailed and closer to the root patterns are examples found in your favorite PEAR or other framework libraries. For example, using PEAR DB is an example of putting a Design Pattern into use (notably the factory method). The Zend Framework also uses various different patterns such as the Singleton and the Adapter patterns.

The Common Parts of a Design Pattern

The Gang of Four pioneered a documentation standard for describing Design Patterns. They used this in their book for each of the patterns that they mentioned. Authors after them have copied this exact format and continued to propagate this form of documentation. I was a little bit less verbose with you because I felt a lot of the sections either reiterated the sections above them or were just there for structure's sake. The introduction to this book mentions the four main parts of each pattern's documentation: the name, the problem and solution, the Universal Modeling Language (UML) diagram, and the code example.

The Name

The name is actually more important in Design Patterns than you may initially guess it is. Proper descriptive naming conventions can go a long way toward explaining the behavior and relationship of the pattern to the project and other patterns.

In the example for this chapter, you saw how Jason mentioned to Steve that he was going to rewrite a portion of the payment-processing system. Since Steve was the senior programmer, he may not have necessarily agreed with the approach that Jason was using, but he certainly could have suggested some patterns to be used in that rewrite's architecture. This way, the entire team would both be familiar with the underlying concepts of the payment system, with Jason specializing in the exact implementation.

Problem and Solution

As mentioned previously, Design Patterns are what emerge from solving the same problem with the same general solution. This section of the description covers the main problem or problems in your project and then shows how this particular Design Pattern is one of the better solutions.

As you may have noticed, I didn't use the phrase "the best solution" because no one can say this definitively. Even if you find what you believe is the best Design Pattern for a particular problem, you're going to have to apply a certain amount of tweaking to it in order for it to fit perfectly into your project.

UML Diagram

The UML diagram will show the general structure of the pattern. In some cases, it may be necessary to generate more than one diagram to show additional implementations of the pattern or to illustrate a complex concept in easier-to-understand segments.

What is UML?

Unified Modeling Language (UML) diagrams should be a staple in your programming arsenal. UML is a standard way to diagram programming actions, objects and use cases. This helps communicate your design when building complex software in PHP. For a quick refresher on UML, visit the `http://Wikipedia.org/wiki/Unified_Modeling_Language` page on Wikipedia.

You may find that the building blocks for generating your own UML diagrams for your project can be loosely based on these generic pattern diagrams. Of course, your method names, class names, and attributes will vary and be more complex than those in the example.

The Code Example

Hands-on PHP programmers are finally rejoicing: the code examples. These are going to be relatively simple examples of the Design Pattern concept put into PHP code. The bonus here in having a PHP-based Design Patterns book is that you don't necessarily need to know another language to see an example of this pattern. (Other books focusing on Enterprise Design Patterns have used Java or C examples, somewhat taking away the effectiveness of the example to a sole-language programmer.)

I continue to reiterate: the code examples are simply that. They are not meant to be plug and play. They may not contain error logging or handling, auditing, or wholly secure programming techniques. This is not to say that I don't appreciate high-quality, secure programming (previous teammate programmers of mine can confirm that I'm a stickler for details), but it would distract from the main concept that I'm trying to explain.

What Design Patterns Are Not

It's important to rein in the explanation of Design Patterns by also talking about what they don't encompass. Up until now, you may have noticed that I've created a pretty large umbrella of coverage for the Design Pattern definition.

Design Patterns Are Not Plug and Play

If you're expecting to flip to the Design Pattern pages of this book and see full examples that you can quickly copy and paste for your next project, you will be sadly disappointed. Design Patterns are not just a simple plug and play solution to your programming project.

Design Patterns are not the actual implementation or even the algorithm for solving the problem. For example, you may create a design such that every house you construct has windows in the south to let in more heat and light. You are not actually doing the constructing with exact measurements and locations of the windows. You just hand over your design to the builder (programmer in our case), and they implement it.

Another analogous way to view Design Patterns is to compare them to musical notes on a scale. You may know all the notes in a minor scale, but playing them exactly in order and in the same tempo does not make an enjoyable song. You can't open up a scale book, grab the scale, play it on guitar, and expect everyone to think you're an amazing song writer. It would be quite boring and wouldn't solve the problem your music is made for: to demonstrate a specific set of emotions via art. In this way, Design Patterns are like those scales in the book. While they are the building blocks of a great solo, it is up to you to apply them, tweak them, and create a great song.

Design Patterns are Maintainable But Not Always Most Efficient

Design patterns don't always lend themselves to the greatest efficiency and speed in applications either. The goal of a Design Pattern is to help you design a solution in an easily repeatable and reusable way. This means the Pattern may not be specifically tailored to your situation but will have greater code maintainability and understandability.

Design Patterns are a Vehicle, Not a Refactoring End

A particular supervisor of mine just finished reading a book by Joshua Kerievsky and came to me with his newly acquired knowledge. He told me that we need to refactor our code base to use all Design Patterns. We had a discussion about what refactoring really meant, especially in our context.

While respecting Kerievsky and not disagreeing, I do feel that a greater distinction should be maintained when coupling Design Patterns to refactoring. Refactoring approaches both creating a more efficient code base and improving the maintainability and clarity of the code. Design Patterns are a great vehicle for your refactoring approach, but shouldn't be the destination. While I'm in favor of starting a project with a highly detailed set of Design Pattern architecture specs, I don't want to force something into a pattern for patterns' sake. Imagine if the first rock bands in existence threw a piano into the mix just because everyone else in music was doing it, and they thought they had to. You wouldn't have that classic guitar-driven rock music that we've come to love!

Design Pattern Demonstration

Most examples of Design Patterns historically have been very sparse and theoretical so as not to have the reader confuse the core concepts with language-agnostic features. Readers who have studied Design Patterns, or even Object Oriented Programming before will be very familiar with the ever-present square, circle, and oval object examples.

The debate rages on about Design Pattern books using simple objects like squares or people in their examples. Purists say you should detail the Design Pattern concepts and practice and give the simplest examples possible so as not to distract from the actual implementation of the pattern. (These are the people that hated story problems in math class because of all the extra information!) In my experience, self-taught PHP programmers prefer to see more thorough examples of the concept in code form. (They probably learned a lot by copy and paste coding when they first started.)

The Design Patterns in this book do contain small to medium-sized examples of PHP code to demonstrate the pattern. This dual-phased approach combines the actual conceptual explanation of the pattern for those who need that particular structure with the example-based pattern demonstration for those who are more hands-on learners.

The reference pages of this book will be more satisfying to the purists, while the case study section at the end will satisfy the code-example-hungry readers. For more information on the references pages, skip to the next section to see how they will be laid out.

Why Use Design Patterns in PHP?

PHP has a very easy beginner's learning curve with the backing of an enterprise-ready engine. Chances are that you ventured into PHP by inserting a few lines of code into an existing HTML document. Simply change the extension from `.html` to `.php`, add your quick snippet of code, deploy it to a PHP server, and you're a bona-fide PHP programmer. Up until the advent of the Zend Certified Engineer (ZCE) certification, there was no real measurement of a PHP programmer's prowess. Even after becoming a ZCE, programmers can still lack some of the essentials for developing enterprise-ready, architecturally sound application software.

As if the example in the beginning of the chapter weren't enough encouragement, more business-class players are coming on board with PHP. PHP's humble roots have left it somewhat devoid of the limelight of major enterprise-level programming languages. However, the hard work of Zend as well as the adoption of PHP by large Internet companies (such as Yahoo! and Amazon) has shown that PHP is enterprise ready. With the introduction of enterprise-level software requirements, enterprise-level methodology is to follow.

PHP now has support for a lot of the building blocks behind the concepts you're going to study. Perhaps during the era of PHP3 or PHP/FI, applying these styles of patterns may have been more difficult if not impossible. Don't get me wrong; there are always patterns in language; it's just that this book and its examples wouldn't have been nearly as useful!

Summary

This chapter discussed the prevalence of patterns in your normal programming by using an everyday programming example. By extending your understanding of patterns, you can make correlations to actual Design Patterns. Examining the realm that Design Patterns encompass, and what they do not, provided a more concise definition. Finally, the case was made for using Design Patterns in PHP by pointing out PHP's support for building base Design Patterns as well as mentioning PHP's position among some of the greater enterprise partners.

Now that you have an understanding of what Design Patterns are, let's move on to discovering what PHP already has available to help you out.

2

Using Tools Already In Your Arsenal

Now that you've got a pretty good idea what Design Patterns are from Chapter 1, you can take a look at your current arsenal and see where they have already infiltrated. After which, you'll learn ways to make it easier to increase that penetration.

Common PHP frameworks and libraries such as PEAR and the Zend Framework were mentioned in the last chapter. In this chapter, you're going to look a bit deeper at those to pull out more details of Design Patterns in use. You'll then touch on an additional framework that you might also have heard of.

PHP 5 introduced a new standard set of classes and functions known as the SPL. After a quick introduction, this chapter examines what functionality may be useful when creating code examples of the Design Patterns for the reference chapters.

Finally, you'll finish up this chapter by looking at features of the Eclipse PDT IDE that can help with Design Pattern creation and duplication.

Patterns in Existing Frameworks

Some of the things that make the most common PHP frameworks so successful are their careful architecture, maintainability, and extensibility. This is all a tribute to the proper use of Design Patterns in their initial architecture. This section pulls out a couple of examples of the use of these patterns for each framework. The goal is to demonstrate even more the proliferation of these patterns throughout your daily programming so that the reference chapters seem less daunting. If you see an example of a Design Pattern being featured in one of these frameworks, feel free to page ahead to that reference chapter to learn more about it.

It is important to reiterate that a Design Pattern is simply a template for constructing your program. Not every Design Pattern–based architecture will be one object to a pattern, nor will it follow the exact book specifications of that pattern. You will very often find classes created with more than one Design Pattern or that the base pattern has been heavily tweaked to fit into the particular context.

Design Patterns in PEAR

PEAR is one of the oldest libraries of PHP extensions. PEAR stands for PHP Extension of Application Repository. The PEAR website's quick summary of PEAR almost screams the potential for being a great example for Design Patterns, specifically this phrasing: "for reusable PHP components." While the newest versions of PHP are no longer bundling PEAR into the core distribution, I'm sure that you've run into PEAR in your existing PHP Programming experience. PEAR seems to be falling slightly behind in the race as other frameworks gain greater traction. However, PEAR still has some great functionality and Design Pattern–centric architecture examples.

To examine the Design Pattern immersion of PEAR, this section reviews various PEAR libraries and indicates which design patterns they implemented during architectural planning. There are hundreds of PEAR classes with undoubtedly more demonstrations of Design Pattern–based design.

PEAR Mail

The PEAR Mail class is an interface created to send mail using various backend systems, including PHP's mail function, sendmail, and SMTP.

In the 1.2.0b1 version of this class, the `Mail.php` file contains an instance of the factory class around line 49. (Chapter 9 defines the Factory Design Pattern.) You'll learn about that particular pattern in the reference pages. The good news is that, if you've used this class, you've already used the Factory pattern in your applications!

PEAR Mail also includes a mock object for testing the e-mail functionality. Using a function to add pre- and post-send handlers, and calling these handlers when executing the send method, is very close to an Observer Design Pattern. (Chapter 13 defines the Observer Design pattern.) Remember, patterns are just the base blueprint for your architecture design. You may find during implementation that you need to modify the pattern to fit your requirements as was done in the mock object here.

PEAR MDB2

PEAR MDB2 is a database abstraction layer for all of PHP's supported relational database management system (RDBMS). MDB2's documentation boasts a heavily object-oriented API that predicts a great potential for Design Pattern–saturated architecture.

When reviewing version 2.5.0b2, I've found that MDB2 uses the Factory pattern again at around line 377 of `mdb2.php`. It looks like PEAR programmers heavily relied on the Factory pattern when creating this repository. MDB2 also protects itself from duplication by using the Singleton pattern around line 484 of `mdb2.php`. (Chapter 16 defines the Singleton Design pattern.)

Finally, a great example of the Iterator pattern can be found in the `iterator.php` file around line 54. (Chapter 11 defines the Iterator Define pattern.) This example is by far the most detailed implementation of a Design Pattern so far. This implementation also extends functionality from the Standard PHP Library, which is discussed later on in this chapter.

PEAR DB DataObject

One of the clearest examples of a Design Pattern put into practice in PEAR is the DB `DataObject`. (Chapter 5 defines the Data Access Object Design pattern.) Instead of pointing to various portions of this class where the patterns are implemented, I suggest that you review the whole structure. From start to finish, this is a great example of a Design Pattern implemented in a solid but not overly verbose way. As explained in Chapter 1, code based on Design Patterns is rarely plug and play. This class pays homage to that notion by requiring the base `DataObject` class to be extended by your own code to be usable.

PEAR Log

The PEAR Log package is an abstract logging framework with hooks for files, databases, syslog, e-mail, Firebug, and the console. Version 1.11.3 uses the standard Factory (line 151 of `Log.php`) and Singleton (line 213 of `Log.php`) patterns. The Log package makes use of the Observer pattern (line 769 of `Log.php`) to handle some of this extensibility.

Design Patterns in the Zend Framework

Zend, the company behind PHP, is best known for the PHP engine. They continue to grow by offering more professional services for PHP and additional software products like the Zend Optimizer and the Zend Studio. With all of this experience, Zend was the perfect organization to aggregate the newest Web 2.0 functionality, Design Patterns and old staples into one framework.

The Zend Framework is a simple, object oriented framework and library built on best practices. You can bet you'll see some of these Design Patterns built into the architecture of this framework! When reviewing the Zend Framework, I'm going to focus on individual design patterns directly and indicate which modules of the framework they're part of. We will be using version 1.6 of the Zend Framework for this book's examples.

The Singleton Pattern in Zend Framework

One of the most common patterns demonstrated in the Zend Framework is the Singleton pattern. Briefly, the Singleton is a Design Pattern that aims to allow only one instance of the base object.

The Auth module uses the `getInstance()` method around line 68 of `Auth.php` to create a Singleton instance. The Feed module uses two functions, `setHttpClient()` and `getHttpClient()` to store a single instance of the connection. The Layout module uses a Singleton pattern to contain only one instance of a Layout. Finally, the `Registry` class also uses its own `getInstance()` method on about line 49 of `Registry.php`. (Some authors have listed Registry as its own Design Pattern, but I humbly disagree and view it as almost a language extension or an organizational pattern.)

The Factory Pattern in Zend Framework

The next most common design pattern in Zend Framework is the Factory pattern. The Factory pattern basically creates an interface to instantiate different objects in a similar way.

The Cache module of Zend Framework has a method named `factory()`, which is responsible for this functionality. This particular method (line 82 of `Cache.php`) demonstrates the Factory pattern well by looking at the exterior usage of the method compared to the complex logic contained within to generate new classes. The Db module also uses a method named `factory()` to create instances of the Db connections. Database abstraction is a great example of the need for the Factory pattern; both Zend Framework and PEAR have proven this. The Uri module is a more traditional example of the Factory pattern. It uses more control structures to determine the proper class to instantiate and return. The `switch` statement is located near line 107 in `Uri.php`.

The Iterator Pattern in Zend Framework

The Iterator Design Pattern is also an important pattern that is implemented in the Zend Framework. The Iterator pattern is simply a design of an object that makes it traversable. Imagine this to be like casting an object's properties to an array in PHP.

The Config module is used to store configuration options, which surely need to be accessed programmatically. The necessity to make some options read-only solidifies the need to create an `Iterator` object instead of just using a plain array in PHP. This is done in PHP by implementing the `Iterator` interface when the `Config` class is created. The Form module is another implementation of the Iterator pattern in which the various elements of the HTML form can be stepped through. The Paginator module is one of the most obvious candidates for iteration, as pagination has the iteration of individual results at its core.

The Adapter Pattern in the Zend Framework

The Adapter Design Pattern has been instrumental in giving the Zend Framework that ease of implementation that it boasts. (Chapter 3 defines the Adapter Design pattern.) The Adapter pattern creates an interface that changes one object's methods to something that another object expects.

A portion of the Db suite of files located in the Zend/Db/Adapter folder contain classes that create a simple structure for calling common functions in databases such as Db2, MySQL, and Oracle. This pattern allows the programmer to call a method like `connect()` without having to worry about the exact DSN and PHP function calls to build it. The InfoCard module has two functions, called `setAdapter()` and `getAdapter()`, located at line 127 and 139 in `InfoCard.php`. This allows each call to the public methods to function the same regardless of the actual logic contained inside of them. The Paginator module, in addition to using the Iterator pattern, also makes use of the Adapter pattern, providing a unified interface for any number of items that need to be stepped through. This is demonstrated clearly in its `factory()` method. (It looks like the Paginator module is very heavily saturated with Design Patterns!)

The Observer Pattern in Zend Framework

Any framework makes heavy use of a plug-in type architecture — the Zend Framework being no exception. The best way to architect this is with the Observer pattern. The Observer pattern is just a way of requesting potential action from other objects when something happens in the source object.

The Filter module provides a method to add actions to the filter stream using the `addFilter()` method on line 51 of `Filter.php`. On line 65, the main `filter()` function runs, passing that value through each of the objects added earlier. The Log module also makes use of the Observer pattern. The `Log()` method sends the action that just happened, or the event, through to various objects waiting to process it. When running the `isValid()` method of the Validate module, you are also engaging functionality created with the Observer pattern. The function `addValidator()` on line 70 of `Validate.php` is the vehicle to add in the objects that will process the event.

Design Patterns in Doctrine

Doctrine is an object relational mapper (ORM) for PHP. This object-oriented library provides an interface for database abstraction. It also features an implementation of the Data Access Object Design Pattern. "Features an implementation" is an understated way of saying that the entire library really is focused on being a Data Access Object pattern.

The main functionality of Doctrine revolves around the ability to create objects that correspond to tables in the database. Instead of accessing this data directly by creating SQL with `Select`, `Join`, and `Union` statements, objects are created with properties that reflect these predefined relationships. Then, complex data manipulation is executed using simple public methods of objects regardless of the actual database engine and language specifics.

The Standard PHP Library

The Standard PHP Library (SPL), developed by Marcus Boerger, is a useful collection of interfaces and classes bundled with PHP as an extension. In PHP 5, this was added as part of the core distribution. The manual states that this set of interfaces and classes is "meant to solve standard problems." At first read, this echoes the explanation given earlier of Design Patterns. Indeed, the library has an assortment of features that does help with your creation of Design Patterns in PHP. Let's review a few of the main players of the SPL to see what you may use in your future pattern-based architecture.

SPL Observer and SPL Subject

The `SplObserver` and the `SplSubject` interfaces are an implementation of the Observer Design Pattern. `SplSubject` contains three method declarations: `attach()`, `detach()` and `notify()`. `attach()`, and `detach()` are used to attach objects to the chain of notification and receive a `SplObserver` object. The `notify()` function is called whenever an action happens that the chain should be aware of. The `SplObserver` interface contains one method, `update()`, which receives only one parameter — an `SplSubject` object. This should be called whenever the `SplSubject`'s value changes.

This may seem very vague and confusing if you're not familiar with the Observer Design Pattern. However, the main thing to remember is the existence of these methods as you continue on to study the Design Patterns. You may find that using some of these methods may jump-start your patterns on your next programming project.

SPL Iterators

When I first ran across SPL iterators, I didn't directly correlate them to what I knew about Design Patterns at the time. Even though they functioned as you would expect from an Iterator Design Pattern, and were even named the same thing, I totally overlooked the intentional architecture. Because of this ease of use, it is perfectly fine to review these before reviewing the actual Iterator Design pattern. After reviewing these interfaces, an understanding of the Iterator should come naturally when it is reviewed in the reference materials in Part II.

Basically, an `Iterator` is an object that provides an interface for traversing some other data structure or object. It is programmer-agnostic of the actual underlying structure. For example, if you were running an online music store and you received your inventory list in both XML and CSV, you could create an object that would read through each of these data sources. The public methods of this object should allow you to travel both forward and backward through the collection of music without having to worry about what type of data structure the incoming list was in.

As the intent of the first part of this book is to give you building blocks to create your own Design Pattern structures, this section only points out the more common or important interfaces and classes used with iteration in SPL. To review the full feature list of the SPL, visit `http://php.net/spl`.

Iterator, RecursiveIterator, SeekableIterator

The `Iterator` interfaces in the SPL allow you to access an object much as you would an array (don't confuse this with the `ArrayAccess` interface, however). The member functions of the `Iterator` interface are `current()`, `key()`, `next()`, `rewind()` and `valid()`. Being familiar with the array functionality built into PHP, you can draw your own conclusions right away on how to use the `Iterator` interface.

The `SeekableIterator` adds on one additional function to the `Iterator` methods: `seek()`. This method allows the object to travel to an absolute position within its storage system. You can closely equate this to accessing an array by defining its index in brackets.

The `RecursiveIterator` defines an easy way to traverse hierarchical data. It contains all of the methods of `Iterator` plus two additional ones: `hasChildren()` and `getChildren()`. Simply put, the `hasChildren()` method notifies the user if there is an additional level below the current access level. The `getChildren()` method returns a collection of objects that contain the same properties as the parent (with an optional additional level of children). This may seem confusingly abstract at first glance. However, just compare it to a programmatic way of accessing a multidimensional array.

DirectoryIterator, LimitIterator, SimpleXMLIterator

In addition to some useful interfaces that SPL provides, there is a collection of classes that can also add useful functionality. Extending these classes can both save time and solidify the pattern-based designs in your programming.

❏   The `LimitIterator` is functionally very similar to a `LIMIT` statement in MySQL. When you provide an existing `Iterator` to it with an offset and a count, the `LimitIterator` confines the traversal to objects to those that fit within the predefined bounds. You may find this useful when creating objects that are responsible for featuring only the top 100 items of a collection even if the collection is much larger. Applying the `LimitIterator` structures the programming to check these bounds.

❏   The `DirectoryIterator` provides a powerful set of methods to loop through a directory on the file system. The common set of `Iterator` methods such as `next()` and `rewind()` are just the tip of the iceberg for managing a set of files. This class also integrates useful functions like `isDot()` and `isLink()`. Additionally, each file that is returned is an instance of the `SplFileInfo` class. (The `SplFileinfo` class is not reviewed here; however, full documentation of its collection of over 25 methods returning file system information is located at `http://php.net/splfileinfo`.) The `DirectoryIterator` is one of the greatest examples of how Design Patterns can provide the basis of a very powerful, extensible, and architecturally sound object.

❑ The `SimpleXMLIterator` is an `Iterator` class that works directly with the SimpleXML extension of PHP. It extends the `SimpleXMLElement` object. As you can predict by the name of the class, it also implements the `Iterator` interface (among other interfaces), providing that familiar `next()`, `rewind()`, `valid()`, and `key()` functionality at the very least. This creative implementation of the `Iterator` pattern is an example of a reusable object that is one of the major goals of our usage of patterns.

Using Eclipse PDT with Patterns

The Eclipse PDT software package is a PHP-centric distribution of the popular Eclipse IDE. With additional features like the PHP perspective, and JavaScript and CSS syntax highlighting, Eclipse PDT is one of the most important tools in my programming arsenal.

The next part of this chapter is based on Eclipse PDT 2.0 in Windows. However, you can use these steps for a standard Eclipse installation as the feature set is common to the core Eclipse distribution. If you use a different IDE and have never tried out PDT, I suggest that you try it out now with this next tutorial. You can acquire the newest PDT package from `http://zend.com/pdt`. If you continue to use a different IDE, you may be able to adapt these steps to fit your own IDE. (Perhaps you may even want to write these up in your own technical blog!)

Code Snippets in Eclipse PDT

One useful feature in Eclipse PDT is the code snippets function. Snippets allow code templates to be created and inserted into your current file. These can range from a simple code comment template to a complex set of function definitions for a reusable interface.

For this example, we're going to use the SPL `Iterator` interface. As you build your own library of Design Pattern based modules, you may find you will need to create more code snippets.

Creating the Iterator Interface Code

When implementing the `Iterator` interface, five methods are required to be part of your object: `current()`, `key()`, `valid()`, `next()`, and `rewind()`. You need to create these stub functions. As you're a very good programmer, you're going to also add documentation (albeit very sparse) to your code as well. This is the base code sample you're going to use:

```
/**
 * Get the current element
 * @return mixed
 */
public function current()
{
}

/**
 * Gets the current key
 * @return mixed
 */
public function key()
```

```php
    {
    }

    /**
     * Checks if current element exists
     * @return boolean
     */
    public function valid()
    {
    }

    /**
     * Moves pointer forward to next element
     */
    public function next()
    {
    }

    /**
     * Moves pointer to first element
     */
    public function rewind()
    {
    }
```

Now that you have the base code to use, it is time to investigate the snippet functionality of Eclipse PDT.

Creating the Snippet

After opening Eclipse, locate the Snippets tab in your current perspective. If you cannot find this tab, it may be necessary to activate it:

1. Click the Window ⇨ Show View ⇨ Other.

2. In the Show View dialog (see Figure 2-1), expand the General folder and click Snippets.

Figure 2-1

3. Click OK. The snippets tab should now be available on this perspective.

Because this is your first snippet, you're going to have to create a category first. To create a new category, do the following:

1. Right-click inside of the Snippet area and choose Customize. The Customize Palette dialog box appears.

2. Click the New button on the top left of the Customize Palette.

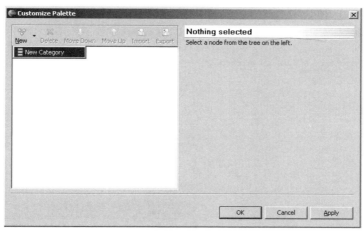

Figure 2-2

3. Click the New Category menu item (see Figure 2-3).

The Create Category dialog box appears.

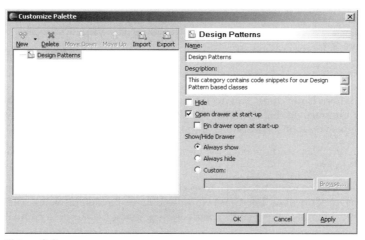

Figure 2-3

4. Fill in the Category name and description if desired.

5. Click the Apply button.

To create a new template:

1. Again, click the New button.

2. Click the New Item menu item.

3. Fill in the name and description (refer to Figure 2-4).

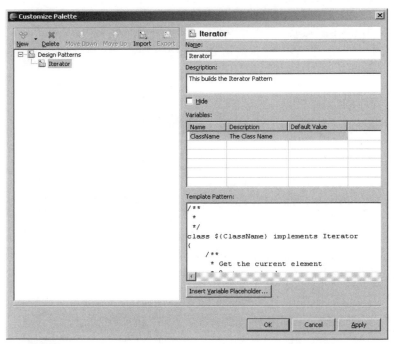

Figure 2-4

4. Paste the code snippet from the previous section into the Template Pattern section. Your template pattern is not done. You need to declare the class and make sure that it implements the Iterator interface. In this example, you don't know your class name. However, the snippets feature allows you to insert variables into the snippet.

5. Under the Variables heading, click the New button. This should insert a generic variable name in the table below.

6. Click under each heading to change the values. For this example, name your variable **ClassName**, describe it as **The Class Name** and leave the default value blank. Variables are inserted into a template by using a $ sign and enclosing the variable name in curly braces.

7. Modify your Template pattern with the class definition. Insert the following above the previous code snippet in the Template pattern:

```
/**
 *
 */
class ${ClassName} implements Iterator
{
```

Don't forget to add the closing curly brace at the very end of the code snippet.

8. Finally, click the OK button.

Using the Snippet

Now, for the moment of truth! When a new PHP file is created in Eclipse PDT and the Snippets tab is showing, it's easy to use the newly created snippet:

1. Position the cursor where you'd like the class definition to start.

2. Double-click the Snippet named Iterator under the Design Patterns category. The Insert Template: Iterator dialog box appears (Figure 2-5). You may notice the variables section shows the ClassName variable with no value.

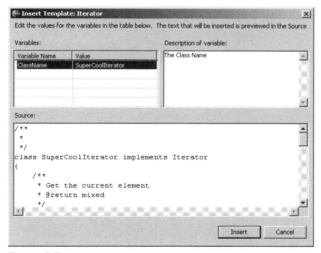

Figure 2-5

3. Click in the table cell, and type in your new class name. The Source box is updated with your new class name after you press Enter.

4. Click the Insert button, and your new template is inserted into your source file.

Summary

This chapter focused on a few tools that already exist in PHP and your IDE that can help jump-start your Design Pattern–based programming. You learned about the Design Pattern immersion in PEAR, the Zend Framework, and Doctrine by looking at both the usage and construction of the individual classes in these libraries. The Standard PHP Library also houses a helpful set of interfaces and classes that provides some necessary building blocks for applying Design Patterns in new architecture. Finally, you created a code snippet in Eclipse PDT to make it easier to stick with these programming best practices by reducing the need to retype code required by the Iterator interface.

The next sections of this book are the reference chapters and focus on the specifics of some of the Design Patterns mentioned so far as well as providing some additional ones to expand your pattern repertoire.

Part II
Reference Material

Chapter 3: Adapter Pattern

Chapter 4: Builder Pattern

Chapter 5: Data Access Object Pattern

Chapter 6: Decorator Pattern

Chapter 7: Delegate Pattern

Chapter 8: Façade Pattern

Chapter 9: Factory Pattern

Chapter 10: Interpreter Pattern

Chapter 11: Iterator Pattern

Chapter 12: Mediator Pattern

Chapter 13: Observer Pattern

Chapter 14: Prototype Pattern

Chapter 15: Proxy Pattern

Chapter 16: Singleton Pattern

Chapter 17: Strategy Pattern

Chapter 18: Template Pattern

Chapter 19: Visitor Pattern

3

Adapter Pattern

In a simple world, no software requirements would ever change. Applications and business would not innovate. Programming would be simple, but boring. Programmers would continue to build applications on top of the same technologies that they did years ago. They would never need to introduce different databases, implement new best practices, or consume different APIs. But these things do change. Luckily, programmers have the Adapter Design Pattern to help update legacy systems with new code and functionality.

Name: Adapter

The Adapter Design Pattern simply adapts one object's interfaces to what another object expects.

Problem and Solution

In an application, you may be a working code base that is architecturally sound and stable. However, new functionality is constantly being added that requires use of these existing objects in a different way than they were originally designed. The roadblock may be as simple as the new functionality expecting a different name of a function. It could also be a bit more complex scenario, where the functionality expects slightly different original object behavior.

The solution is to build another object, using the Adapter Design Pattern. This `Adapter` object works as an intermediary between the original application and the new functionality. The Adapter Design Pattern defines a new interface for an existing object to match what the new object requires.

For the most part, no existing functionality is lost; it's just used or consumed in a different way. You can equate this to an electrical adapter that receives a three-pronged grounded connection and conforms to a two-prong socket. The adapter transparently forwards the alternating current from the prongs but provides a different interface for the grounding functionality. In most common electrical adapters, the grounding functionality is not lost but is instead provided via a grounding wire that should be connected to the screw on the electrical socket container. In the same way, the Adapter Design Pattern aims to help object-oriented code; it creates conversions for the object interfaces.

While it may be tempting to modify the existing code to work in the way the new functionality expects, you should create an adapter object instead. Quite often, it is suggested that a quick tweak to an existing object is the fastest and most cost effective way to accomplish this task. I argue that speed and cost are rarely an issue when creating the adapter object. No real new functionality is being created. By the time the original object was changed and tested against regression, a quick adapter class with a few lines of code could have been created with no possibility for regression.

The best solution still is to create an `Adapter` object. This affords the possibility of parallel development on both the new functionality and the existing code base. If your job is to integrate the new functionality and you accomplish this by editing the existing code base, you may find yourself at odds with the team who is developing new functionality in those initial classes. They may be adding additional private methods and expecting them to be called by the public methods that were originally available with the last stable release. The last thing you want to create is a complex merging scenario or a forked code base.

The Adapter Design Pattern is also a great solution for changes to a data source. Two common problems concern database engine changes and data file format changes:

❑ The project may need to change the database engine for any number of reasons. A common scenario involves an application created with MySQL migrating to a larger database like Oracle. Other times, licensing restrictions and costs require a different engine to be used; for example, Postgres, when the product finally goes to distribution. If you're not already using a database abstraction layer, you will need to create `Adapter` objects to intercept calls to the legacy database functionality and make those compatible with the new database. Interestingly enough, if you examine the code of some database abstraction libraries, you'll see them as nothing but a collection of adapters as well.

❑ When working with third-party data providers, the data files provided may change format. Your vendor may have been providing data in CSV format for years but will be migrating to an XML document. An adapter can be created that will take the XML and give it in a consumable format to the stable CSV processing objects.

Basically, whenever there is a problem that requires the continued stability of the main platform and doesn't disrupt the existing application flow, the Adapter Design Pattern could be used in developing the solution.

UML

This Unified Modified Language (UML) diagram details a class design using the Adapter Design Pattern (see Figure 3-1).

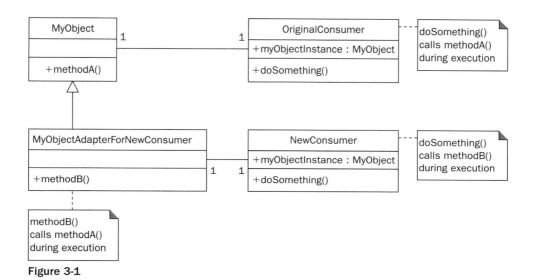

Figure 3-1

Note the following about this figure:

❑ The MyObject class contains a public method called methodA(). OriginalConsumer acquires an instance of MyObject and calls methodA() during its doSomething() function.

❑ The NewConsumer class is introduced. Its doSomething() function expects to call a public method of the MyObject instance called methodB() during execution.

❑ The MyObjectAdapterForNewConsumer is created by extending the MyObject class. It then provides a public method called methodB() as expected by NewConsumer. In this simple example, all methodB() does is call methodA().

Code Examples

In the original code base of the project, an object exists that handles all of the error messages and codes called errorObject. The original programmers didn't think their code would ever generate any errors, so they designed the system to output the errorObject's error information directly to the console.

In this example, a *404:Not Found* error is being generated. You are going to assume that the error message content and code may change, but the text will always stay in the same format.

```php
class errorObject
{
    private $__error;

    public function __construct($error)
    {
        $this->__error = $error;
    }

    public function getError()
    {
        return $this->__error;
    }
}

class logToConsole
{
    private $__errorObject;

    public function __construct($errorObject)
    {
        $this->__errorObject = $errorObject;
    }

    public function write()
    {
        fwrite(STDERR,$this->__errorObject->getError());
    }
}

/** create the new 404 error object **/
$error = new errorObject("404:Not Found");

/** write the error to the console **/
$log = new logToConsole($error);
$log->write();
```

In this scenario, a new network admin has been brought into the project. Best practice suggests that a network log for monitoring software should be installed. The package the admin chose requires the errors to be logged to a multicolumn CSV file. The CSV format calls for the first column to be the numeric error code. The second column should be the error text.

This new software package is familiar with the errorObject class. The vendor has provided code to implement the proper logging format! Unfortunately, that code was created from a different version of the errorObject than the one the current project is using. The new errorObject had two additional public methods, called getErrorNumber() and getErrorText(). The logToCSV class expects to use those.

```php
class logToCSV
{
    const CSV_LOCATION = 'log.csv';

    private $__errorObject;

    public function __construct($errorObject)
    {
        $this->__errorObject = $errorObject;
    }

    public function write()
    {
        $line = $this->__errorObject->getErrorNumber();
        $line .= ',';
        $line .= $this->__errorObject->getErrorText();
        $line .= "\n";

        file_put_contents(self::CSV_LOCATION, $line, FILE_APPEND);
    }
}
```

There are two solutions to this problem:

❑ Alter the existing code base's errorObject

❑ Create an Adapter object.

Because of the need to keep these public interfaces standard, creating an Adapter object is the best solution.

In this adapter object, the existing errorObject functionality must be present. In addition, the getErrorNumber() and the getErrorText() public methods must be available. In the legacy logToConsole, the getError() method is called to get the error message. The adapter should make use of that method to get the error message from the parent class and then translate that output to be used by the two new public methods.

```php
class logToCSVAdapter extends errorObject
{
    private $__errorNumber, $__errorText;

    public function __construct($error)
    {
        parent::__construct($error);

        $parts = explode(':', $this->getError());

        $this->__errorNumber = $parts[0];
        $this->__errorText = $parts[1];
    }

    public function getErrorNumber()
```

```
    {
        return $this->__errorNumber;
    }

    public function getErrorText()
    {
        return $this->__errorText;
    }
}
```

Finally, to implement this adapter, the code is updated to use the adapter instead of the original errorObject. Then, the logToCSV class can receive the adapted class instead of the original errorObject so that the legacy code works as the logToCSV class expects.

```
/** create the new 404 error object adapted for csv **/
$error = new logToCSVAdapter("404:Not Found");

/** write the error to the csv file **/
$log = new logToCSV($error);
$log->write();
```

Remember, implementing an Adapter object is both best practice and a headache saver when one object's interface needs to be translated for use by another.

Builder Pattern

Software complexity is an interesting thing. The requirements for software are complex as are the functionality of a software package or product. Even the code that makes up the software is complex. The focus of the Design Pattern approach is to provide maintainability, architectural strength and reduced complexity. With the host of complex objects making up most software repositories, solutions involving the Builder Design Pattern have their work cut out for them.

Name: Builder

The Builder Design Pattern defines the design of an object that handles the complex building of another object.

Problem and Solution

When an object is instantiated, it is technically a complete object. Some objects can be used in this capacity and are ready to propagate throughout the code flow. However, other objects are more complex in nature. They may require additional public methods to execute to be considered "complete" and available for the rest of the application.

It is important to understand what the word *complex* means in this context. Generally, complexity is the actual logic contained within methods of a class. However, when I refer to a complex object in connection to object instantiation, it means the level of steps that are required to create that complete object. The actual logical steps in each of the executed methods have no bearing on whether these classes are complex.

When creating complex objects, a common architecture decision revolves around the creation of the constructor. Some programmers think that any constructor should execute the proper logic to create the whole object. Others recognize that it makes sense to break up some of that logic into additional methods. Constructors designed in that fashion are basically a list of methods to call on instantiation. Neither of these solutions are very flexible. In fact, they are fundamentally wrong solutions.

It may be necessary to construct an object based on the results of a set of business logic. In this particular example, the base business decision rules have already been written and tested. Because of the results, only certain parts of the object must be created. In fact, if all parts of it are defined fully, it may cause other unforeseen results down the line. I realize this is vague. Let me give a better example.

In ABC Co, widgets are loaded into the inventory system before they are fully priced and inventoried. No matter if it's an initial load of a widget or the generation of an HTML page with widgets, their descriptions, and prices, the same widget object is created. The HTML page process does not show any widgets that have a NULL value for their product ID because those aren't for sale. They have not yet been entered into the inventory system. Both new and existing inventory requests are routed the same way through the code. By the time the data gets to the widget object, it's known if the widget data is for a new inventory item or for an existing one. Now, with what you know about the HTML page process, you must decide how to create the widget object. You would not want any of your new inventory widgets to accidentally show up on the website for sale. The solutions are as follows:

❑ **Wrong solution:** Duplicate the business logic inside the widget object constructor. Right now, this may be as simple as a quick conditional statement to determine the type of data, but this solution is wrong. With time, the chance grows that the business logic to determine if a widget is new or for sale may change. What if a third status is introduced, such as "Inventoried" but no price has been defined? This would require you to change the logic in both the other code and this object's constructor.

❑ **Wrong solution:** Set all the default values by calling all the methods in the constructor on widget object creation. These may include methods to set the price, description, and product ID. However, there is a potential issue here as well. You know that your HTML page process will be looking for product IDs of not NULL. If you assign a default value to this product ID, the HTML page will pick it up. Once again, the temptation to call all these methods, except for the product ID setter, is there. It's easier to just put a quick conditional statement around that method making sure not to assign the property on new widget creation. However, this is also not the proper solution.

❑ **Best solution:** Create a new object based on the Builder Design Pattern. This object is responsible for interpreting those results from the business logic and calling only the required functionality to build the complete widget object. Even if the required types of information or the business rules change, the main code flow will still deal with the Builder object in the same way. You will only need to modify the Builder object — in only one place. This saves both time and complexity in your main code base.

Another way to prove the benefits of the Builder Design Pattern is by examining interactions with third-party applications, a common one being a database wrapper. In the example, if you're using version 1.0 of the database wrapper class, you may be required to call the setUsername(), setPassword() and setHostName() methods to have a complete instance of that object. Each time you create a connection to the database, your code contains the instantiation of the wrapper followed by three function calls.

In version 1.1, the third party makes the setDatabase() method mandatory. This means that every single instance of the database wrapper instantiation in your code base now needs to be altered to have an additional method call.

The best solution when implementing the wrapper with those complex creation steps is to create a database wrapper Builder class. Then, when version 1.1 is released, only the Builder class needs to be modified.

Remember, the complexity of multiple method calls may not seem so bad the very first time, but it's a slippery slope. If these methods need to be called continually, a Builder object should be created.

UML

This Unified Modified Language (UML) diagram details a class design using the Builder Design Pattern (see Figure 4-1).

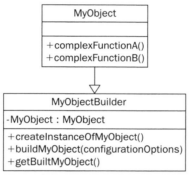

Figure 4-1

Note the following concerning this figure:

❑   The MyObject class has two methods to completely finish the construction of the object. Both complexFunctionA() and complexFunctionB() need to be executed in order to have a complete MyObject object.

❑   The MyObjectBuilder class contains a method called createInstanceOfMyObject(). This class is responsible for creating a simple instance of the MyObject class. Note how no configuration options have been used to further construct it. It also stores the instance privately in that instance of the MyObjectBuilder class.

❑   The buildMyObject() method takes a parameter of configurationOptions. This is used to call both complexFunctionA() and complexFunctionB() of the MyObject object stored in the MyObjectBuilder object.

❑   The getBuiltMyObject() method returns the private instance of MyObject inside the MyObjectBuilder object, completed and built properly.

Code Example

The project contains a class that creates the complex product object. This class contains three methods to completely form it. If each of these methods is not called when creating a new product object, attributes of the class will be missing and the program will halt. These methods are setType(), setColor(), and setSize(). The initial version of this code was designed to create the object followed by the execution of each of these methods.

```php
class product
{
    protected $_type = '';
    protected $_size = '';
    protected $_color = '';

    public function setType($type)
    {
        $this->_type = $type;
    }

    public function setSize($size)
    {
        $this->_size = $size;
    }

    public function setColor($color)
    {
        $this->_color = $color;
    }
}
```

To create a complete product object, the product configurations need to be passed individually to each of the methods of the product class:

```php
// our product configuration received from other functionality
$productConfigs = array('type'=>'shirt', 'size'=>'XL', 'color'=>'red');

$product = new product();
$product->setType($productConfigs['type']);
$product->setSize($productConfigs['size']);
$product->setColor($productConfigs['color']);
```

Having to call each one of these methods when an object is created is not best practice. Instead, an object based on the Builder Design Pattern should be used to create this product instance.

The productBuilder class is designed to accept those configuration options that are required to build the product object. It stores both the configuration parameter and a new product instance on instantiation. The build() method is responsible for calling each of the methods in the product class to fully complete the product object. Finally, the getProduct() method returns the completely built product object.

```php
class productBuilder
{
    protected $_product = NULL;
    protected $_configs = array();

    public function __construct($configs)
    {
        $this->_product = new product();
        $this->_xml = $configs;
    }

    public function build()
    {
        $this->_product->setSize($configs['size']);
        $this->_product->setType($configs['type']);
        $this->_product->setColor($configs['color']);
    }

    public function getProduct()
    {
        return $this->_product;
    }
}
```

Note that this `build()` method hides the actual method calls from the code requesting the new product. If the `product` class changes in the future, only the `build()` method of the `productBuilder` class needs to change. This code demonstrates the creation of the `product` object, using the `productBuilder` class:

```php
$builder = new productBuilder($productConfigs);
$builder->build();
$product = $builder->getProduct();
```

The Builder Design Pattern is meant to eliminate the complex creation of other objects. Using the Builder Design Pattern is not only best practice but it also reduces the chances of having to repeatedly alter pieces of code if an object's construction and configuration methods change.

5

Data Access Object Pattern

The simplest web widget to the most complex online e-commerce website have one thing in common: they deal with data. So much of programming revolves around data access and manipulation. With the massive proliferation of the Internet, cheaper storage devices, improved understanding of analytics, and greater expectations for information access, data is being leveraged in more interesting and unique ways. The Data Access Object Design Pattern aims to help construct objects that can work easily (transparently) with all of this data.

Name: Data Access Object

The Data Access Object Design Pattern describes the creation of an object that provides transparent access to any data source.

Problem and Solution

For those who have learned PHP and MySQL together hand in hand, the Data Access Object Design Pattern is a new and exciting concept. This Design Pattern aims to solve two specific problems: repetition and data source abstraction.

Programming typically can be a lot of repetition. This was especially true before more popular frameworks started being released. Most PHP programmers can count into the double digits the number of CRUD (create, read, update, delete) applications they've had to make. One of the major portions of repetition in the standard create/update application is the data source manipulation. For the rest of the discussion, I'm going to stop generalizing the data source and refer to it as SQL.

In the application, a SQL statement has to be written to create the entity in the database. Next, an additional SQL statement must be written in order to provide updates to any of the individual features of that entity. The repetition involved in creating these SQL statements is not only boring but also not best practice.

Instead, an object based on the Data Access Object Design Pattern should be created. This Data Access Object (DAO) encapsulates an intelligent way of creating those SQL calls, reducing the complexity and repetition of the entity creation and updating process. It should be written in such a way that the consumers of this object are not aware of the actual table structures or database engine used. Methods that are invoked from this object should take logical parameters and handle the creation of the SQL statements.

An added benefit of the Data Access Object is the database abstraction layer it affords. Now, the main processing code of the application no longer has to be aware of the database engine or table relationships. Calling those public methods of the object can return any type of data regardless of the underlying SQL required.

A good way to picture this is with a relational database structure where a non-normalized table is joined to another table to provide a certain result set. If a database administrator modifies the table structure to be fully normalized, each of the SQL statements throughout all of the logic modules in the application will need to be modified to add an additional join table. Using the Data Access Object, only the methods that provide this information need to be edited. Imagine another situation in which the actual table structure changes. A column may be named something else or an additional column may be added. The Data Access Object is once again the only place that code needs to be edited. (SQL purists will argue that an added table column should not affect the queries at all. They would say that named columns in the SQL statement should be used. I agree. This won't help if a column name is changed, however!)

It is always a concern that programmers not over architect the Data Access Object. Once the full power of these types of objects is contrasted with the ease of use, the temptation to add more functionality is almost overwhelming. I encourage simplicity in the Data Access Object, however. Do not add in extra functionality that is unproven or unneeded.

A good way to manage simplicity in the Data Access Object classes is to create parent-child relationships. First, create the base parent object. This object should be responsible for database connections, executing queries abstractly, and communicating with children. A good way to start out with the Data Access Object Design Pattern is to associate child classes in a one-to-one relationship with tables in the database. These child classes hold vital information such as the table name and the primary key. Additionally, child classes may contain specific public methods that execute the parent queries in such a way that makes sense only to the child. For example, a child class named `userAddress` may contain a function named `getAddressesByZip()`. Having that method in the parent DAO class would make no logical sense and destroy the abstractness that the parent is hoping to achieve.

When working with entities that reference specific database information, it is best practice to create a Data Access Object.

UML

The following Unified Modified Language (UML) diagram details a class design using the Data Access Object Design Pattern (see Figure 5-1) and is further explained in the following list:

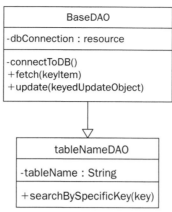

Figure 5-1

❑ The BaseDAO class is an abstract class that the tableNameDAO class extends. BaseDAO has a private method to connect to the data source named connectToDB(). This stores the connection in the private instance variable dbConnection. BaseDAO contains two public methods, named fetch() and update().

❑ The fetch() method expects to receive a parameter called keyItem. This references the primary identifier of the data source that is expected to be returned. This method will perform the proper database calls and return the result set.

❑ The update() method expects to receive a parameter called keyedUpdateObject. This is an object or array that contains keys and values to update the database with. In this function, the columns and values are extracted and the update is applied.

❑ The tableNameDAO class directly correlates to a table in the database. The tableName variable stores the exact table name. This private variable is used to create the database calls in fetch() and update(). As an example of additional features that a Data Access Object can possess distinct from the base object, the searchBySpecificKey() function is diagramed. This method expects to receive a variable named key. This method would create the proper database combination of calls to the parent data access object class to obtain the specified style of return.

Code Example

In this example, a user entity is the focus. The user has a row in a MySQL database that contains information specific and unique to each user. The functionality must allow us to return a user by their primary key or by a search on their first name. Additionally, you must be able to perform updates to any field in the user entity's row.

From these requirements, two classes are needed. The first should be the base Data Access Object with methods to fetch data and update data:

```php
abstract class baseDAO
{
    private $__connection;

    public function __construct()
    {
        $this->__connectToDB(DB_USER, DB_PASS, DB_HOST, DB_DATABASE);
    }

    private function __connectToDB($user, $pass, $host, $database)
    {
        $this->__connection = mysql_connect($host, $user, $pass);
        mysql_select_db($database, $this->__connection);
    }

    public function fetch($value, $key = NULL)
    {
        if (is_null($key)) {
            $key = $this->_primaryKey;
        }

        $sql = "select * from {$this->_tableName} where {$key}='{$value}'";
        $results = mysql_query($sql, $this->__connection);

        $rows = array();
        while ($result = mysql_fetch_array($results)) {
            $rows[] = $result;
        }

        return $rows;
    }

    public function update($keyedArray)
    {
        $sql = "update {$this->_tableName} set ";

        $updates = array();
        foreach ($keyedArray as $column=>$value) {
            $updates[] = "{$column}='{$value}'";
        }

        $sql .= implode(',', $updates);
        $sql .= "where {$this->_primaryKey}='{$keyedArray[$this->_primaryKey]}'";

        mysql_query($sql, $this->__connection);
    }
}
```

The first thing to note is that this class is an abstract class. Obviously, this means that this class must be extended in order to be used. On instantiation, the private method called __connectToDB() is executed with the proper credentials. This simply stores that database connection inside of the object. This will be referenced whenever a new query is executed. It is important to store this connection internally in the class and reference it with each query call because it is quite possible that more than one database connection could be open at the time. This Data Access Object should be referencing its own connection solely. Generally, in more scalable models, interfaces are created to share connections.

The next method is the public fetch() method. This accepts one required parameter and one optional one. The required $value parameter is used in the MySQL query in the select statement specification. The optional $key parameter defaults to the primary key of the table. If the parameter is set, however, a more flexible query will be executed, possibly returning more results. Finally, a results array is created, populated with results, and returned. It is important to note how abstract this method is: it doesn't know the table name, key, or value that it will be querying ahead of time. This is some of the strength that the Data Access Object lends to the code.

The last method in the class is the public update() method. Once again, its construction is interesting because of the abstractness of the query it builds. This particular method expects the keyed array to have the primary key of the entity as an array element in order to successfully update the table row.

This abstract class is extended by any child class. Our class is referencing the user entity by pointing to the userTable MySQL table. It also needs to have more specific functionality that only makes sense in the user entity context.

```
class userDAO extends baseDAO
{
    protected $_tableName = 'userTable';
    protected $_primaryKey = 'id';

    public function getUserByFirstName($name)
    {
        $result = $this->fetch($name, 'firstName');
        return $result;
    }
}
```

Since this class extends the baseDAO object, it has access to all of those parent functions. This child class is where the table name and the primary key are defined. These directly correlate to a MySQL table in the database. At the very least, those two protected variables are the only things that need to be defined to have a functioning Data Access Object child entity. However, part of the functionality requirements is to be able to search the user table via first name. The public method getUserByFirstName() accepts a name parameter to accomplish this requirement. The result is obtained by calling the parent fetch() method and defining a column that should be queried.

Here is an example of the Data Access Object being used:

```
define('DB_USER', 'user');
define('DB_PASS', 'pass');
define('DB_HOST', 'localhost');
```

```
define('DB_DATABASE', 'test');

$user = new userDAO();
$userDetailsArray = $user->fetch(1);

$updates=array('id'=>1, 'firstName'=>'aaron');
$user->update($updates);

$allAarons = $user->getUserByFirstName('aaron');
```

The first section of code is defining the database credentials. (In a production system, there would obviously be a more secure and flexible way of providing these credentials.) A new userDAO is created. The first bit of information requested is the first user. Now you have an array with all of the details from the user entity with a primary key of 1. Next, an update is defined. The user entity with an id of 1 will have its first name updated to "aaron." Finally, an array is built of all the users that contain a first name of "Aaron."

In order to reduce repetition and give an abstract layer to data, creating an object based on the Data Access Object is best practice.

6

Decorator Pattern

One of the scariest phrases a programmer can hear is "This is a living requirements document." The client specifies that development needs to begin and continue throughout the requirements-gathering and specification creation phases. Even after these are complete, chances are that the client will come back and ask for just a few tweaks here and there. Since those changes seem small to the client, they do not expect the timeline for deployment to change with the addition of the enhancements. If not handled correctly, even these small tweaks can generate headaches. Whenever base functionality needs to be modified slightly, the Decorator Design Pattern is the optimal pick.

Name: Decorator

The Decorator Design Pattern is best suited for altering or decorating portions of an existing object's content or functionality without modifying the structure of the original object.

Problem and Solution

When just beginning to learn about Object Oriented Programming, the first hurdle usually is understanding the parent-child relationship through inheritance. As time goes on, this method of programming becomes more familiar and easy. When faced with new challenges, even seasoned object-oriented programmers can jump immediately to extending an object to add more functionality. However, as with everything that is great, it's only healthy when used in moderation.

There is a limit to the amount of class hierarchy that a code base should have. If objects start requiring too many children to become functional, the code sacrifices both programmer comprehension and maintainability. Generally, I try not to ever have more than three parent-child relationships for one object. I find when more parent-child relationships are created, the code starts to become confusing and unwieldy. Besides, printing a UML diagram representation of any object in your application hopefully should not require legal-sized paper.

Another reason to be careful when generating complex class hierarchies is PHP's limitation of extending only one class. If a more comprehensive extension model existed in PHP, there might be less chance of creating unwieldy object relationships.

I don't wish to deter you from the usage of class extension, however. There are many times when the proper solution to the problem is extending the object. Even some examples of Design Patterns in this book require objects to be extended. However, for some problems, classes based on the Decorator Design Pattern are a much better solution.

The Decorator Design Pattern fits a niche in which programmers find themselves spending a lot of their time: quick and small changes with little impact to the rest of the application. The goal of a class designed with the Decorator Design Pattern is to apply incremental changes to a base object without having to overwrite any of the existing functionality. Decorators are built in such a way that one or more should be able to be inserted directly into the main code execution stream, modify or "decorate" their target object, and affect no other code stream.

Some programmers suggest that objects based on the Decorator Design Pattern are best made by extending existing objects. The Decorator then provides additional methods or possibly rewrites existing methods. This not only borders on some of the base concepts of an Adaptor Design Pattern, but it really does undo one of the main purposes of the Decorator Design Pattern. Decorators can provide a quick, noninvasive modification to the content or functionality of an object without modifying the structure of the object. In this particular case, extending an object adds additional functionality and modifies that base structure. The main code stream has to be modified in all places that require that new functionality to include the new child class. The instantiation of that parent needs to be replaced with the child's class name instead.

One situation where the Decorator Design Pattern can be useful is passing user input to external systems. Imagine a process that uploads a user's file, associates the user internally in a database to the proper user ID, and finally deposits them on a network storage device. The file system on the network storage device allows mixed case filenames, so this process is pretty simple. Later, a new network storage device is introduced with a legacy file system. This requires all filenames to exist in uppercase only. When files are physically moved to the drive, this happens automatically. However, internally, the object is still storing the mixed-case filename. The tight coupling is gone and may cause instability in the system.

The best solution for this scenario is to introduce an object based on the Decorator Design Pattern. This object modifies the user file management object directly after each file moves to the physical storage space but before the information logs to the database. Passing a reference to the object allows the Decorator to modify the internal data, rewriting each filename into uppercase. Then, the user file management object continues to process the data insertion. It is very important to notice that the base object structure is not modified at all by introducing this new requirement and Decorator solution.

Another example of a good time to use a Decorator Design Pattern based object is when processing blog output. Generally, a standard set of markup conditions exists: changing image links to actual images, finding links and turning them into clickable anchors, and applying visual styles such as bold or italics. If the blog content becomes more specialized, it may require additional items to be captured and modified. Extra features could be added to form a better user experience. Examples of these decorations include changing an address into a clickable link to a map and applying a style to a brand name to fit into an advertising theme. Adding so many features in this way would make a class's hierarchical architecture way too large. These small modifications can best be executed by creating those objects based on the Decorator Design Pattern.

When requirements are introduced that require small changes to the content or functionality of an application without compromising the stability of the existing code base, it is best practice to create a Decorator object.

UML

This Unified Modified Language (UML) diagram details a class design using the Decorator Design Pattern (see Figure 6-1).

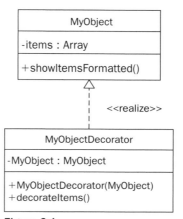

Figure 6-1

Note the following about this figure:

❏ The `MyObject` is the base class with the existing functionality. It contains a public array named items and a public method named `showItemsFormatted()`.

❏ `showItemsFormatted()` is responsible for taking the items array, formatting them using predefined functionality, and presenting output.

❏ The `MyObjectDecorator` class contains a private instance of `MyObject` and two public methods, named `MyObjectDecorator()` and `decorateItems()`.

❏ The `MyObjectDecorator()` method represents the constructor. It takes a parameter of type `MyObject` and stores it internally.

❏ The `decorateItems()` method modifies the items array of the `MyObject` instance.

Code Example

In this example, the application is processing compact discs (CDs). It must have a method to add tracks to the CD and a way to show the track list from the CD. The client has specified that the CD track list should be displayed in a single line with each track being prefixed by the track number.

```
class CD
{
    public $trackList;

    public function __construct()
    {
        $this->trackList = array();
    }

    public function addTrack($track)
    {
        $this->trackList[] = $track;
    }

    public function getTrackList()
    {
        $output = '';

        foreach ($this->trackList as $num=>$track) {
            $output .= ($num + 1) . ") {$track}. ";
        }

        return $output;
    }
}
```

The CD class contains a public variable called $trackList, which will store an array of tracks added to the CD object. The constructor initializes this variable. The addTrack() method simply adds a track to the CD object's trackList array. Finally, the getTrackList() method loops through each of the tracks on the CD and compiles them into a single string in the format that was specified.

To use this CD object, the following code is executed:

```
$tracksFromExternalSource = array('What It Means', 'Brr', 'Goodbye');

$myCD = new CD();

foreach ($tracksFromExternalSource as $track) {
    $myCD->addTrack($track);
}

print "The CD contains
```

This works fine for this example. However, the requirements have changed slightly. Now, each track in the output needs to be in uppercase for just this instance of output. Because its best practice not to modify the base class or create a new parent-child relationship for such small changes, an object based on the Decorator Design Pattern is created.

```
class CDTrackListDecoratorCaps
{
    private $__cd;

    public function __construct(CD $cd)
```

```
    {
        $this->__cd = $cd;
    }

    public function makeCaps()
    {
        foreach ($this->__cd->trackList as &$track)
        {
            $track = strtoupper($track);
        }
    }
}
```

The class CDTrackListDecoratorCaps is very simple. The __construct() method simply adds the instance of the CD class to an internal private variable named $__cd. While, initially, this may seem cryptic and maybe even an impossible way to modify the base object by a true Decorator, PHP's handling of objects by reference makes it possible. Even though the instance is stored internally and privately, any modifications to it will immediately be available to the main code flow.

The makeCaps() method exists in the decorator to perform the decoration or modification that is needed. In this case, it loops through each of the tracks and executes PHP's strtoupper() function on them.

To add the Decorator to the mix, the new CDTrackListDecoratorCaps class is added:

```
$myCD = new CD();

foreach ($tracksFromExternalSource as $track) {
    $myCD->addTrack($track);
}

$myCDCaps = new CDTrackListDecoratorCaps($myCD);
$myCDCaps->makeCaps();

print "The CD contains the following tracks: " . $myCD->getTrackList();
```

Only two additional lines were added to the main code flow to accomplish this small change. $myCDCaps is created by instantiating CDTrackListDecoratorCaps with a reference to the existing CD object. Next, the functionality is executed by calling the makeCaps() function.

To make small modifications to content or functionality of existing objects without modifying their structure, the Decorator Design Pattern should be used.

7

Delegate Pattern

One of the strongest features of Object Oriented Programming is its dynamic nature. With today's push of more available features, mash-ups and constantly evolving standards, dynamic code is gaining a whole new meaning. Whether its new file storage or streaming standards, a new social networking site or a fresh take at some of the existing Internet pioneer's APIs, web programming continues to mutate. Legacy ways of handling decisions are no longer effective when confronted with the enormous number of options available today. The Delegate Design Pattern is made for taking complex decisions out of the loop by moving smart objects into their place.

Name: Delegate

The Delegate Design Pattern removes decisions and complex functionality from the core object by distributing or delegating them to other objects.

Problem and Solution

Most PHP programmers have started out working with a very procedural type of programming. This style of programming relies heavily on flow control based on conditional statements. Object Oriented Programming provides some avenues to move beyond traditional conditional statements to create a more polymorphic code stream. One of the ways to implement this is by creating objects based on the Delegate Design Pattern.

The Delegate Design Pattern focuses on removing complexity from core objects. Instead of designing an object to rely heavily on executing specific functionality by evaluating a conditional statement, the object can delegate the decision to different objects. This can be as simple as having an intermediate object to process the decision tree to as complex as having objects instantiated dynamically to provide the desired functionality.

It is important not to view the Delegate Design Pattern as a direct competitor to the conditional statement. Instead, the Delegate Design Pattern helps form the architecture in such a way that conditional statements aren't needed to invoke the proper functionality. They're encouraged to reside in the actual methods, where they can be tasked to process business rules.

An example of when the Delegate Design Pattern should be used is when providing multiple formats for a specific piece of data. Imagine an archive at an open source code repository. When the visitor intends to download a portion of that code, they have the choice of two compression methods. The files are compressed and then sent to the browser. In this particular example, I'm going to refer to .zip and .tgz files.

Traditionally, a file collection and downloading object would be made. It would have methods to gather together the requested files and store references to them internally. Then, a method named specifically for that type of compression might be called. If the type was ".zip," the generateZip() method would be called.

Objects based on the Delegate Design Pattern should be used instead of these custom-named functions. The generateZip() method's functionally should be transferred to a Delegate class that executes that functionality against the base object's file list. This not only reduces the complexity of the base object, but it also provides greater maintainability of the code. If the future brings a new compression type such as .dmg, only a new Delegate object needs to be created. The stable base object does not need to be edited.

When an object contains individual portions of complex but independent functionality that must be executed based on a decision, it is best practice to use objects based on the Delegate Design Pattern.

UML

This Unified Modified Language (UML) diagram details a class design using the Delegate Design Pattern (see Figure 7-1).

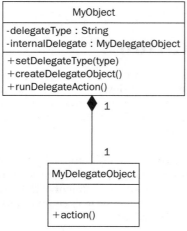

Figure 7-1

Looking at this figure, you'll note that:

❑ The base class `MyObject` is aware that it will be using objects based on the Delegate Design Pattern. It contains a private string `delegateType` and a private instance of `MyDelegateObject`, called `internalDelegate`.

❑ The `setDelegateType()` method receives a parameter named type. This is stored in the `delegateType` string.

❑ The `createDelegateObject()` method will create an instance of a delegate object named after the `delegateType` variable. It then stores the instance internally by assigning it to `internalDelegate`.

❑ The `runDelegateAction()` method is responsible for running the `action()` method of the `internalDelegate` object.

❑ `MyDelegateObject` contains the logic responsible for this particular action. The `action()` method is run by `MyObject` to accomplish the feature.

Code Example

This particular website has a feature to create playlists from MP3 files. These could come from the visitor's hard drive or from locations on the Internet. The visitor has the choice to download the playlist in either M3U or PLS format. (The code example will only show the creation of the playlist for brevity.)

The first step is to create the `Playlist` class:

```php
class Playlist
{
    private $__songs;

    public function __construct()
    {
        $this->__songs = array();
    }

    public function addSong($location, $title)
    {
        $song = array('location'=>$location, 'title'=>$title);
        $this->__songs[] = $song;
    }

    public function getM3U()
    {
        $m3u = "#EXTM3U\n\n";

        foreach ($this->__songs as $song) {
            $m3u .= "#EXTINF:-1,{$song['title']}\n";
            $m3u .= "{$song['location']}\n";
        }
```

```
            return $m3u;
        }

    public function getPLS()
    {
        $pls = "[playlist]\nNumberOfEntries=" . count($this->__songs) . "\n\n";

        foreach ($this->__songs as $songCount=>$song) {
            $counter = $songCount + 1;
            $pls .= "File{$counter}={$song['location']}\n";
            $pls .= "Title{$counter}={$song['title']}\n";
            $pls .= "Length{$counter}=-1\n\n";
        }

        return $pls;
    }
}
```

The `Playlist` object stores an array of songs, which is initialized by the constructor.

The `addSong()` public method accepts two parameters, a location of the MP3 file and the title of the file. These are formed into an associative array and then added to the internal songs array.

The requirements state that the playlist must be available in both M3U and PLS formats. For this, the `Playlist` class has two methods, `getM3U()` and `getPLS()`. Each of them is responsible for creating the proper header to the playlist file and looping through the internal song array to complete the playlist. Then, each function returns the playlist in string format.

The current code stream to execute this functionality contains the familiar `if`/`else` clause:

```
$playlist = new Playlist();
$playlist->addSong('/home/aaron/music/brr.mp3', 'Brr');
$playlist->addSong('/home/aaron/music/goodbye.mp3', 'Goodbye');

if ($externalRetrievedType == 'pls') {
    $playlistContent = $playlist->getPLS();
}
else {
    $playlistContent = $playlist->getM3U();
}
```

A new instance of the `Playlist` object is created. Two song locations and titles are added. Then, an `if`/`else` clause is created. If the type is "pls," the `getPLS()` method is executed and its output is put into the `$playlistContent`. Otherwise, the `$externalRetrievedType` probably contains "m3u," which is caught by the `else` portion of the statement.

The Sales team for this website found out about five more playlist formats that are available. Consequently, they started selling the features of the software before it was even created. At this point, the programmers still don't know which new playlist formats were sold.

In the meantime, the code can be modified to use the Delegate Design Pattern. The aim is to eliminate that potentially unwieldy if/else statement. Also, as more formats are added, the initial Playlist class could become extremely large.

The newPlaylist class is aware of the fact that it will be using the Delegate Design Pattern. PHP's ability to dynamically create class instances based on a variable will also be helpful.

```php
class newPlaylist
{
    private $__songs;
    private $__typeObject;

    public function __construct($type)
    {
        $this->__songs = array();
        $object = "{$type}Playlist";
        $this->__typeObject = new $object;
    }

    public function addSong($location, $title)
    {
        $song = array('location'=>$location, 'title'=>$title);
        $this->__songs[] = $song;
    }

    public function getPlaylist()
    {
        $playlist = $this->__typeObject->getPlaylist($this->__songs);
        return $playlist;
    }
}
```

The constructor of the newPlaylist object now accepts the $type parameter. In addition to initializing the internal songs array, the constructor now dynamically creates a new instance of the specified delegate from $type and stores it internally in the $__typeObject variable.

The addSongs() method is the same as the initial Playlist object. The getM3U() and getPLS() methods are replaced by the getPlaylist() method. This method executes the getPlaylist() method of the internally stored delegate object. It passes the song array to that object so that that object can create and return the proper playlist.

The two methods previously part of the Playlist object have been moved to their own delegate objects:

```php
class m3uPlaylistDelegate
{
    public function getPlaylist($songs)
    {
        $m3u = "#EXTM3U\n\n";

        foreach ($songs as $song) {
            $m3u .= "#EXTINF:-1,{$song['title']}\n";
```

```
                $m3u .= "{$song['location']}\n";
            }

            return $m3u;
        }
    }

    class plsPlaylistDelegate
    {
        public function getPlaylist($songs)
        {
            $pls = "[playlist]\nNumberOfEntries=" . count($songs) . "\n\n";

            foreach ($songs as $songCount=>$song) {
                $counter = $songCount + 1;
                $pls .= "File{$counter}={$song['location']}\n";
                $pls .= "Title{$counter}={$song['title']}\n";
                $pls .= "Length{$counter}=-1\n\n";
            }

            return $pls;
        }
    }
```

Each of the delegate classes is basically just a repackaging of the original methods from the base
Playlist class. Each delegate object has an identical named public method called getPlaylist(),
which accepts the songs parameter. This makes it simple and dynamic for the base object to create and
access any of the delegators.

The code to execute this new delegate-based system is much simpler:

```
$externalRetrievedType = 'pls';

$playlist = new newPlaylist($externalRetrievedType);
$playlistContent = $playlist->getPlaylist();
```

When the additional playlist formats are announced, new classes based on the Delegate Design Pattern
can be created without having to modify this code.

To remove complexity from the core object while making the process dynamic to add more functionality,
the Delegate Design Pattern should be used.

8

Façade Pattern

If application programming were simple, anyone could do it. There would be no need for books like this, software development would be even less glamorous, and the industry would need to evolve to a different business model to survive. But programming is not simple. It is actually quite complex. While acknowledging this complexity, superior programmers strive to simplify their systems. They opt to remove complexity at every chance, using any available Design Pattern, including the Façade Design Pattern. When they hear the term *façade*, most people will picture the false fronts of older buildings. Others may think of a sly person putting up a façade in a potentially difficult situation. The façade is this person's attempt to deceive those around them. The person's actions, feelings or reactions seem very simple, hiding the complexity they may be experiencing. In the same way, the Façade Design Pattern is designed to make dealing with complex components appear deceptively simple.

Name: Façade

The Façade Design Pattern hides complexity from a calling object by creating a simple façade interface in front of the collection of required logic and methods.

Problem and Solution

A reoccurring theme throughout this book seems to be making an effort to remove complexity from the code. But, it's not necessarily complexity in code that we're trying to remove. It's the coupling of different objects that is the aim of this simplicity. Project architects should tip their hat to the programmer of a complex subsystem, appreciate its complexity, quality, and execution, and then plug it into their overall project. As interior component logic becomes more complex, however, the exterior interaction seems to follow suit. The goal of the Façade Design Pattern is to rein in the exterior intricacies and provide a simple interface to harness the power of said component. What makes the Façade Design Pattern unique is that it's designed to combine or couple multiple related components into that simple usable interface.

Put into more practical terms, Façade Design Pattern–based classes may provide a public interface to execute a logical business request. This individual business request may require multiple technical logic steps to be executed in order to complete. Business processes are not always as simple as their name implies. For example, the process may be titled "Make Shared Files Available on Network." From their point of view, the programmer knows that they must execute the following technical processes: "Create File Share," "Move File to File Share," and "Apply Proper Permissions to File." The Façade Design Pattern provides that interface called "Make Shared Files Available on Network" by calling each one of those technical requirements first.

Another reason to use objects based on the Façade Design Pattern is to interface with third-party solutions. Remember, it is continually stressed that the object-oriented project should be just a collection of related objects. Because of this architecture, the lead programmer may find it more prudent to use a third-party object.

Imagine providing a search web page for an application. This search page first searches all of the data it has available itself for the search term. If there are fewer than 10 results, it makes a call to a third-party service, such as Google, to retrieve additional results. These results are appended to the bottom of any results the application found internally. The Search Façade object returns the results to the calling view object. Internally, the Search Façade object will call methods to query the internal database. After which, it will determine if it needs to make a web service call to Google. If so, it will also parse those results to make one homogeneous result set to return.

If the benefits of this architecture are not immediately clear, think about the next step of the application's evolution. The Yahoo! search engine begins to return better results than its Google counterpart. The external web service request needs to be modified to call Yahoo!'s API now.

In a traditional approach, every time a request for results was created, the Google API would need to be replaced. However, with a Search Façade object in place, you don't need to modify anything on the calling view object. Instead, a Yahoo! Search class is created. Then, the Search Façade's method is modified to use the Yahoo! Search class instead of the Google Search class.

To hide the complex group of methods and logic required to execute a step of the business process, a class based on the Façade Design Pattern should be used.

UML

This Unified Modified Language (UML) diagram details a class design using the Façade Design Pattern (see Figure 8-1).

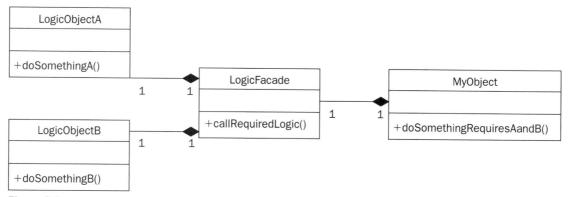

Figure 8-1

For this diagram, note the following:

❏ The MyObject class contains a public method called doSomethingRequiresAandB(). This is just one step in the execution of the MyObject class. doSomethingRequiresAandB() creates a new instance of the object LogicFacade. It calls the public method named callRequiredLogic(), which is named abstractly enough for MyObject.

❏ The callRequiredLogic() method inside the LogicFacade class is then responsible for creating an instance of LogicObjectA and calling the doSomethingA() method. It also is responsible for creating an instance of LogicObjectB and calling the doSomethingB() method.

❏ All of these actions are passed back through the LogicFacade class so that they are available to MyObject.

Code Example

The website passes its inventory to a different system in the company nightly as part of a required audit. This other system will accept the request via a post to its web service. It is an older system, however, and works with only uppercase strings. The code needs to acquire CD objects, apply uppercase to all their properties, and create a well-formed XML document to be posted to the web service.

The following is a simple example of a CD class:

```
class CD
{
    public $tracks = array();
    public $band = '';
    public $title = '';

    public function __construct($title, $band, $tracks)
    {
        $this->title = $title;
        $this->band = $band;
        $this->tracks = $tracks;
    }
}
```

When a new CD is instantiated, the constructor adds the title, band, and track list to the CD object. To build the CD object, the steps are pretty simple:

```
$tracksFromExternalSource = array('What It Means', 'Brrr', 'Goodbye');
$title = 'Waste of a Rib';
$band = 'Never Again';

$cd = new CD($title, $band, $tracksFromExternalSource);
```

To format the CD object for the external system, two additional classes will be created. The first one will be used to prepare the properties of the CD object. The required format is uppercase. The other class will be responsible for building an XML document out of the CD object. This class will return a string of the entire document.

> It is important to note that two classes will be created for maximum reusability. It may be tempting to combine both of these steps into one class, but that may require uncoupling in the future.

```
class CDUpperCase
{
    public static function makeString(CD $cd, $type)
    {
        $cd->$type = strtoupper($cd->$type);
    }

    public static function makeArray(CD $cd, $type)
    {
        $cd->$type = array_map('strtoupper', $cd->$type);
    }
}

class CDMakeXML
{
    public static function create(CD $cd)
    {
        $doc = new DomDocument();

        $root = $doc->createElement('CD');
        $root = $doc->appendChild($root);

        $title = $doc->createElement('TITLE', $cd->title);
        $title = $root->appendChild($title);

        $band = $doc->createElement('BAND', $cd->band);
        $band = $root->appendChild($band);

        $tracks = $doc->createElement('TRACKS');
        $tracks = $root->appendChild($tracks);

        foreach ($cd->tracks as $track) {
            $track = $doc->createElement('TRACK', $track);
```

```
            $track = $tracks->appendChild($track);
        }

        return $doc->saveXML();
    }
}
```

The `CDUpperCase` object has two public static methods. The first one, named `makeString()`, accepts the CD object and a string parameter called `$type`. It simply applies the `strtoupper()` PHP function to the CD instance's public variable, named after the content of `$type`. The other method, named `makeArray()`, functions similarly to `makeString()`. It applies the `strtoupper()` method to each of the items in the CD object's public array, named after the content of `$type`, using the `array_map()` function. Since the CD object is passed in by reference in PHP, no return variables are defined. This dynamic execution of each of these methods allows this class to be used in the future in case the CD expands to include more public properties.

The `CDMakeXML` object has only one public static method, named `create()`. This accepts the CD object and is responsible for returning a fully formed XML document from the CD content. Simply, it creates elements for the title, band, and tracks using uppercase tag names.

At first glance, the programmer may want to implement the functionality in this way:

```
CDUpperCase::makeString($cd, 'title');
CDUpperCase::makeString($cd, 'band');
CDUpperCase::makeArray($cd, 'tracks');
print CDMakeXML::create($cd);
```

While this is one way to solve the problem, it is not the best way. Instead, a `Façade` object should be made for the web service call:

```
class WebServiceFacade
{
    public static function makeXMLCall(CD $cd)
    {
        CDUpperCase::makeString($cd, 'title');
        CDUpperCase::makeString($cd, 'band');
        CDUpperCase::makeArray($cd, 'tracks');

        $xml = CDMakeXML::create($cd);

        return $xml;
    }
}
```

The `WebServiceFacade` object has only one public static method, called `makeXMLCall()`. This accepts the CD object and returns an XML document. The steps used to create the XML document previously were just moved into this `Façade`'s method. Now, instead of the four lines listed previously, only one is needed:

```
print WebServiceFacade::makeXMLCall($cd);
```

When the next step in the application process contains many complex logical steps and method calls, it is best practice to create an object based on the Façade Design Pattern.

9

Factory Pattern

The largest `switch`/`case` statement I've ever seen in an object-oriented program had more than 20 conditions. Upon execution, this block of code was executed one time for each condition. Each condition was responsible for creating a new object. This object was used to communicate with external consumers of the application's API. After performing some routine troubleshooting on one of the classes, I investigated the interface it implemented. To my surprise, each of the classes referenced in that `switch`/`case` statement implemented the same interface! The next time a new condition was being added to that `switch`/`case`, I suggested we move to the Factory pattern. As indicated earlier, the names of Design Patterns are very important. They not only provide uniformity to referencing each Design Pattern, but they also key into what the pattern exactly does. In the case of the code I was looking at, the Factory Design Pattern was a perfect match for this assembly line of class creation.

Name: Factory

The Factory Design Pattern provides a simple interface to acquire a new instance of an object, while sheltering the calling code from the steps to determine which base class is actually instantiated.

Problem and Solution

As PHP continues to grow and evolve as a language, its features continue to provide easier avenues for development, using proven Design Patterns. One feature of PHP that has been particularly helpful is the ability to create new instances of classes based on the content of a variable. This dynamic approach to object instantiation is one of the building blocks of my approach to the Factory Design Pattern in PHP.

Classes based on the Factory Design Pattern help reduce conditionally based complexity in the main code stream. Throughout applications, objects are called in many different ways. Changing just one thing about an object's creation can cause ripples through the rest of the application. Think of instantiating one of five objects to perform some sort of functionality. One method would be to create a conditional to determine which object to instantiate. This might be a complex if/else statement or a switch/case statement. This functionality can be used in many places in the application but can cause code duplication. Then, add a sixth object to the mix or change the name of one of the existing five, and all instances of this code need to be modified and tested again. The Factory Design Pattern helps eliminate this headache by providing a simple interface to create any of these objects. The way the Factory object is called stays the same no matter if objects are changed or other objects are added.

A practical example of this can be observed when showing a blog entry. This particular blog is very popular and has many different ways of providing its content to consumers. These include the standard web browser, RSS feed, mobile delivery, and the REST API. The code stream or controller that actually retrieves the proper blog entry does not need to be concerned with the view that is being consumed. It simply will request a new view object from the view creation Factory. Once it has that instance of that view object, it can pass the article object into the view. Finally, it calls the rendering method that executes the view object. Throughout the whole process, because of the usage of that Factory object, the main code stream does not have to deal with figuring out which is the right view object to create. It blindly calls the Factory and is presented with the correct object to work with.

The creation of different objects is not the only thing that the Factory Design Pattern can be used for, however. Another reason to use a class based on the Factory Design Pattern is when you are working with collections of items. In this case, the collection of objects consists of the same base object, but each object has different characteristics.

A great example of using a Factory class to manage a collection of objects is an inventory system. A music shop may have an application that shows its guitar inventory. The view was originally created to work with a single guitar object to determine its brand and model, its color, and the number of strings. To show multiple results in the inventory, a Guitars Factory object could be used. It could accept a collection of IDs from the database on instantiation. It would then have a public method called getGuitar(). This would return a guitar object created from a single ID. In this case, the Factory continually creates a new guitar object from the collection and returns them uniformly using a public method.

When you need steps to determine which type of object to create, you should use a class based on the Factory Design Pattern to retrieve the new instance.

UML

This Unified Modified Language (UML) diagram details a class design using the Factory Design Pattern (see Figure 9-1).

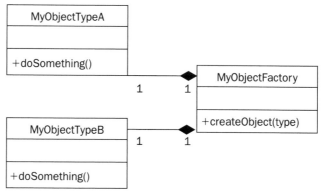

Figure 9-1

Note the following about this figure:

❑ Two base classes exist: `MyObjectTypeA` and `MyObjectTypeB`. Both have a public method called `doSomething()`, which executes the logic of that object in its own unique way. Their public interfaces and return types are identical.

❑ The `MyObjectFactory` class exists to create an instance of either one of these base classes and return it to the code stream. `MyObjectFactory` has one public method, named `createObject()`. This accepts a parameter called `type`. This helps determine which of the two base classes should be created. The `createObject()` method then returns an instance of the requested type class.

Code Example

For the mastering process of a CD, the application needs to compile the required information into the CD object. This object will be passed on to an external vendor, who will process the actual CD creation. The CD object needs to contain the title, the band name, and the track list.

This simple CD class contains methods to add the title, band, and track list:

```
class CD
{
    public $title = '';
    public $band = '';
    public $tracks = array();

    public function __construct()
    {}

    public function setTitle($title)
    {
        $this->title = $title;
    }

    public function setBand($band)
```

```
    {
        $this->band = $band;
    }

    public function addTrack($track)
    {
        $this->tracks[] = $track;
    }
}
```

In order to make a complete CD object, the process is always the same. Create an instance of the CD class, then add the title, band name, and track list:

```
$title = 'Waste of a Rib';
$band = 'Never Again';
$tracksFromExternalSource = array('What It Means', 'Brrr', 'Goodbye');

$cd = new CD();
$cd->setTitle($title);
$cd->setBand($band);
foreach ($tracksFromExternalSource as $track) {
    $cd->addTrack($track);
}
```

Some artists are now releasing additional content on their CDs that can be used on the computer. These CDs are called enhanced CDs. The first track written to the disc is a data track. The mastering software recognizes the data track by its label of 'DATA TRACK' and will create the CD accordingly.

The enhancedCD class is similar to the regular CD class. It has the same public methods. However, it does add the first track to the disc in the constructor automatically:

```
class enhancedCD
{
    public $title = '';
    public $band = '';
    public $tracks = array();

    public function __construct()
    {
        $this->tracks[] = 'DATA TRACK';
    }

    public function setTitle($title)
    {
        $this->title = $title;
    }

    public function setBand($band)
```

```
        {
            $this->band = $band;
        }

        public function addTrack($track)
        {
            $this->tracks[] = $track;
        }
    }
```

After seeing these similarities and recognizing that there are only two possible CD types, it may be tempting to just create a conditional statement. If the type is an enhanced CD, create a new instance of the enhancedCD class. Otherwise, create the generic CD class. However, there is a better solution. The Factory Design Pattern should be used.

The CDFactory class uses PHP's ability to dynamically instantiate a class from a variable. The create() method accepts the type of class requested and returns a new instance of it:

```
    class CDFactory
    {
        public static function create($type)
        {
            $class = strtolower($type) . "CD";

            return new $class;
        }
    }
```

Now, the class creation and execution is changed to reflect the usage of the Factory class:

```
    $type = 'enhanced';

    $cd = CDFactory::create($type);
    $cd->setBand($band);
    $cd->setTitle($title);
    foreach ($tracksFromExternalSource as $track) {
        $cd->addTrack($track);
    }
```

The last thing one might consider is the name of the existing CD class. To make it uniform, it may make sense to change its name to standardCD. Make sure that this won't damage other functionality anywhere else in the code. It would be best to change any new instantiation of the CD to use the CDFactory class.

When requesting an instance of a class that requires some logic and steps to determine its base, it is best practice to use a class based on the Factory Design Pattern.

10

Interpreter Pattern

Whether you loved or hated math class, those concepts equipped you to be where you are now. Even as early as algebra, core ideas were absorbed preparing you for your programming career. Algebra revolves around using variables to hold unknowns. Substituting values into the equation provided an interpretation of the variables to obtain the final result. Programming languages, like PHP, provide another form of interpretation. PHP generally is referred to as an interpreted language because its core installation does not compile the code ahead of time. PHP has also been referred to as a templating language. As more elaborate applications are created, this templating and interpreting becomes more advanced. More often than not, this template approach exists to allow the team to create entities in a less technical and complex way. The Interpreter Design Pattern is made to review these entities and provide a replacement for or interpretation of them to that template.

Name: Interpreter

The Interpreter Design Pattern analyzes an entity for key elements and provides its own interpretation or action corresponding to each key.

Problem and Solution

The Interpreter Design Pattern is one of the few extremely common design patterns you may have been using often without realizing it. This style of design is not limited to just the creation of classes. The base concepts of the Interpreter Design Pattern are used throughout most of the programming algorithms created.

To understand how the Interpreter Design Pattern works, consider the processing of a macro language. The commands that are written for each macro are, in themselves, collections of more commands. The shorthand macro language makes it easier for a programmer to create something without having to worry about the exact syntax of other system commands. In some cases, this is also done to boost security: the programmer is not given direct access to the system commands. Instead, wrapper methods are written to execute the system commands in a sort of sandbox. The macro language is interpreted and translated into a set of commands to be executed.

Another way to think of this is by examining a template system. Specific predefined keywords or symbols are defined to represent something else. The template processor takes the code, interprets each keyword to reference a specific set of instructions, and executes those.

Building systems based around the Interpreter Design Pattern allows third parties or users greater flexibility over how to present and retrieve data that the system provides. Instead of predefining method names or specific constants to represent a type of data retrieval, a set of keywords can be used to retrieve that data.

For example, a third-party consuming a web service could dictate the values they wish to retrieve in the order they wish by sending a keyword-laden request. Perhaps this request mimics an XPath query in the way it's constructed. The class based on the Interpreter Design Pattern would then retrieve each bit of information that each key symbolizes in the order in which they were requested. The interpretation of these keywords is done piecemeal; therefore, it does not require a complex set of predefined data set orders. For a CD, the request may be in this form: "band title track4." The interpreter knows to return the band name, the CD title and the title of track number 4 to the requester. The next request could be "track3 title" which would send back the third track's name and the title of the CD.

The most common use of the Interpreter Design Pattern is in PHP/HTML template systems. HTML documents are created with specific placeholders in their body. These placeholders reference a function or property of the processing object or another template or file on the file system. These template systems are used often when working with large collections of similar data, such as user profiles. A base template is created with keywords referencing the user's name, hometown, and picture. The processing class then interprets each one of these keys as a request for user data and acts accordingly. In similar fashion, the header, navigation, and footer information for a website may be duplicated throughout the entire site. The base template is created with a key to be interpreted as the requested page's output. The processing object is responsible for interpreting that key to mark the placement of the current request's output.

Processing requests using keys to reference functionality should be handled by an object created using the Interpreter Design Pattern.

UML

This Unified Modified Language (UML) diagram details a class design using the Interpreter Design Pattern (see Figure 10-1).

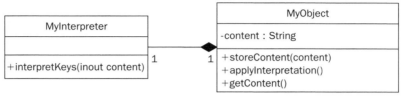

Figure 10-1

Note the following about this diagram:

MyObject deals with content that needs to be interpreted. It has a private string called content to store the content it needs to work with.

The storeContent() method accepts one parameter, named content. This is the content pre-interpretation. It is then stored internally in the MyObject object.

applyInterpretation() is called next. It creates an instance of MyInterpreter. MyInterpreter has one public method named interpretKeys(). This method accepts the parameter named content. applyInterpretation() and passes its internal content to interpretKeys(). The MyInterpreter class executes the interpretation on the content and then returns it to MyObject. Then applyInterpretation() replaces the internal content variable.

MyObject, finally, provides the content via the getContent() after interpretation.

Code Example

The website in this example has decided to jump on the bandwagon to merge the CD buying experience and social networking. Users who sign up for the website can have their own profile page. They'll be able to add advanced functionality like HTML, widgets, and listings of their favorite CDs.

In the first iteration, users can create their profile and add their favorite CD title to their profile. The first piece of functionality is the User class:

```
class User
{
    protected $_username = '';

    public function __construct($username)
    {
        $this->_username = $username;
    }
```

```
            public function getProfilePage()
            {
                //In lieu of getting the info from the DB, we mock here
                $profile = "<h2>I like Never Again!</h2>";
                $profile .= "I love all of their songs. My favorite CD:<br />";
                $profile .= "{{myCD.getTitle}}!!";

                return $profile;
            }
        }
```

Most of the User class is mocked up for this example. When creating an instance of the User class, the username is assigned to the protected $_username variable. In a non-mock example, some logic may be placed here to query the database and initialize the User object with the proper values. The getProfilePage() function is also a mock method. It returns a hard-coded profile. The important portion of this example to note, however, is the {{myCD.getTitle}} string. This represents the template language that will be interpreted later. The getProfilePage() just returns what the user has specified as their profile page.

In order to retrieve CD information for the user, a new object is created, called userCD:

```
        class userCD
        {
            protected $_user = NULL;

            public function setUser($user)
            {
                $this->_user = $user;
            }

            public function getTitle()
            {
                //mock here
                $title = 'Waste of a Rib';

                return $title;
            }
        }
```

Once again, this example is heavily mock based. The setUser() method accepts the user object and stores it internally. It could probably create an instance of a CD object and store it internally in a more robust example. The getTitle() method would retrieve the title from the CD and return it.

It is important to note the similarity between the name of the getTitle() method and the template language that was specified in the user's profile. This will be used by the interpreter class:

```
        class userCDInterpreter
        {
            protected $_user = NULL;

            public function setUser($user)
```

```
        {
             $this->_user = $user;
        }

        public function getInterpreted()
        {
             $profile = $this->_user->getProfilePage();

             if (preg_match_all('/\{\{myCD\.(.*?)\}\}/', $profile,
                 $triggers, PREG_SET_ORDER)) {
                 $replacements = array();

                 foreach ($triggers as $trigger) {
                     $replacements[] = $trigger[1];
                 }

                 $replacements = array_unique($replacements);

                 $myCD = new userCD();
                 $myCD->setUser($this->_user);

                 foreach ($replacements as $replacement) {
                     $profile = str_replace("{{myCD.{$replacement}}}",
                     call_user_func(array($myCD, $replacement)), $profile);
                 }

             }

             return $profile;
        }
    }
```

The userCDInterpreter class contains the setUser() method. This accepts a User object and stores it internally. The only other method of the userCDInterpreter class is the public function named getInterpreted().

❑   First, the getInterpeted() method gets the profile from the User object that is stored internally. Next, it parses the profile for any interpretable key language that can be processed. If any is found, an array of replacements is built. After that, a unique set of replacements is generated.

❑   The next step is to create a new CD based on the userCD object. This object is created, and the User instance is passed into it.

❑   Finally, each of the replacements is looped through. A method named after the content of the $replacement variable belonging to the userCD instance is called. Its output is used to replace the interpreted placeholder in the profile. After each of these interpretations is complete, the profile is returned.

To actually perform this interpretation and generate a templated output is now very simple:

```
$username = 'aaron';

$user = new User($username);
$interpreter = new userCDInterpreter();
$interpreter->setUser($user);

print "<h1>{$username}'s Profile</h1>";
print $interpreter->getInterpreted();
```

The user instance is created, a class based on the Interpreter Design Pattern is created, and the interpretation is executed.

When a set of instructions is referenced by keywords or a macro language, it is best practice to use a class based on the Interpreter Design Pattern.

11

Iterator Pattern

One of the most valuable things a computer can do is execute a repetitive task. Always doing it the same way without becoming "bored" or getting tired, a computer can chug along doing the same thing over and over. This is one of the many reasons why computers became mainstream, affordable, and a staple in the household. Their ability to do simple things repetitively is amazing: anything from simple math to playing music on repeat or helping to correct a misspelled word in this book over and over. Computer programming languages manage repetition through a construction called a loop. Looping is used in almost every program and action now, without our even realizing it. From a programming point of view, however, not all objects are the same when it comes to looping. Some require complicated hash table access. Others can be handled like an array. Because of this complexity in object interface, a common method of looping through items had to be established. This is where the Iterator Design Pattern stands alone.

Name: Iterator

The Iterator Design Pattern helps construct objects that can provide a single standard interface to loop or iterate through any type of countable data.

Problem and Solution

One of the most convincing proofs that these Design Patterns make sense is their appearance in the continued refactoring of any of the older code a programmer creates. I fondly remember creating my first data-driven site. It used flat files to handle the data and was pretty clunky and slow. When I learned MySQL, I migrated all of the data into a few database tables. I still had to write multiple queries to return my data. When I progressed to an object-oriented refactor, I started creating data objects from those MySQL queries. I still created each individual object by hand and then accessed them later. Finally, the last step I remember was creating an object that created objects for a page. It had a method to get the next object from the list. Little did I know it — I was on the edge of actually implementing a Design Pattern: the Iterator Design Pattern.

The Iterator Design Pattern helps fashion objects to handle these collections of data or other objects. When creating a class based on the Iterator Design Pattern, a set of interfaces is created in order to provide a unified approach to managing these collections. For example, some objects dictate the mere creation of themselves as evidence that they are complete and available to the collection. Other objects may require additional building before they are available to be processed as part of the collection. The class based on the Iterator Design Pattern will provide those unified public methods to access the collection. Inside the class, however, logic is applied to determine which object is returned from the collection next.

Sometimes a data set may seem simple. The programmer may not be able to predict a situation where it might change, so he/she opts to leave the code as is and not create an Iterator. This is often the case with calls to the database. MySQL queries are created, and the simple fetch array command is executed. However, leaving a procedural approach like this in the code is not the best solution.

An Iterator object should be created to deal with the MySQL result set. It may be as basic as providing a MySQL query to the class constructor and then looping through the result sets by calling the public methods of the object. Other, more complex, examples of the Iterator may feature additional parameters being sent to the Iterator. Perhaps a different set of MySQL queries is executed, depending on these conditions. No matter what, however, the exterior code stream just deals with the same public methods to obtain the next items in the collection.

Another example of a great use for a class based on the Iterator Design Pattern involves dealing with the file system. Looping through the file system to present a list of available files is a common theme in programming. Examples using this approach include providing a list of files to download and applying plugins dynamically to a modular code base. A class based on the Iterator Design Pattern is created. Next, it accesses the file system and provides the file information back to the calling code. This could be in the form of a string of the file path or perhaps a file object. The Iterator may have logic to help determine which types of files to return. For example, the download page may only want to present Zip files for download, ignoring any of the other meta data and files in the directory. The Plugin system may be looking to include only files ending with ".inc," which is transparently handled by the Iterator. In all cases, that Iterator provides the same public methods to the exterior code stream to retrieve the file information. As mentioned in Chapter 2, the Standard PHP Library has an extensive set of classes based on the Iterator Design Pattern. Visit http://php.net/spl for more information on these classes and interfaces.

With the extensive amount of information available on the Web and the ever-increasing demand to aggregate and present sets of data, programmers are facing new challenges. Now, instead of having just one entity type to loop through and provide in a cumulative view, various other entities are being injected. The Iterator Design Pattern provides a welcome tool for this challenge.

Imagine a scenario in which a social networking site wants to display user status changes publicly to a web page. Every minute, it runs a cycle that retrieves all of the status changes from the database. An Iterator object is created to loop through each of these status changes and provide useful information such as user ID and status content.

A new way of updating the status is introduced. This comes in the form of txt messages added to a queue. Now, in addition to querying the database, the txt message queue also needs to be checked and looped through. A new Iterator can be created to handle the txt messages. Now, after one Iterator is finished returning content, a new one can be created dynamically, like the txt message iterator, and provided to that external code stream. Because of the objects created from the Iterator Design Pattern and their common public methods, no other code needs to be modified.

When dealing with countable data that needs to be traversed, creating an object based on the Iterator Design Pattern is the best solution.

UML

This Unified Modified Language (UML) diagram details a class design using the Iterator Design Pattern (see Figure 11-1).

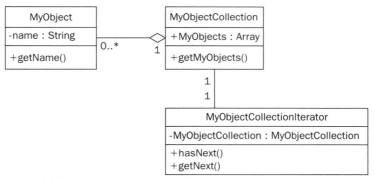

Figure 11-1

For the figure, note that:

❑ MyObject is the base object, which can be collected into countable collections. MyObject has a private string called name. This is used to represent the uniqueness of that particular object. The public method getName() provides the interface to determine what the name of the object is by retrieving it from the private name.

❑ MyObjectCollection represents a class that manages collections of the object MyObject. The MyObjects array holds the collection of the objects. getMyObjects() provides the logic to create the collection and store the objects in the MyObject array.

❑ The MyObjectCollectionIterator provides the interface to iterate over the objects stored in the MyObjectCollection. It has two public methods. hasNext() will let the caller know if there is another item left in the MyObjectCollection collection of MyObjects. The getNext() method will return the next MyObject from the array in MyObjectCollection.

Code Example

Part of the example website's job is to show all the CDs from a particular artist or band. This information is stored in a MySQL database. Some visitors may want to search the database by the band name and get a summary of all the CDs that particular artist has released. This is the perfect example of the Iterator Design Pattern in practice.

First, our semi-standard CD class:

```
class CD
{
    public $band = '';
    public $title = '';
    public $trackList = array();

    public function __construct($band, $title)
    {
        $this->band = $band;
        $this->title = $title;
    }

    public function addTrack($track)
    {
        $this->trackList[] = $track;
    }
}
```

In this example of the CD class, you're using public variables for the band, title, and track list. The constructor creates the instance and assigns the band and title internally. The addTrack() function accepts the $track variable and uses that to add to the track list.

The next class to make is the Iterator. In this example, the SPL Iterator is being implemented. Because of that, you're required to have the current(), key(), rewind(), next(), and valid() public methods.

```
class CDSearchByBandIterator implements Iterator
{
    private $__CDs = array();
    private $__valid = FALSE;

    public function __construct($bandName)
    {
        $db = mysql_connect('localhost', 'user', 'pass');
        mysql_select_db('test');

        $sql = "select CD.id, CD.band, CD.title, tracks.tracknum, ";
        $sql = "tracks.title as tracktitle ";
        $sql .= "from CD left join tracks on CD.id=tracks.cid where band='";
        $sql .= mysql_real_escape_string($bandName);
        $sql .= "' order by tracks.tracknum";
        $results = mysql_query($sql);

        $cdID = 0;
        $cd = NULL;

        while ($result = mysql_fetch_array($results)) {
            if ($result['id'] !== $cdID) {
                if (!is_null($cd)) {
                    $this->__CDs[] = $cd;
                }
                $cdID = $result['id'];
```

```
            $cd = new CD($result['band'], $result['title']);
        }

        $cd->addTrack($result['tracktitle']);
    }

    $this->__CDs[] = $cd;
}

public function next()
{
    $this->__valid = (next($this->__CDs) === FALSE) ? FALSE : TRUE;
}

public function rewind()
{
    $this->__valid = (reset($this->__CDs) === FALSE) ? FALSE : TRUE;
}

public function valid()
{
    return $this->__valid;
}

public function current()
{
    return current($this->__CDs);
}

public function key()
{
    return key($this->__CDs);
}
}
```

Compared to most of the classes used in the examples, this one is pretty verbose. However, to properly illustrate the Iterator, especially the implementation of the SPL Iterator, this is necessary. While the code is lengthy, it's not that complex.

The CDSearchByBandIterator class is designed to return an object that can be accessed by using some of the PHP array functions. It is important to note that every Iterator does not need to implement the SPL Iterator. However, in this example, it made the most sense to me.

There are two private variables, $__CDs, which is an array that contains the collection of CD objects, and $__valid, which is used by the array access functions. Basically, this just stores whether there is an available object in the collection to work with.

The __construct() method takes one parameter named $bandName. On instantiation, a connection to the database is created. Then, a query is created to return a MySQL result set of all the CDs and tracks whose band column matches $bandName.

The storage of the CDs and tracks is normalized. This means that for the result set that is retrieved, there will be many rows of the same CD, with the same title but different track names. If the relationship were one row of data to one CD object, a novice programmer might be even more tempted not to create an Iterator object.

Since you're expecting to deal with CD objects, the next portion of the constructor loops through all of the results and creates individual CD objects. Whenever there is a change in the CD ID, which is stored in $cdID, the current CD object stored in $cd is added to the internal result array. Then a new instance is created. After determining if a new CD should be created, the result set's track title is added to that object. The end result, after constructing the CDSearchByBandIterator, is a complete class with an array of CD objects whose band matches the name that was searched.

The public next() and rewind() methods function similarly. First, the matching action using PHP's built-in array methods is executed on the internal instance of $__CDs. If that function is unable to perform that action on the internal array, it will return FALSE. Using a simple conditional, the function is performed, and its result is compared and added to the internal $__valid variable.

The public valid() function is pretty straightforward. Implementing the Iterator class is required. All it does is provide the value of the internal $__valid variable.

The final two public methods are current() and key(). Predictably, they also execute the corresponding internal PHP methods for array access against the internal collection of CD objects.

To use this class, the code is pretty familiar. The CDSearchByBandIterator functions like an array. As it's traversed, it returns the CD objects that the code is expecting.

```php
$queryItem = 'Never Again';

$cds = new CDSearchByBandIterator($queryItem);

print '<h1>Found the Following CDs</h1>';
print '<table><tr><th>Band</th><th>Title</th><th>Num Tracks</th></tr>';
foreach ($cds as $cd) {
    print "<tr><td>{$cd->band}</td><td>{$cd->title}</td><td>";
    print count($cd->trackList) . '</td></tr>';
}
print '</table>';
```

When working with a collection of countable and traversable data, it is best practice to create an object based on the Iterator Design Pattern.

12

Mediator Pattern

Complex intertwined, or "spaghetti," code just doesn't get the respect it deserves. The extensive coupling, managed interdependencies, and monolithic code streams are a testament to the beauty, hard work, and sheer brilliance of the programmer. I can't believe "spaghetti" code gets such a bad rap. Programmers, from novice to experienced, will have picked up on my sarcasm by now. However, very often, this is the mindset that one has to acquire in order to not go crazy when working with a software application. Additional features, scope creep, and too many cooks in the kitchen can lead to this interwoven repository of code. The term *object oriented* seems to be lost. Chances are that this cluster of inseparable code was once a very sleek, fast, and modular system. But similar objects within the system started finding out too much about each other, applying updates to each other, and generally being too tightly coupled. But there is hope. When many similar objects need to accept changes, without being tightly coupled, the Mediator Design Pattern is there to lend a hand.

Name: Mediator

The Mediator Design Pattern is used to develop an object that communicates or mediates changes to a collection of similar objects without them interacting with each other directly.

Problem and Solution

When objects start becoming too tightly coupled, the benefits of Object Oriented Programming start to disappear. While still working with objects, the style begins to shift towards procedural. The code base starts to become monolithic and cumbersome. Before the solutions can be applied, this particular problem needs to be investigated further. It is important to understand the underlying causes. The same problems that the Mediator Design Pattern solves can slowly creep into other instances of the code.

When objects that are not specifically designed to deal with each other start realizing relationships, a problem has begun. Now, there are times when objects are created to work with child objects or collections. This is a perfectly fine architectural choice. However, when interchangeable objects or objects not based on the same framework start to have interdependencies, problems develop — usually when an object is updated or its interface changes or when an update needs to be applied to an object. It may be tempting to add a new method to update similar objects with the same information. However, by adding this method, the object is gaining an understanding of and relationship with another object that it need not be coupled to. The most immediate consequence comes from the other object's public methods changing. Now, not only is the other object being modified, but this unrelated object's method needs to be updated.

Objects based on the Mediator Design Pattern provide a much needed hub for communication between these related but uncoupled objects. A similar but unrelated object gets affected by a change. It mentions that change to the Mediator object. The Mediator object then mediates with all other objects that could accept this change by applying it to them. The initial changed object does not know how many, if any, other objects are acquiring the same change. Other similar objects don't know the source of the update, just that they should apply it themselves.

A human example of this behavior can be demonstrated by the employees and the boss. One employee decides to learn a new skill set at their home by themselves. While they are learning this new skill set, they are not communicating with any other employee. Once finished, they tell the boss about their new skill. The boss decides it's a good idea and notifies all the other employees that they should also learn this new skill set. They go and learn the new skill set in their own way.

Another way to see the Mediator Design Pattern in action might be with a sales system. This sales system is used to sell guitars at a music shop. Each guitar in inventory is accessed by creating a guitar object. On the sales management screen, the owner has the option to apply a discount to that particular guitar. Since vendors tend to run special promotions, the owner also has the ability to select a check mark to apply the discount to all guitars of this brand. If that option is checked, the update is applied normally. However, the Mediator is notified that this change has happened and that it should be applied to every other guitar object.

When changes to a source object should be communicated to other related but uncoupled objects, an object based on the Mediator Design Pattern should be used to manage the updates.

UML

This Unified Modified Language (UML) diagram details a class design using the Mediator Design Pattern (see Figure 12-1), which is described in the following list:

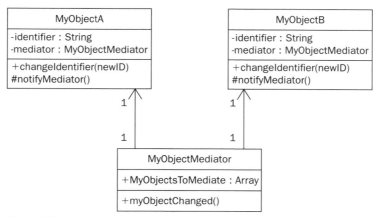

Figure 12-1

❑ Two similar classes exist in this diagram: `MyObjectA` and `MyObjectB`. Both classes appear the same externally. They may differ in their identifier, represented by the private variable named `identifier`. Both function similarly.

❑ During object creation, an instance of `MyObjectMediator` gets stored internally. Then, if a change is requested of the object by calling the public method `changeIdentifer()`, the parameter `newID` is applied to the object by updating the private identifier string. Then, the protected method `notifyMediator()` is called to apply the mediation to the rest of the objects.

❑ `MyObjectMediator` is a hub for a list of objects. These are stored in the array `MyObjectsToMediate`. When `MyObjectMediator` is notified, the `myObjectChanged()` method is executed. This is responsible for parsing the array `MyObjectsToMediate` and applying the change to each of the other objects.

Code Example

The example website allows bands to come in and manage their music collection. It also allows them to update their profile, change information about their band, and update their CD information. Recently, artists were allowed to upload a collection of MP3s as well as ship CDs from the website. Because of this, the website needs to keep CDs and their MP3 counterparts in sync with each other.

The initial version of the website allowed the band to change its band name from the profile page or from an individual CD itself. The CD object had a method that would accept the band change and update it in the database:

```
class CD
{
    public $band = '';
    public $title = '';

    public function save()
```

```
    {
        //stub - writes data back to database - use this to verify
        var_dump($this);
    }

    public function changeBandName($newName)
    {
        $this->band = $newName;
        $this->save();
    }
}
```

This simple class just demonstrates that the CD object can have a band and title. Then, the function changeBandName() takes a new band name parameter. It sets it in the object and then calls the save() method. For demonstration purposes, the save() method is just a stub. You dump the instance to verify that the changes have been made.

With the addition of our MP3 archive, another similar object needs to be created to work with that archive. The artist must also be able to change their band name on the MP3 archive page. The band name must also then change in the CD that is associated with it.

The Mediator Design Pattern should now be used. First, the CD class is modified in order to take advantage of this. Then, the MP3 archive class is created similarly:

```
class CD
{
    public $band = '';
    public $title = '';
    protected $_mediator;

    public function __construct($mediator = null)
    {
        $this->_mediator = $mediator;
    }

    public function save()
    {
        //stub - writes data back to database - use this to verify
        var_dump($this);
    }

    public function changeBandName($newName)
    {
        if (!is_null($this->_mediator)) {
            $this->_mediator->change($this, array('band'=>$newName));
        }
        $this->band = $newName;
        $this->save();
    }
}

class MP3Archive
```

```
{
    public $band = '';
    public $title = '';
    protected $_mediator;

    public function __construct($mediator = null)
    {
        $this->_mediator = $mediator;
    }

    public function save()
    {
        //stub - writes data back to database - use this to verify
        var_dump($this);
    }

    public function changeBandName($newName)
    {
        if (!is_null($this->_mediator)) {
            $this->_mediator->change($this, array('band'=>$newName));
        }
        $this->band = $newName;
        $this->save();
    }
}
```

The first change that was made to the CD object was adding a protected variable called $_mediator. This stores the instance of the Mediator object. The constructor was added. When creating an instance of the CD, a new Mediator object should be passed into the class. Notice, however, that the default value for the variable is null. This allows you to create the object without a Mediator in the instance that you're using it for read-only functionality. It also ensures you don't create infinite loops when using the Mediator object to update the other classes. Next, the changeBandName() method was modified. It checks to see if the Mediator object exists and is not null. If so, it calls the Mediator's change() method, passing in the instance of itself and a keyed array of items that will change.

This happens before the update is applied to the object itself. It's important for the Mediator to get a snapshot of the item before it changes.

The MP3Archive is almost identical to the CD object.

The Mediator needs to be created next:

```
class MusicContainerMediator
{
    protected $_containers = array();

    public function __construct()
    {
        $this->_containers[] = 'CD';
        $this->_containers[] = 'MP3Archive';
    }

    public function change($originalObject, $newValue)
```

```
{
    $title = $originalObject->title;
    $band = $originalObject->band;

    foreach ($this->_containers as $container) {
        if (!($changedObject instanceof $container)) {
            $object = new $container;
            $object->title = $title;
            $object->band = $band;

            foreach ($newValue as $key=>$val) {
                $object->$key = $val;
            }

            $object->save();
        }
    }
}
}
```

The Mediator object knows about each type of Music Container that it will be mediating. The constructor is used to build this internal array of objects it will mediate. In the future, if a new container is created, the only change that is required in this class is to add a new element to the protected $_containers array.

The change method accepts the original object and the new values. First, the title and band name are retrieved from the original object. Next, all of the containers are looped through. If $originalObject is not an instance of that container, that container is created. The reason the container is compared to the original object is to reduce duplication. The changes will be processed to the original object after the mediator is done. A copy of the original object does not need to be created and modified, so it is skipped in the loop.

If the container is created as a new object, the title and band name are set from the original object. Finally, any of the changes from $newValue are looped through and applied to the new object. The object is then saved.

After this whole process, the original object then applies its own updates and saves itself.

To use the new Mediator object, the code is simple:

```
$titleFromDB = 'Waste of a Rib';
$bandFromDB = 'Never Again';

$mediator = new MusicContainerMediator();
$cd = new CD($mediator);
$cd->title = $titleFromDB;
$cd->band = $bandFromDB;

$cd->changeBandName('Maybe Once More');
```

When working with uncoupled objects that have similar properties that need to stay in sync, using an object based on the Mediator Design Pattern is best practice.

13

Observer Pattern

Forming a company around the creation of open source software was something that was largely unheard of a decade ago. Now, there are many successful companies who base their survival on the same open source software that they help to create. They've come up with a business model that works. Imagine what the first few hurdles were when this concept initially came out:

❑   These companies wanted to keep providing open source software and not take over the code base.

❑   They had licensing restrictions to worry about if they continued to work with that particular code base.

❑   Their goal was to keep the community involved. They wanted to provide a vehicle to keep the existing strong group of individuals involved.

These companies possessed a great amount of talent that was familiar with the code base. Because of this, they settled on adding additional features to the application as a way to generate a profit. With each new piece of functionality that is added, however, existing users of the software should not be forced to update the full software package again. But these companies definitely didn't want to provide a forked version of the software either. Finally, it became clear: create a plugin system. That way, the company could continue to develop custom proprietary software for a profit, while encouraging other community members to contribute even more functionality via this avenue. Because of the plugin system, the end users could determine what features they wanted in addition to the core package. When new functionality needs to be added to a code base without the core objects being aware of it, the Observer Design Pattern can be of use.

Name: Observer

The Observer Design Pattern facilitates the creation of objects that watch the state of a target object and provides state targeted functionality that is uncoupled from the core object.

Problem and Solution

The clearest example of the Observer Design Pattern is the plugin system. Because a good portion of the applications that I worked on were managed by a core team of developers, I didn't see many reasons to create a plugin-based code base. In fact, I was quite reluctant to even explore the Observer pattern further. But the plugin system is only the most common example of the Observer Design Pattern in use. There are many other ways to implement it.

The core concept of the Observer Design Pattern solves a very common problem. Software applications continually need new features to stay viable. But, how can additional functionality be added to the application without having to completely refactor some of the core objects? The Observer Design Pattern lays out the blueprint to solve this issue from the object's initial creation.

First, it's important to understand that the Observer Design Pattern is based around state changes. A *state change* is simply an object being transformed from one thing to another. This could be very simple such as an internal method being called that alters the object's properties. It could also be a more involved process such as a complete logic path; for example, balancing an inventory object after selling some merchandise based on another object. In either example, state changes are happening to the object.

The core object that is based on the Observer Design Pattern is responsible for communicating these state changes to other classes that are assigned to observe and understand them. These other observing classes may either take external actions or modify the core object, depending on how they were designed to handle the state communication.

When designing an Observable class, the core object, it is important to communicate very verbosely. On every notable state change, the Observable class should notify any object that is listening that it has changed. It should also include what type of change has occurred. While there might not be any observing class that "cares" now, additional iterations of the software application may add in new functionality that is looking for that specific state change. The observing classes should be configured to take action only on notifications that match their action criteria.

Another thing to remember is that the Observable class, which is generating all of these notifications, doesn't know or care if they're being acted upon. The loose coupling method here allows the Observable class to just perform its logic process from start to finish. Anything that the observing classes are doing is not known by the Observable class, giving the whole group that uncoupled architecture.

As mentioned before, plugin systems are the first example of the Observer Design Pattern that programmers think of. But, as mentioned in the first chapter, PHP is enterprise ready. Message queuing is a big part of larger systems because of their size. Developing classes based on the Observer Design Pattern in PHP can help facilitate this architecture as well.

One very common example of the Observer Design Pattern in practice comes from e-commerce websites. When a visitor purchases a client's item, the sale is applied to the inventory and the stock. The sale process can implement the Observer Design Pattern to watch for successful sales. When a successful sale is completed, not only will the main processing of the credit card and the inventory adjustment be applied, but the sale object will also notify any observers about what item was sold. Clients may have opted to receive an e-mail immediately when an item is sold. They may want to actually ship the item or prepare their own inventory list. The "sale complete" notification is sent to an observing class, which takes the information and sends the e-mail to the client. Not only is this a great way to handle this activity, but it also allows for extensibility of the notification system. Perhaps in the future, clients may want to be notified via a `txt` message. This would be as simple as adding in another observing class. The sales system would not need to be changed.

Another example of the Observer Design Pattern in use involves building a cache. For every new blog post, an entry appears on an RSS feed to be consumed by RSS readers. The first way that novice programmers approach building this RSS feed is by creating a script that searches for the top entries on each load. Then, it formats its results in an RSS document. High-traffic sites will suffer if this design is used. Instead, they build static RSS documents, which also contain expiration information. This creates a nice cacheable system for providing the data to RSS readers. To update that cached RSS resource, an observing class could be used. The successful blog post should notify any observers that it has completed. The observing class will take that information and create a new RSS resource. Then, the cache is updated. This keeps the cache fresh, while also reducing the server's load. Instead of regenerating the cache periodically, even if there are no changes, the cache is updated only when it's observed that it needs to be updated.

When adding features to software that are activated by an action or state change but are loosely coupled, objects based on the Observer Design Pattern should be created.

UML

The following Unified Modified Language (UML) diagram details a class design using the Observer Design Pattern (see Figure 13-1) that is discussed in the following list:

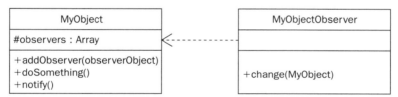

Figure 13-1

❑ `MyObject` is the Observable object. It contains a protected array of observers called `observers`. The public method `addObserver()` takes an instance of an observer and stores it in the array.

❑ The `doSomething()` public method is called. `doSomething()` applies a state change to the `MyObject`. It then calls the `notify()` public method, which loops through the array of observers.

❑ `MyObjectObserver` has a public method called `change()`, which accepts an instance of `MyObject`. This particular observer then does something with the content of the `MyObject`. The `notify()` method of `MyObject` directly calls this method when it encounters it in the array of observers.

Code Example

The music website has some social networking type features available to the visitors of the website. The newest feature to integrate is an activity stream, which shows the most recent purchases on the home page. The hope is that people will click through to recent purchases, possibly buying their own copy.

The first step to putting the sales of CDs into the activity stream is having a CD object that is based on the Observer Design Pattern:

```php
class CD
{
    public $title = '';
    public $band = '';
    protected $_observers = array();

    public function __construct($title, $band)
    {
        $this->title = $title;
        $this->band  = $band;
    }

    public function attachObserver($type, $observer)
    {
        $this->_observers[$type][] = $observer;
    }

    public function notifyObserver($type)
    {
        if (isset($this->_observers[$type])) {
            foreach ($this->_observers[$type] as $observer)
            {
                $observer->update($this);
            }
        }
    }

    public function buy()
    {
        //stub actions of buying

        $this->notifyObserver('purchased');
    }
}
```

The constructor simply assigns the title and band name to the public variables of $title and $band.

The attachObserver() public method takes two parameters. The first is the $type parameter. Because there are many types of state changes that a CD can have, the type of notification is further specialized by having the $type parameter. The second parameter is the Observer class that will be added to the protected $_observers array. Note, the $type variable determines the key of the first level of the array. Then all types of observers of that $type are added to that particular level sequentially.

The public method notifyObserver() accepts one parameter, called $type. This is used to acquire the proper key of the protected $_observers array. Each one of the observers is accessed. Its public update() method is executed with a parameter of the current instance of the object.

The buy() method simply has a stub comment for the process to purchase the CD. Once this is done, the notifyObserver() method is called with the type set to "purchased."

Next, an observer to publish this information to the activity stream is required:

```
class buyCDNotifyStreamObserver
{
    public function update(CD $cd)
    {
        $activity = "The CD named {$cd->title} by ";
        $activity .= "{$cd->band} was just purchased.";
        activityStream::addNewItem($activity);
    }
}
```

This class has one public method, called update(), which accepts the CD instance. It simply builds the content that you'll publish to the stream. It gathers this information from the CD instance.

The last two things to detail are the activityStream class and the way we initiate the CD sale with observers:

```
class activityStream
{
    public static function addNewItem($item)
    {
        //stub functions
        print $item;
    }
}

$title = 'Waste of a Rib';
$band = 'Never Again';
$cd = new CD($title, $band);

$observer = new buyCDNotifyStreamObserver();
$cd->attachObserver('purchased', $observer);

$cd->buy();
```

The activityStream class contains the public method addNewItem(). This simply prints the $item parameter to the screen. In a full example, it might write it to a database or a cacheable XML file.

To execute the sale, the code is pretty straightforward:

1. A new CD is created using the $title and $band.

2. A new observer instance of buyCDNotifyStreamObserver is instantiated. This is added to the CD object by using the attachObserver() method. It is dictated as a "purchased" type of observer.

3. The CD is bought.

When creating objects whose core functionality may contain actionable state changes, creating other classes to interact with the target object based on the Observer Design Pattern is best practice.

14

Prototype Pattern

There is one particular thing that I've been reminded of over and over again while programming in object-oriented languages. This reminder peaks its head above all the rest with its ever-insistent mentions in most books and articles. What is the point that no object-oriented programmer should forget? Keep your objects small, modular, uncoupled, and streamlined. There are two times when one might find contradictory objects, however:

❑　When inheriting code from someone else. Sometimes you just don't have the time or budget to refactor this code into something that you find more acceptable.

❑　When code just can't be slimmed down any further. This is pretty concrete. The expense comes in when this object has to be uniquely created and used multiple times in one code stream.

In situations where a resource intensive object needs to be created often, the Prototype Pattern provides a welcome route to faster execution.

Name: Prototype

The Prototype Design Pattern creates objects in such a way that an initial object or prototype can be copied and cloned more efficiently than creating a new instance.

Problem and Solution

As applications become more advanced, the core objects seem to follow suit. While it still may be a fully modular approach to creating these standard objects, the path to build a proper object has perhaps grown tenfold. Other times the code base is not as perfectly streamlined as the programmer would wish. Either way, some objects start to become expensive to create. The extra time needed to construct this object or the amount of memory it consumes is the expense that should try to be avoided. A good way to recognize this is that it seems like it might be simpler to create a new type of object that mimics the behaviors of a core object without all of the complexity. When it starts becoming obvious that the cost for creating these objects is becoming prohibitive, there are two ways to move forward. The first is refactoring. As alluded to earlier, there might become a point where refactoring is no longer practical or even possible. The other path to investigate involves modifying the objects so that they can be duplicated using the Prototype Design Pattern.

The Prototype Design Pattern maps out a way to reduce the expense of creating complicated objects. It does this not by removing the intricacies of the object itself but by creating an interface to preserve those properties through duplication. The Prototype Design Pattern is useful, especially when complex objects will not change their state throughout the code stream. That is to say, the initial state that they hold when created will always be the same during this one session. However, each individual copy may be able to take on different and individual characteristics. A good example of this would be an object that has rendered a large XML document to protected properties of itself. Further along in the code, some properties may be modified but most of the nodes will stay the same.

The levels of implementation of the Prototype Design Pattern range from simply creating a duplicate to an elaborate cloning method. You may find that some objects' initial state easily translates to a unique version of that object. For others it is more difficult. Imagine an object that has a unique identifier, such as a Globally Unique Identifier (GUID), as a base property. During the duplication process, it won't need to modify every other property. It will need to acquire a new GUID, though.

To understand the actual benefit of using the Prototype Design Pattern, picture a group of employees working in a factory in a sparsely populated area. When the workload increases, new employees are needed. To acquire new workers, the factory needs to train new individuals. The ramp-up time is pretty expensive. During that time, more and more work is queuing. Wouldn't it be easier to just copy one of the hardworking employees into a new worker clone? This is precisely what the Prototype Design Pattern is detailing. That exemplary worker is the Prototype that all new employees should be made from.

A good technical example showing the merits of the Prototype Design Pattern is a Community Library book catalog system. The application may be made for each library in a 50-library system. Each software application is deployed in the same way. The dynamic portion of it is the actual library branch's name and location. This information is stored in an XML file on the file system after deployment. Because this shared group of libraries provides interloan capability, they all need to be aware of which books are checked out. It makes most sense to have this information in one central storage system such as a MySQL database. When a book is viewed by a patron on the system, they can choose to check it out. They may even check out multiple ones. Before they can leave with their books, the system needs to update the central database with the checkout information. The first thing that happens is a prototype book object is created. It grabs the library information from the file system. Then, for each individual book that is in the queue to be checked out, a clone of that initial prototype book object is created. It still has the information from the XML file that was initially retrieved. Then, it receives the custom information, such as the book title or ISBN. The book object based on the Prototype Design Pattern saves queries of the file system to retrieve that information from the XML file. It can be reasonably assumed that during checkout, that information will not change and, therefore, can be applied to the prototype object similarly to a cache.

Another way to understand the benefits of the Prototype Design Pattern is more abstract. Imagine an object that has a significant amount of setters and getters. To build this object requires a painstakingly detailed set of steps. Many different setters need to be called in a particular order to complete the object.

Instead of executing this series of events identically whenever a new object is needed, it may make more sense to build that initial object based on the Prototype Design Pattern. Then, the first instance still retains the labyrinthine composition. Objects that will actually become part of the logic in the main code stream will just be duplicates of that initial prototype, thus reducing the number of times this complex process needs to occur.

When objects whose creation is expensive need to be created multiple times, it may be more efficient to build objects based on the Prototype Design Pattern.

UML

This Unified Modified Language (UML) diagram details a class design using the Prototype Design Pattern (see Figure 14-1). Refer to the following list:

❑ The `MyObject` class has been assembled using the Prototype Design Pattern. It has one public method called `requestClone()`. This method is used to generate a copy of the `MyObject` instance.

❑ The `ClonedObject` object represents a copied instance of the `MyObject` class. Note that, since it is an exact duplicate, it also has the `requestClone()` public method.

❑ Many instances of `ClonedObject` can be created by calling the `requestClone()` method of `MyObject`.

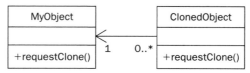

Figure 14-1

Code Example

The music sales website has made a deal with many of the artists on the site to create "mix tapes" of their band's music. Currently, this functionality is restricted to all of the available tracks from only one band. To start creating a variety CD, there are many avenues. The most popular is the option that is available when a visitor is viewing a band's CD page. A link exists to start the process of building a new mix CD. The process sends an ID that corresponds to that specific CD whose band has tracks that will be used.

The first building block of the process is the CD class. Generally, to construct a CD object, the information is retrieved from the database that matches the ID that was requested:

```
class CD
{
    public $band = '';
    public $title = '';
    public $trackList = array();
```

```php
    public function __construct($id)
    {
        $handle = mysql_connect('localhost', 'user', 'pass');
        mysql_select_db('CD', $handle);

        $query = "select band, title, from CDs where id={$id}";

        $results = mysql_query($query, $handle);

        if ($row = mysql_fetch_assoc($results)) {
            $this->band = $row['band'];
            $this->title = $row['title'];
        }
    }

    public function buy()
    {
        //cd buying magic here
        var_dump($this);
    }
}
```

This class has the standard public properties of the $band, $title, and $trackList.

The constructor takes the ID in the form of the $id parameter and executes a query against that database. When that specific CD is found, the band and title are assigned to the public properties $band and $title, respectively.

One additional function named buy() exists. This is simply a stub method to display this instance of the CD for the example. In the production code, this method might be tasked to process the CD and send it off for purchase.

The next class that needs to be created represents the Mix CD entity. This particular object will take advantage of PHP's cloning ability:

```php
class MixtapeCD extends CD
{
    public function __clone()
    {
        $this->title = 'Mixtape';
    }
}
```

Since the MixtapeCD is really just a specialized CD, it extends the CD object.

When PHP's clone command is executed, the magic method __clone() is executed on the object. In the MixtapeCD object, the title property of the initial CD is being overwritten. This MixtapeCD is no longer coupled to a band and title CD combination. It is now still associated with the $band, but has a new title: 'Mixtape.'

This particular example will showcase a user ordering two mixes based on this band:

```
$externalPurchaseInfoBandID = 12;
$bandMixProto = new MixtapeCD($externalPurchaseInfoBandID);

$externalPurchaseInfo = array();
$externalPurchaseInfo[] = array('brrr', 'goodbye');
$externalPurchaseInfo[] = array('what it means', 'brrr');

foreach ($externalPurchaseInfo as $mixed) {
    $cd = clone $bandMixProto;
    $cd->trackList = $mixed;
    $cd->buy();
}
```

The $bandMixProto object is created from a new instance of the MixtapeCD. The parameter $externalPurchaseInfoBandID is passed in to be used in the query that is actually executed from the CD constructor.

Once that Prototype is created, the track lists for the mix CDs that this visitor can be looped through. For each instance of the foreach() loop, $cd is assigned a new clone of the original $bandMixProto. Then, that particular track list is added to the object. Since cloning was used, each new loop does not require a new query to the database. All that information is stored already and is available to the cloned object the same way it was to the original. Finally, the $cd is bought by executing the buy() public method.

When working with objects whose creation is expensive and whose initial configuration stays relatively the same through new instances, using duplicate classes made with the Prototype Design Pattern is best practice.

15

Proxy Pattern

My first foray into the world of AJAX was filled with both exciting triumphs and frustrating moments. I stumbled across this new technology that was going to revolutionize the way that I designed and created my web pages. I was so excited to be able to use this tool to move from web pages to web applications. The first thing I attempted to do was make a mash-up of weather and upcoming bands. I wanted to know if I went to an outdoor show, if I'd need a jacket. I initially designed the project to read the XML feeds using PHP on the server side. Once I knew it could be done, I wanted to migrate the functionality to the browser side so I could take advantage of the cool effects of the AJAX object. As you probably know, I ran into a snag right away. The XML feeds would just not load with my AJAX request. The `XMLHttpRequest` object was not able to load cross-site requests. It wasn't immediately clear to me how I could accomplish retrieving this data from these remote sites. Finally, I came across the solution, which involved designing a proxy PHP object to retrieve the remote data and provide it locally. When working with data and objects that require special attention or access considerations, the Proxy Design Pattern can help.

Name: Proxy

The Proxy Design Pattern builds an object that is positioned transparently within two other objects in order to intercept or proxy the communication or access.

Problem and Solution

The Proxy Design Pattern has always seemed like second nature to me. I remember hiding in my parent's basement, on the old computer, and reading some material about security exploits and penetration testing. The one thing that everyone harped on over and over was to use a proxy. Whenever a security exploit was tested, the use of a proxy was expected to provide a layer of anonymity between the tester and the target system. A proxy, by design, accepts and then retransmits the data it receives. In this case, the hope was that the origin of the test was shadowed by the intermediate usage of proxies.

Other more upright and common implementations of proxies exist, however. Proxy servers, which work as a web resource cache, are in place on some corporate networks. The internal network browsers communicate directly to the proxy server. It then checks its cache to determine if it has the resource on its local disk. If it does, it replies with that. Otherwise, it forwards the request transparently. Other networks take this a step further by installing a content-filtering proxy. This watches the traffic for websites that are against company policy. If the proxy finds a website that employees should be restricted from viewing, it stops the attempt. All other requests are sent transparently through. From the browsers' point of view, they don't know they're surfing through a proxy — well, that is until they try to go to a restricted page!

The Proxy Design Pattern is the building block for an object that can intercept communication between two or more other objects. The exterior interface of the `Proxy` object is identical to the class it belongs to. Calling objects cannot tell the difference between the original object and the `Proxy` object. At the core of the Proxy Design Pattern, there are any of three objectives. These are there to provide access, to incur expense only on demand, and to persist storage.

Granting access to a specific resource can be a tricky undertaking. Various business rules may need to be applied. Credentials need to be verified or retrieved. Identities or even locations need to be verified and validated. As with good object-oriented design, the base object should not be concerned with who can access it. It should only be a container of programming that accomplishes the task. This is where the Proxy Design Pattern fits nicely. A `Proxy` object can step in and determine access restrictions based on other exterior properties. For example, a `Proxy` object may dictate that the current user does not have the proper authority to execute the command and refuse the execution. Access conditions are not restricted only to credential validation, however. In a distributed and segmented network, certain resources may exist outside the standard reach of the current set of objects. The `Proxy` object can intercept these requests and act as that bridge to connect to the remote systems.

Some objects have a great deal of expense in their creation. It may be from many remote calls to a database or just a giant memory footprint. If it is possible not to instantiate that object right away, an object based on the Proxy Design Pattern might be created. This Proxy object will request the creation of the expensive object only when needed. It may be a situation where the whole code execution may be able to finish without actually needing to create that object. Other times, it may make more sense to create the larger object later when other object's memory spaces have been deallocated.

Finally, `Proxy` objects can work as a method of persistent storage. Whenever a caching method is put into place, the basis of this is an object created using the Proxy Design Pattern. The Proxy will determine if it has a store of the object from a previous request. If it does, it will provide that resource. If not, it will forward the initial request transparently.

One particularly common example of the Proxy Design Pattern can be seen with web interfaces to external devices. Consider the web application that controls a cable box and TV for remote viewing. When it receives the request from the web page to change to Channel 5, a specific `Proxy` object intercepts this request. Depending on the type of TV, it may send a sequence of `'0005<enter>'` or simply `'5<enter>'` to the remote receiver. Without the Proxy intercepting the communication, the TV could ignore the single "5" that was sent because it wasn't in a format that it expected.

Another example of the Proxy Design Pattern in action can be examined in access restrictions to publishing information. A particular social networking site allows users to create a profile page. They can either keep it private or publish it publicly. This system is fully tested and in good working order. No one wants to edit any of the code. Then, a new memo is passed throughout the company. No company employee is allowed to create a profile and publish it publicly. The programmers have been tasked with creating a system to keep employees from publishing their profiles publicly. They decide to create a

Proxy object that intercepts the request to publish the profile. If the user is in a list of employees, the request is stopped. Otherwise, it gets forwarded. The publishing object is blissfully unaware that it is being filtered by a proxy.

When communication between two objects needs to be filtered or enhanced, this can be accomplished by an object based on the Proxy Design Pattern.

UML

This Unified Modified Language (UML) diagram details a class design using the Proxy Design Pattern (see Figure 15-1). Note the following concerning this pattern:

❑   MyObject is the base object that clients normally interact with. It has one public method, called doSomething().

❑   MyProxyObject is the Proxy for MyObject. It contains one public method, named doSomething(), and one protected one, named provideProxyFeature().

❑   When MyProxyObject is substituted in for MyObject, the doSomething() method still can be called. MyProxyObject executes the provideProxyFeature() method before possibly forwarding the request to the doSomething() method of MyObject.

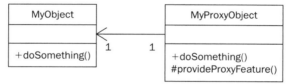

Figure 15-1

Code Example

Because the web site is so great, sales have grown at the CD store. Expansion is inevitable. The website has been executing normal sales every day. The good working code is simple. First, you have the object that represents a CD that a visitor can purchase:

```
class CD
{
    protected $_title = '';
    protected $_band = '';
    protected $_handle = null;

    public function __construct($title, $band)
    {
        $this->_title = $title;
        $this->_band = $band;
    }

    public function buy()
```

```
    {
        $this->_connect();

        $query = "update CDs set bought=1 where band='";
        $query .= mysql_real_escape_string($this->_band, $this->_handle);
        $query .= "' and title='";
        $query .= mysql_real_escape_string($this->_title, $this->_handle);
        $query .= "'";

        mysql_query($query, $this->_handle);
    }

    protected function _connect()
    {
        $this->_handle = mysql_connect('localhost', 'user', 'pass');
        mysql_select_db('CD', $this->_handle);
    }
}
```

The constructor builds the CD by assigning its two parameters, $title and $band, to the protected variables $_title and $_band, respectively.

The other public method is called buy(). This executes the sale. The first step is calling the protected _connect() method. _connect() creates a connection to the local MySQL database using the proper credentials. Next, buy() creates a query to update the CD row and set it to bought. Finally, the query is executed, and the CD purchase is complete.

The current code to buy a CD is pretty streamlined:

```
$externalTitle = 'Waste of a Rib';
$externalBand = 'Never Again';

$cd = new CD($externalTitle, $externalBand);
$cd->buy();
```

A new instance of the CD is created. Then the public method buy() is executed, and the CD is bought.

Because you have had such great sales, you've expanded your server capacity. You now need to access data from the Dallas, Texas, location. This will require a Proxy object acting in an access capacity. It needs to intercept the connection to the local database and connect to the Dallas Network Operations Center instead.

The Proxy object simply extends the base CD object. It replaces functionality, however:

```
class DallasNOCCDProxy extends CD
{
    protected function _connect()
    {
        $this->_handle = mysql_connect('dallas', 'user', 'pass');
        mysql_select_db('CD');
    }
}
```

The protected _connect() method is being overwritten by this Proxy object. Instead of connecting to the localhost, it is now connecting to the dallas host. The calling code has no idea it's actually working with a Proxy. The calling code is now only slightly modified:

```
$externalTitle = 'Waste of a Rib';
$externalBand = 'Never Again';

$cd = new DallasNOCCDProxy($externalTitle, $externalBand);
$cd->buy();
```

When there is a need to intercept communication between two objects, using a new object based on the Proxy Design Pattern is best practice.

16

Singleton Pattern

My boss came to me one day and told me customers were complaining about the website being slow. I decided to do a few tests on the responsiveness of the website under a heavy load. I started out with 25 concurrent users. This was enough to crash the MySQL server. Through trial and error — and a very upset networking team — I was able to find that magic number where the website started showing strain. Six simultaneous users were all it could handle. Obviously, my boss told me to find out why. I was eager to solve this problem, too. The page I tested was rendering content from a Content Management System, which was nothing too complicated. After some investigation, I found out that two specific database systems were queried to build the front page. However, each page opened up more than ten connections to the same MySQL server and two to the same DB2 server. I examined the queries that were used to build these pages and discovered that their state did not need to persist throughout the whole page. The connection was opened, the information retrieved, and the link was then abandoned. Later on, a new connection was forced open for a new query. The only good news was that the code base was using an object-oriented approach to connect to the databases. After some refactoring, the objects used only one shared database connection to each type of server. Instead of generating a new connection whenever the database was called, I forced the objects to reuse themselves. To accomplish this, I used the Singleton Design Pattern.

Name: Singleton

The Singleton Design Pattern is used to restrict the number of times a specific object can be created to a single time by providing access to a shared instance of itself.

Problem and Solution

The Singleton Design Pattern is one of the most used Design Patterns I've seen. This particular architecture type provides leverage to object-oriented design that exists normally only in global and procedural programming. Objects created from the Singleton Design Pattern will normally only allow one instance of themselves to be created. On the initial instantiation, the object stores itself internally. Then, it provides a reference to that stored instance. On each new request for a new object, it simply checks its storage. If it already has an instance of itself, it returns that reference. Otherwise, it follows the new object request detailed previously.

Singletons that allow only one instance of themselves are the most common. They are considered exclusive to the one runtime. They should not be allowed to generate clones of themselves.

Design Patterns are great base blueprints for architecting objects. However, as I keep reiterating, they do provide flexibility. Another type of object that exists restricts the number of copies of itself allowed at any one time. The initial architecture is based on the Singleton Design Pattern but is slightly modified. For example, this object may store up to five instances of itself. If a sixth is requested, it may have to wait or just provide a reference to one of the initial five that was created. This type of architecture is especially useful in queued requests.

Regardless of the type of Singleton being designed, there is one base characteristic that needs to be applied. The constructor of the object should be a protected method. This will not allow anything but the class itself to create an instance of it. Then it can make a public method to actually create, store, and provide that instance.

Objects based on the Singleton Design Pattern provide a welcome object-oriented defense to the use of global variables. Many PHP packages have been guilty of having a strong object-oriented core but still making use of the $GLOBALS array. The most common reason they implement the global variable usage is for configuration options. Instead, a configuration object could be created as a Singleton. Whenever a configuration option was required, the code would request a new configuration object. If there was no existing one stored internally, a new instance would be created. This constructor could have logic that is executed to determine and make available all the configuration options. Then, the requesting object could make use of the object to retrieve the configuration options. Since this is a reference to one instance that all requests will be using, an object could update the configuration options on demand and make it available to other requesters. This would completely replace the use of a global variable for configuration options. As an added bonus, since this is an object and not a normal variable, security measures could be added to restrict certain configuration options from being modified after initial instantiation.

The most common use of the Singleton Design Pattern is for architecting database connection objects. The database access object may be responsible for creating a connection to the database on instantiation. Then, whenever a particular method of the object is called, it uses the connection it has created. Since creating a connection to a database server can be expensive (time consuming and resource intensive), the code should make as few as possible. For the most part, the database connection's state no longer needs to be preserved after the data is retrieved. With both of these concerns in mind, it makes the most sense to make the database access object a Singleton. Then, each time a new instance of the object is requested for a new query, you can be assured that the object will be reused and no additional connections will be made.

When making multiple instances of an object should be prohibited, that object should be created using the Singleton Design Pattern.

UML

This Unified Modified Language (UML) diagram details a class design using the Singleton Design Pattern (see Figure 16-1). The following list details this pattern:

❏ MyObject is designed as a Singleton. The constructor named MyObject() is a protected method.

❏ The public method getInstance() is responsible for checking the protected variable named instance. If instance contains an instance of MyObject, it would simply return that instance. However, if instance is NULL, getInstance() will execute the protected MyObject() to construct a new MyObject. Then, it will store that instance of MyObject in the instance variable. Finally, it will return that instance variable.

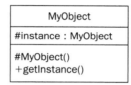

Figure 16-1

Code Example

Visitors to the CD Website can purchase more than one CD at a time. In fact, they're encouraged to do just that. You should provide a shopping cart for them to store their purchases in. Since you work with a live inventory, it is important to update the inventory listing as soon as the CDs are purchased. To do this, you need to connect to the MySQL database and update the quantity for that CD. With your object-oriented approach, you could potentially create multiple connections to the database that are not needed. Instead, the inventory connection is based on the Singleton Design Pattern:

```
class InventoryConnection
{
    protected static $_instance = NULL;

    protected $_handle = NULL;

    public static function getInstance()
    {
        if (!self::$_instance instanceof self) {
            self::$_instance = new self;
        }

        return self::$_instance;
    }

    protected function __construct()
```

```
    {
        $this->_handle = mysql_connect('localhost', 'user', 'pass');
        mysql_select_db('CD', $this->_handle);
    }

    public function updateQuantity($band, $title, $number)
    {
        $query = "update CDS set amount=amount+" . intval($number);
        $query .= " where band='" . mysql_real_escape_string($band) . "'";
        $query .= " and title='" . mysql_real_escape_string($title) . "'";

        mysql_query($query, $this->_handle);
    }
}
```

The first public method of the InventoryConnection class is a static method called getInstance().
This checks to see if the protected static variable named $_instance has an instance of the class itself.
If it does not, then a new instance of the class itself is assigned to the $_instance variable. Then,
regardless of if the new instance needed to be created or not on this particular call, the last step is to
return the instance from that protected $_instance variable.

The constructor is a protected method. This does not allow any other object besides this one to call it.
__construct() makes a connection to the database and stores the instance locally in the protected
$_handle variable.

The public method updateQuantity() takes three parameters. The band name, the title and the
number to change the quantity by are used in a MySQL query that is created. Finally, the object executes
the query using the internally stored handle.

InventoryConnection whenever a CD is purchased:

```
class CD
{
    protected $_title = '';
    protected $_band = '';

    public function __construct($title, $band)
    {
        $this->_title = $title;
        $this->_band = $band;
    }

    public function buy()
    {
        $inventory = InventoryConnection::getInstance();
        $inventory->updateQuantity($this->_band, $this->_title, -1);
    }
}
```

The CD object is pretty standard. However, the buy() method is of interest. First, it calls the getInstance() method of InventoryConnection to obtain an instance of that class. Once that instance is received, it subtracts one from the quantity of that specific CD by calling the updateQuantity() method of the InventoryConnection object.

The sample code to use these objects is probably pretty familiar:

```
$boughtCDs = array();
$boughtCDs[] = array('band'=>'Never Again', 'Waste of a Rib');
$boughtCDs[] = array('band'=>'Therapee', 'Long Road');

foreach ($boughtCDs as $boughtCD) {
    $cd = new CD($boughtCD['title'], $boughtCD['band']);
    $cd->buy();
}
```

In this example, the $boughtCDs array represents the items from the visitor's cart. The code loops through each of the purchased CDs. First, it creates a new CD object. Then, it requests to buy() that CD. Since this can happen one too many times, it is a good thing that the InventoryConnection object is a Singleton. It would not be a good idea to open up a new connection to the database for each CD purchased.

When the instantiation of an object should only be allowed to happen one time during the code stream, using the Singleton Design Pattern is best practice.

17

Strategy Pattern

The worst few months of my career were completely unavoidable. I tackled a big project with a large code base. New requirements kept popping up, and I did what any inexperienced junior programmer would do: I just added on to my objects. My classes started becoming monolithic. I kept obliterating my unit tests. As luck would have it, I was just learning about object inheritance in PHP. From then on, I started creating more but smaller classes, each extending others to add additional functionality. My problem went from having a few single giant classes to having way too many smaller classes to keep track of. The issues continued. If it wasn't the sheer size of the list of objects in my repository, it was the convoluted naming scheme I had to develop to keep those objects organized. I found that there was also a lot of bloat in my classes. There were methods that were not called in most instances of the class. My next refactoring step involved removing some of this logic from these base classes and adding it to individual classes that would only be created when need be. This is where the Strategy Design Pattern really shines.

Name: Strategy

The Strategy Design Pattern helps architect an object that can make use of algorithms in other objects on demand in lieu of containing the logic itself.

Problem and Solution

The beauty of Object Oriented Programming can sometimes be disfigured by its incorrect usage. Many programmers can grasp the modularization of individual entities as objects. But object-oriented architecture does not stop at just entity architecture. Any task, whether it's the creation of the entity or a modification to said entity, can be encompassed in an object. The Strategy Design Pattern is a great example of taking the object-oriented approach to this next level.

The Strategy Design Pattern details the construction of an object so that it is lighter weight by removing complex logic from itself. Instead of holding a set of logic internally, the object can invoke algorithms from other classes on the fly.

When first examining the Strategy Design Pattern, programmers may mistake the construction of this functionality for standard object inheritance. One of the most common uses of Object Oriented Programming consists of building objects that extend each other. This way, the core object is smaller, with all child objects having additional sets of logic.

Functionally, this can cause a headache. Imagine an object that has multiple children, each of which modify the base object in a specific way. If there is just one single instance of the modification to take place, extending a child class may seem the easiest route to take. The problem comes in when that particular object needs to have multiple modifications. Since the parent/child relationship is already made, a new instance of the object would need to be created to add a new child's functionality to the base object. For example, a base object might have a public property. One child object may want to make that property capital letters. Another child object may want to translate it into a different language. Chaining multiple children together to the base parent object will most likely also be clunky or impossible. Each child's method names would have to be distinct so as to not overwrite another child's functionality.

The Strategy Design Pattern takes the approach of removing the functionality from the parent object, much as in the parent/child relationship. However, instead of building objects that extend the parent, the logic is modified to be a self-contained algorithm. This class, then, is a complete object, whose sole use is executing that functionality. When architected properly, the parent object can choose which one of the logic objects it wants to use to modify itself during runtime. Besides the obvious benefits of the base object being lighter weight, the other Strategy objects are now more reusable and flexible.

The Strategy objects can be reused with various different types of base objects. These replace building a complex set of inherited classes with the potential to duplicate code among each different type of base object's child classes. Since the Strategy object is a self-contained algorithm, it should be able to take an object that it knows little to nothing about and apply its changes. The only level of coupling comes when specific algorithms require a specific object to complete. In general, this is an acceptable level of dependency.

An example of a great use for the Strategy Design Pattern is calculating shipping charges. A specific item may be represented by an object in the code. The object has certain properties such as length, width, height, and weight. When the purchase method is invoked on the object, additional protected methods may be executed to determine the shipping charges by calling the U.S. Postal Service (USPS) API. If another item becomes available for sale, there would most likely be code duplication in those protected methods. Instead, that calculation is pulled out and created as a Strategy object. The USPS Shipping Strategy object accepts an object that communicates its physical properties. The Strategy object calls the API and applies the shipping charge to the base object. This same Strategy object can now be used on either of the items available for sale. Additional items will also make use of this Strategy object. As an added bonus, having the shipping calculation as a Strategy object adds additional flexibility for future expansion. If the site decides to start shipping via the United Parcel Service (UPS), a new Strategy object is created. None of the original objects needs to be modified. The main calling code will then just determine if a USPS Strategy or a UPS Strategy should be applied to that object to update the shipping charges.

Another way to use the Strategy Design Pattern involves creating pattern replacements. Imagine an object that holds the profile information for a user of the website. Placeholders exist in the profile information to display the user's favorite instant messaging client information. The Profile object would have a method that sets the type of instant messaging vendor the user prefers. Then, the corresponding Strategy object would be applied to the Profile object. It would recognize the placeholder and replace it with a link to interact with the user. It could even be as complex as retrieving status information from an API of that service. Since the Profile object uses the Strategy Design Pattern, it can execute faster and with a lighter footprint. Instead of needing to encompass the simple functionality for one instant messaging vendor and the complex bloated logic to display another, it contains neither. It retrieves those values at runtime by instantiating only the Strategy objects it needs.

When objects can remove algorithms from themselves and place them in other self-contained objects to be invoked only when needed, the Strategy Design Pattern should be used.

UML

This Unified Modified Language (UML) diagram (see Figure 17-1) and following list detail a class design using the Strategy Design Pattern.

❑   MyObject contains a public property called name. This represents the property of MyObject that normally accepts modification. The public method setName() receives one parameter, called name. This is assigned to the MyObject name property.

❑   MyObjectStrategy is the self-contained algorithm object. It has one public method, named change(). This accepts a parameter of MyObject. change() and executes that specific logic against the MyObject by modifying its public name variable.

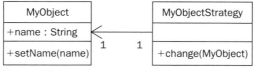

Figure 17-1

Code Example

The website works heavily with AJAX. From time to time, it's necessary for the CD object to generate an XML version of itself. This is returned to the JavaScript front end to be processed.

The CD object is:

```
class CD
{
    public $title = '';
    public $band = '';

    public function __construct($title, $band)
```

```
    {
        $this->title = $title;
        $this->band = $band;
    }

    public function getAsXML()
    {
        $doc = new DomDocument();
        $root = $doc->createElement('CD');
        $root = $doc->appendChild($root);
        $title = $doc->createElement('TITLE', $this->title);
        $title = $root->appendChild($title);
        $band = $doc->createElement('BAND', $this->band);
        $band = $root->appendChild($band);

        return $doc->saveXML();
    }
}
```

The constructor takes two parameters, the $title and $band, and assigns them to the public properties of the class. The getAsXML() public method creates a new DomDocument. It then builds each individual node and adds it to the DomDocument. Finally, the saveXML() method is called, which returns a string representation of the XML file. This is sent as the return parameter from the getAsXML() method.

To use this, the code is pretty straightforward:

```
$externalBand = 'Never Again';
$externalTitle = 'Waste of a Rib';

$cd = new CD($externalTitle, $externalBand);

print $cd->getAsXML();
```

A new developer has joined the team. He has some great experience with AJAX and says that you could be doing this a little bit better. Additional flexibility is needed for the website's AJAX functionality, including being able to generate the CD as a JavaScript Object Notation (JSON) entity.

The first implementation of the CD will not be flexible enough to generate this new output type. Additionally, you know that you may need to keep creating more types of representations of the CD object for other uses. Some web services may require a different format besides XML or JSON. This is the perfect time to use the Strategy Design Pattern.

The first step is to modify the CD object to remove the XML functionality. It should also be able to execute any Strategy objects that you create:

```
class CDusesStrategy
{
    public $title = '';
    public $band = '';

    protected $_strategy;

    public function __construct($title, $band)
```

```
    {
        $this->title = $title;
        $this->band = $band;
    }

    public function setStrategyContext($strategyObject)
    {
        $this->_strategy = $strategyObject;
    }

    public function get()
    {
        return $this->_strategy->get($this);
    }
}
```

The first part of the CDusesStrategy class is relatively similar to the CD class earlier. There are two additional public methods and one protected property, however. The setStrategyContext() accepts one parameter, named $strategyObject. This object is stored in the object by being assigned to the protected $_strategy variable. This will hold an instance of a Strategy object. The other public method, get(), can be thought of as replacing the getAsXML() method from the CD class. It's name is much more abstract because it applies the Strategy object. The Strategy object stored in the protected $_strategy variable has a get() function of its own, which is executed here. It is important to note that an instance of this base class is being passed into the Strategy object.

Next, the Strategy objects for the XML and JSON formats need to be created:

```
class CDAsXMLStrategy
{
    public function get(CDusesStrategy $cd)
    {
        $doc = new DomDocument();
        $root = $doc->createElement('CD');
        $root = $doc->appendChild($root);
        $title = $doc->createElement('TITLE', $cd->title);
        $title = $root->appendChild($title);
        $band = $doc->createElement('BAND', $cd->band);
        $band = $root->appendChild($band);

        return $doc->saveXML();
    }
}

class CDAsJSONStrategy
{
    public function get(CDusesStrategy $cd)
    {
        $json = array();
        $json['CD']['title'] = $cd->title;
        $json['CD']['band'] = $cd->band;

        return json_encode($json);
    }
}
```

The CDAsXMLStrategy class has only one public method, named get(). Earlier, it was noted that this method was called from the CDusesStrategy get() method. This get() method accepts an instance of CDusesStrategy. Then, the logic is pretty much the same as the logic of the getAsXML() method from the CD object, except that it uses $cd instead of $this.

CDAsJSONStrategy is designed nearly identically to the CDAsXMLStrategy class. The obvious difference is the construction of the $json array instead of a DomDocument. The information is retrieved from the $cd variable, which is that instance of CDusesStrategy. Finally, the encoded JSON version of the CD is returned.

Executing the code using these Strategy objects is not complicated:

```
$cd = new CDusesStrategy($externalTitle, $externalBand);

//xml output
$cd->setStrategyContext(new CDAsXMLStrategy());
print $cd->get();

//json output
$cd->setStrategyContext(new CDAsJSONStrategy());
print $cd->get($cd);
```

As is probably familiar, a new instance of a CD is created by instantiating CDusesStrategy. For the XML output, the setStrategyContext() method is called. It is sent a new instance of the corresponding Strategy object. It is important to note that any new functionality now comes in the method of a new Strategy object that is assigned using setStrategyContext().

When it's possible to create interchangeable objects made of self-contained algorithms to be applied to a base object, it is best practice to use the Strategy Design Pattern.

18

Template Pattern

The phrase "too many cooks in the kitchen" has been used by me a few times when examining a new code base. Whether because of time constraints or to use developers' strengths in areas where they excel, there are often times when a set of similar functionalities in development are broken up between programmers and teams. Unfortunately, this sometimes generates inconsistencies in the public interfaces of some of the programming. Superiorly architected code bases dictate base classes to build individual functionality from. To create these base classes, which enforce a specific set of interfaces and behavior, the Template Design Pattern is the way to go.

Name: Template

The Template Design Pattern creates an abstract object that enforces a set of methods and functionality that will be used in common by child classes as a template for their own design.

Problem and Solution

Some programmers do not immediately see a need to implement the Template Design Pattern. Generally, these are programmers who rely heavily on the inheritance of objects without understanding the actual intent of inheritance. Their catch-all answer to a parent method's not doing everything that they need it to do is to simply overwrite it. While some of this theory is used in the Template Design Pattern, it provides a more robust solution.

The Template Design Pattern creates a class that is intended to be used as a parent for another class. It is designed to enforce the existence of certain functionality and methods in the child classes. The `Template` object is a bit leaner than other classes with less bundled functionality. In most cases, it also strongly discourages or restricts instantiation of itself directly. This usually is achieved by making the class abstract.

Generally, the `Template` object defines a shared public method that is common to the goal of any other child class. Inside of that method, it calls the basic steps of the design by requesting other methods belonging to the object. These methods, which will belong to a child object, are either required or optional. If they are required, the class will define that the child class needs to have them. If they are optional for the child class, the `Template` class may create them as a stub so as not to disable the operation of the shared public method. Another way to accomplish the inclusion of an optional method is to check for the method's existence, and if it exists, invoke it.

Child classes then extend the `Template` object to accept that design or template themselves. They are responsible for creating any required methods that the `Template` object defines. Since these methods are predefined in the `Template` object, any child object can be assumed to have all of them and function externally the same way. The internal logic of the method is specified by each individual object in its own way. Basically, the abstract steps that the Template object defines are now detailed in-depth in the child object.

The Template Design Pattern is a little bit different from most design methodologies. This particular pattern defines a concrete set of steps in the parent object, giving much of the control to the parent. This contrasts with a lot of the other patterns that rely on child classes to give added structure and direction to the object. This is to say that most patterns define an individual or peer-to-peer approach. The Template Design Pattern heavily emphasizes the parent/child relationship. Another way to think about it is that the `Template` object is the coach of a football team. The coach defines what the play is and what team members will be involved. The coach tells the quarterback to retrieve the ball from the center and then to throw it down field to a receiver. It's up to quarterback, or the child of the coach, to know how hard and high to throw it in order for the open receiver to catch the ball.

One place that the Template Design Pattern could be used is in a social networking site. This example features a base `Template` object called an Entity. *Entities* can be created, shared, or deleted. To promote the social aspect of the website, entities can also be created publicly and shared with everyone on the site. In the social network, entities can be links, blogs, or pictures. The base `Entity` object is an abstract `Template` class. It contains three abstract methods called `create()`, `share()`, and `delete()`. These will be the responsibility of the child classes to define. The `Entity` class also has a public final method called `generatePublicly()`, which uses two of the abstract methods. First, it may call `create()`. Then, it retrieves a list of the owner's friends and calls `share()` with each one. A child class, such as the `Blog` object, will then extend the base `Entity`. It will need to define the logic inside of the `create()`, `share()`, and `delete()` methods. Later, when a new blog is being created for a member of the site, the `Blog` object's inherited `generatePublicly()` method is called. This is a perfect example of setting up a framework for new items added in the future to function the same. Adding new functionality won't require any additional changes to the calling logic or to the base `Entity` class.

Another example of the Template Design Pattern in use is an online banking website. A bank can deal with many different types of accounts. In general, all accounts function the same way. They accept deposits, provide payments, and possibly have additional logic to increase or decrease the balance. This could be low-balance fees on a checking account or interest on deposits on an investment account. The base account is created as a `Template` object. This object might have a final method called `applyAdjustment()`. This would call the abstract method it defines, named `retrieveAdjustmentOnBalance()`. Then it would either call the abstract `add()` or `subtract()` method. In the case of a checking account, the child class `Checking` will extend the main template. Its `retrieveAdjustmentOnBalance()` may generate a 10-dollar fee if the balance of the account is below

$100. Then, when the parent `Template` object calls the `subtract()` method, it will apply that fee to the total balance of the account. There is an even more important reason to generate these Template-based children when it comes to certificate of deposit accounts. When interest is added to the account using the `add()` method, the owner could be e-mailed a new statement at the request of that child's `add()` method.

When it is important to generate a strict set of guidelines for behavior while making the actual logic separate and flexible, the Template Design Pattern should be used.

UML

The following Unified Modified Language (UML) diagram details a class design using the Template Design Pattern (see Figure 18-1). The following list details this pattern:

❏   The `MyTemplate` class has two public methods. The first is the final public method, named `doCalculation()`. This method will call the other method named `logicA()` to apply logic during the calculation. In `MyTemplate`, the method should be abstract.

❏   The `MyObject` class extends the `MyTemplate` class. It actually contains the logic that the `logicA()` method in `MyTemplate` referred to.

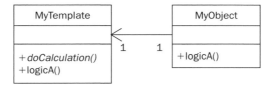

Figure 18-1

Code Example

The e-commerce website has expanded. Visitors to the website can now order many new items, including cases of cereal endorsed by the band. Who knew that these would be in high demand! Now, you can create classes that can hold the price for themselves as well as add tax. You used to be able to apply a flat tax — but now with food sales — each class has to hold the tax for itself. Additionally, some items are pretty large. For example, some of the cases of product require a premium to cover handling. This is added to the final purchase price.

This particular example will differ from most by having more structure. Generally, the simplest version of a class demonstrating a design pattern is created. Best practices, such as enforcing access using interfaces, are generally skipped. However, for this particular design pattern, the controls are so strongly specified that I thought it would be best to illustrate it with a more structured approach using abstract classes and methods.

The first step is to define a base class using the Template Design Pattern to process any of the sale items:

```
abstract class SaleItemTemplate
{
    public $price = 0;

    public final function setPriceAdjustments()
    {
        $this->price += $this->taxAddition();
        $this->price += $this->oversizedAddition();
    }

    protected function oversizedAddition()
    {
        return 0;
    }

    abstract protected function taxAddition();
}
```

The SaleItemTemplate is a simple class. It is an abstract class, so it enforces the requirement to be extended. The public property $price is set to 0. The one public method it defines is setPriceAdjustment(). This method is final so as not to allow it to be overwritten by any of the children. It enforces the modification of the price by calling both taxAddition() and oversizedAddition().

The protected method oversizedAddition() exists in this template class because it's optional that the child classes define it. Most items won't be oversized, so it does not make sense to create an oversizedAddition() method in each that would return 0.

Finally, the abstract protected method taxAddition() exists. Each child object could either be taxable or not. Whereas only some items will need to define surcharges for being oversized, many more need to define whether they are taxable or not. Therefore, this method is created as abstract to enforce its creation in the child element.

The next step is to modify our CD object from its normal state as well as create a new cereal object:

```
class CD extends SaleItemTemplate
{
    public $band;
    public $title;

    public function __construct($band, $title, $price)
    {
        $this->band = $band;
        $this->title = $title;
        $this->price = $price;
    }

    protected function taxAddition()
    {
        return round($this->price * .05, 2);
    }
```

```
}

class BandEndorsedCaseOfCereal extends SaleItemTemplate
{
    public $band;

    public function __construct($band, $price)
    {
        $this->band = $band;
        $this->price = $price;
    }

    protected function taxAddition()
    {
        return 0;
    }

    protected function oversizedAddition()
    {
        return round($this->price * .20, 2);
    }
}
```

The CD object extends the SaleItemTemplate. Its constructor sets the band, title, and price to the object. Since the taxAddition() method was defined as abstract in SaleItemTemplate, it has to be defined in the CD class as well. Here, the taxAddition() figures 5 percent tax on the price of the object and returns that amount.

The BandEndorsedCaseOfCereal object also extends the SaleItemTemplate. Its constructor sets the band and price similarly to the CD object. Next, it defines the taxAddition() method by necessity. In this case, since the item is food related, there is no tax. The taxAddition() method returns 0. However, a case of cereal is a pretty large item. In order to account for this, a surcharge of 20 percent will need to be added to the total price. The protected method oversizedAddition(), which exists in BandEndorsedCaseOfCereal, overwrites the one defined in the Template. It returns 20 percent of the current price.

The following code demonstrates how these classes are used:

```
$externalTitle = "Waste of a Rib";
$externalBand = "Never Again";
$externalCDPrice = 12.99;
$externalCerealPrice = 90;

$cd = new CD($externalBand, $externalTitle, $externalCDPrice);
$cd->setPriceAdjustments();

print 'The total cost for CD item is: $' . $cd->price . '<br />';

$cereal = new BandEndorsedCaseOfCereal($externalBand, $externalCerealPrice);
$cereal->setPriceAdjustments();

print 'The total cost for the Cereal case is: $' . $cereal->price;
```

Both examples create a new child class that extends the `Template` object. They call the `setPriceAdjustments()` method, which applies the possible changes to the public `$price` property. Then, the output shows the adjusted price of the item.

When creating an object where the general steps of a design are defined but the actual logic is left to be detailed by a child class, using the Template Design Pattern is best practice.

19

Visitor Pattern

Society keeps driving for more features and more value with everything they obtain. The days of being happy with a simple set of features or the "classic" item is nearly gone. Programming and applications are not immune to this trend. Companies are finding that the demand for new features is so intense that extra programmers are needed. They have independent consultants come visit the main office and request to have the application "made better." Each consultant is basically told the same thing — create a new feature — and they provide the same product: the finished feature. However, internally, they all take different routes to accomplish this goal. In this same way, some sets of objects are designed to visit the application logic and "make it better" in their own unique way. This is where the Visitor Design Pattern becomes useful.

Name: Visitor

The Visitor Design Pattern constructs distinct objects containing an algorithm that, when consumed by a parent object in a standard way, apply that algorithm to the parent object.

Problem and Solution

The Visitor Design Pattern helps take the complexity out of base objects. Basically, it is a separation of the algorithm from the object that it applies to. This seems to be a common goal of a lot of the design patterns in this book. However, the Visitor Design Pattern tackles this in a unique way.

The name Visitor has been given to this design pattern for a reason. While some other approaches to designing self-contained algorithm classes apply themselves externally, the Visitor object is designed to be incorporated into the object it intends to modify. After visiting or entering the object, a standard method call is executed with an instance of the base class being sent into that Visitor class. Because of this, the Visitor Design Pattern enforces a unified way of accessing these visiting objects' logic. Basically, each Visitor is asked the same thing, but what they do internally to accomplish the task is different.

One of the major benefits of this design pattern is the ability to add new functionality to an object without modifying that object. If the base object is built to accept Visitors, any new bit of logic can be applied through the Visitor acceptance method. Unit tests on the base object never need to be changed. Any new functionality is in the form of Visitors who are distinct from the base object and have their own testing methods. This provides a great flexibility for future development: any new feature set will be constructed as a visit with its own unique flavor.

Visiting objects in PHP will only be able to modify the public properties of an object, however. They also will only be able to access the public methods. Private and protected properties and methods are still out of scope.

One example that can make use of objects based on the Visitor Design Pattern is a blog. After the proper request is placed, an object representing the blog entry will be created. Normally, public properties are retrieved by the view class and used to display the item. The blog entry object contains an author property, which contains the username of the author. Since the owner of the blog website now wants to use full names, a Visitor object is created. It visits the blog object, which calls the Visitor's visit method, passing the reference to itself into the Visitor. The Visitor then does a query based on the username to retrieve the full name. This is then applied to the author property of the blog object. The visit is then over. Later on, Visitors might have noticed that all entry times are in Coordinated Universal Time (UTC). A new Visitor can be created to visit the blog object and change the public timestamp property to the time zone that the author is from. In both examples, the base object's properties were modified. However, the class itself was never changed.

Another example of the Visitor Design Pattern in action is an open source code serving website. An object is created to represent the code file to be downloaded. It contains public properties such as the project name, the location on the server, and the author. Since the demand for these open source code files is so high, additional mirrors are brought in after the site launched. The file object needs to provide the file from one of three new mirrors. Since the file object has been functioning flawlessly, it may make sense not to modify it. Instead, a new Visitor can be constructed that creates a random selection between the source and the three additional mirrors. Then, when it visits the file object, it modifies the location object to replace the original link with one that belongs to a mirror. As time goes on, there is an initiative to accept only files that are compressed in Tarred and GZipped file (TGZ) format. All of the files on all mirrors are compressed into that archive. New files are accepted only in that format. Now, a new Visitor is created to check if the public file location property actually exists. If it doesn't, it will check to see if the TGZ version exists. If so, it'll modify that location property to point to the newly compressed TGZ.

One of the things that I try to reiterate as often as possible is that Design Patterns are a base for projects. They can always be modified and enhanced. Additionally, the design itself is a proven method — but the applications are just theoretical. When considering the Visitor Design Pattern, the standard approach may be to consider Visitors to be something that always apply a set of functionality to an object. However, it could also be possible to create a Visitor with a different intent. In the previous example, the Visitor could have been created to apply updates to the database when the new TGZ file was found. Once all files have been converted, it may be removed from the equation again. I just want to stress that the design is the most important thing — the actual usage can vary.

When creating functionality that is enclosed in exterior classes that can be applied to a main class in a standard way, the Visitor Design Pattern can be used.

UML

This Unified Modified Language (UML) diagram details a class design using the Visitor Design Pattern (see Figure 19-1). Note the following about this diagram:

- ❏ The MyObject class can be visited. It is the base class. It has one public method called acceptVisitor(). This method accepts a parameter called Visitor. Internally, the acceptVisitor() class calls the public method visit() from the Visitor parameter object that it is passed. It passes in an instance of itself.

- ❏ The MyVisitor class is the Visitor in this diagram. All Visitors are required to have the public method visit(). This method accepts an instance of MyObject. The visit() method may call additional logic, such as the protected doSomething() method. This is the unique portion of the visiting class.

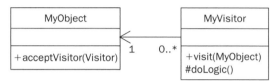

Figure 19-1

Code Example

For auditing, each new CD purchase on your e-commerce website must be logged. This information is then archived. In the case that there are ever any inconsistent inventory counts, the log file can be examined to see if a CD was actually purchased.

In order to accomplish this, the CD object must accept Visitors:

```php
class CD
{
    public $band;
    public $title;
    public $price;

    public function __construct($band, $title, $price)
    {
        $this->band = $band;
        $this->title = $title;
        $this->price = $price;
    }

    public function buy()
    {
        //stub
    }

    public function acceptVisitor($visitor)
```

```
    {
        $visitor->visitCD($this);
    }
}
```

The CD object receives the band, title, and price of the CD on instantiation. The constructor applies each of those to the public $band, $title, and $price properties.

The CD also has a public method called buy(). In this example, the purchase logic is left out. This stub method is for demonstration purposes.

The CD has one more public method, called acceptVisitor(). This method is required in order to comply with the Visitor Design Pattern. It accepts an instance of a Visitor from the $visitor parameter. Inside the method, the Visitor's public visitCD() method is called. It is passed an instance of the CD class, using the $this variable.

The logging Visitor contains the following code:

```
class CDVisitorLogPurchase
{
    public function visitCD($cd)
    {
        $logline = "{$cd->title} by {$cd->band} was purchased for {$cd->price} ";
        $logline .= "at " . sdate('r') . "\n";

        file_put_contents('/logs/purchases.log', $logline, FILE_APPEND);
    }
}
```

The class contains the one public method that is called from the CD class: visitCD(). This accepts a parameter called $cd, which is an instance of the CD object. Next, the $logline variable is created by combining a log message with some of the CD object's public methods. It is important to note that the logging could have been done inside of the buy() method. However, if the logging style was changed or additional logging was requested, the CD object would need to be modified again. This would not be optimal. Finally, the $logline variable is written to the log file.

To purchase this CD and log the sale, the following code is used:

```
$externalBand = 'Never Again';
$externalTitle = 'Waste of a Rib';
$externalPrice = 9.99;

$cd = new CD($externalBand, $externalTitle, $externalPrice);
$cd->buy();
$cd->acceptVisitor(new CDVisitorLogPurchase());
```

The CD object is created with the properties of the CD to be purchased. The buy() method is then called. Finally, the CD accepts a Visitor object in the form of a new CDVisitorLogPurchase being passed into the acceptVisitor() method of the CD class. This last call is where the logging is actually being executed.

A new study was released that said that Visitors who view the home page are actually looking for discount CDs instead of the standard-priced ones. Because of this, it was decided that the front page should have a live updated list of CDs that were purchased that were discounted. A discounted CD is considered to be a CD that is under $10.

To accomplish this task, a new Visitor is created:

```
class CDVisitorPopulateDiscountList
{
    public function visitCD($cd)
    {
        if ($cd->price < 10) {
            $this->_populateDiscountList($cd);
        }
    }

    protected function _populateDiscountList($cd)
    {
        //stub connects to sqlite and logs
    }
}
```

The `CDVisitorPopulateDiscountList` class also has the public `visitCD()` method. As with all of the Visitors created, this one also accepts an instance of the CD object using the parameter `$cd`. If the price property of the CD is less than 10, the protected method `_populateDiscountList()` is called. That function is passed an instance of the CD.

The `_populateDiscountList()` method is only invoked when the main visiting logic has determined that the CD qualifies as a discount CD. This particular example shows this method to be a stub method. However, in a real working class, this may be writing out the CD's details to a SQLite database or an XML file, which would be accessed by the front page.

The purchasing code has this new Visitor added:

```
$cd = new CD($externalBand, $externalTitle, $externalPrice);
$cd->buy();
$cd->acceptVisitor(new CDVisitorLogPurchase());
$cd->acceptVisitor(new CDVisitorPopulateDiscountList());
```

When objects containing algorithms to be applied to an object in a standard way are required, using the Visitor Design Pattern is best practice.

Part III
PHP Design Case Study

20

Requirements Analysis

I've always found that programmers in the open source world, especially when immersed in PHP, benefit from hands on teaching. While I would love to visit each reader's house, crack open some drinks, and program PHP, that's not really feasible. Instead, I'm going to further the analysis of PHP Design Patterns with a case study.

This particular case study will be broken up into several parts as the book introduction says. First, in this chapter, I'll examine the requirements. I'll try to rule out any assumptions and ask any other questions I can of the stakeholders of this case study. Chapter 21 will be the analysis of the features compared to what Design Patterns that were detailed in the reference chapters. The final chapters (Chapter 22 and 23) will cover the code creation, using the Design Patterns and Unified Modeling Language (UML) diagrams that I developed.

Completing this book with a case study is very important. In addition to providing a sort of "hands-on" training tool, there are three other important things that I hope you gather:

❑   First, it is important to follow along in a requirements analysis. There is a careful balance to maintain between flying by the seat of your pants and analyzing a project to death. I aim to show where the balance should fall with this analysis.

❑   The second thing to observe is the pre-programming analysis. Back in the book's introduction, I mentioned my distaste for those who jump right into programming using lack of time as an excuse. As with the requirement analysis, the programming planning is also a balance. It is critical to attain the proper ratio of time spent designing before programming to the actual time spent programming. The horror stories I have about projects going over time and over budget because of a lack of design in the beginning are sadly numerous.

❑   The final thing that I want to demonstrate is a real programmer's approach to programming the application. One thing that frustrated me about other books was their lack of complete application creation. They show a lot of code snippets and examples but never put together a completed project.

I also plan to approach the last segment of the case study in a somewhat controversial manner — I plan to make mistakes. My experience has shown me that the first round of the code base is never perfect. It usually will go through a few refactorings before it is released or even built upon further. Most books that do feature a completed project seem to have perfect code the first time around. Maybe the authors are better programmers than I? Chances are, however, that they've refactored their code before it hit the book. I plan to put in enough rough code to show value in the refactoring while not wasting your time. I think it's important to demonstrate the flexibility of Design Patterns by analyzing if the one I'm using makes the most sense. In some cases, it may make sense to change the code slightly and swap out the architecture to an object built with a different Design Pattern. This controversial approach to allowing "mistakes" in the code will come to a complete and accurate finale I assure you. The last version of the code will be the final architecture, fully working and accurate.

Now that you know what you're in for, let's talk a bit more about the actual content of the case study. To premise this situation, I want to detail a bit of background information for the example. I will be coding for the fictional ACME Company. I will have a direct supervisor who is my one and only point of contact. (Those who have been in the industry for a while right now are probably chuckling. Who really has just one point of contact during a project? But, the case study is about the project, not the business practices. I get to take these liberties!) He will be the one who supplies the requirements, is responsible for answering any of my questions, and makes any final decisions. I will be the only programmer on this project. This means that not only am I the lead architect, but I will also be creating the code as well. The project will be an online contact manager.

The first step in the case study is to review the requirements document that the boss presents.

Initial Requirements

The following sections will be the requirements document that my boss at ACME Company gave to me for the Contacts Manager.

Executive Summary

ACME Company will be shifting all of its employees' contacts to an online web page. This online contact manager will be accessible via Internet Explorer or a mobile phone. The contact manager will hold most features of the company's current e-mail system's address book. The online contact manager will be accessible to any company employee using their own credentials.

Scope

The following table contains the scope items:

Scope	Scope Items
In Scope	❏ Creating an online contact system
	❏ Separating user accounts with distinct credentials
	❏ Providing an interface for Internet Explorer
	❏ Providing an interface for a mobile browser
	❏ Method to import contacts from existing e-mail system
	❏ Allow contact information to be used directly via links.
Out of Scope	❏ Keeping the old and new contacts systems in sync and up to date
	❏ Using the same credentials as the network

Assumptions/Constraints

The assumptions and constraints that should be made are that the project:

❏ Will not incur any additional licensing costs.

❏ Must make use of the existing web server only.

Detailed Requirements

The following section details the objective specifics for the project.

Website Availability

The website should be available to the entire Internet. It should not be restricted to the company intranet. The website should be able to be viewed using Internet Explorer as a web browser. Employees using smart phones should be able to access the web page via their phone's browser as well.

Contact Information

A contact should be able to be created, updated, or deleted on the website. Each contact should have the following information available:

❏ First, Middle, and Last Names

❏ Personal E-Mail Address

❏ Personal Address

❏ Personal Phone/Cell phone

❏ Business Name

❏ Business Title

❏ Business E-Mail Address

❑   Business Address

❑   Business Phone/Extension/Cell Phone

❑   Business Social Network URL

❑   Instant Messenger Name

❑   Website

Contacts should appear on the application with a label of their First, Middle, and Last names.

Contact Sync

The website should be able to take the existing contact information from the company e-mail system and import it directly into this system.

Initial Requirements Analysis

The boss at ACME Company presents me with the preceding requirements document. While it's a good starting point, I still have plenty of questions. The next step is to consider my approach.

There are two ways to approach a requirements document that you have questions about:

❑   Create a list of questions and send them back to the stakeholders. Then one of three things will happen. You may receive answers back, you may just receive an updated requirements document, or you may receive answers back with direction to update the requirements document yourself.

❑   Gather the questions together and send them off to the stakeholders with a stipulation: you plan to update the requirements document for their review based upon the answers to these questions. This second way is usually the way that I try to approach the analysis. This way, everyone is clearly informed of what the next steps in the process are.

I should really interject a reminder here: this book is about Design Patterns and not business practice. However, some of these steps are required steps to make good decisions when choosing the Design Patterns for the PHP application. Without getting the clarification that is needed, the architecture may suffer. It may take longer to make the right decisions. Or, even worse, it's possible to make too many assumptions and create a wholly inaccurate architecture. I want to make sure to get clear requirements in the first step of the case study in order to make the rest of the project run smoother. As an added bonus, detailing my thought process may help you learn from my process how to perfect your own analysis process.

In this example, I've already alerted my boss that I'm going to approach this project by creating a list of questions and then updating the requirements document. In the next sections, I'm going to review the requirements document and break out my list of clarification points. For brevity's sake, I'm going to include the "answer" or "response" from the boss in each section.

Size/User Scale

The first thing I want to know about is the size of this application and the scale that is planned for growth. How many employees will be using it at first? What will that grow to? Will it be opened up to more companies? I did note that there is a constraint to not increase licensing costs and to use our current web server. This will impose some limits. It is my responsibility to determine if the predicted scale can be hosted on the existing hardware.

❏ **Question**: How many users in the company will be using this application in total? How many users do you predict will be using it at one time? Are there any planned hires coming up? Are there any plans to make it immediately available to other companies or individuals besides the ACME Company?

❏ **Answer**: Our company employs two shifts of 25 employees. Our growth is steady — about two new employees every quarter. We have no immediate plans to release the software to anyone else. If it is super-successful, it's not out of the question to sell access to it.

After reviewing this answer, I can make some assumptions.

First, the company has 50 total employees. At any one time, half of them should be using the software. The company also plans on growing two employees every quarter. Because I don't know which shift those employees will be placed in, I'll plan on them all being added to one shift. This gives us 33 users at a time in the next year. In my experience, management has a tendency to round numbers of total employees either under or over. I'm going to safely move my assumption to 40 users at one time, with 80 total initial users.

Next, as far as the initial design is concerned, they plan to keep the distribution in house and small. It's not out of the question that this application will need to scale immensely, but it seems to be predictably small for a while. What I've learned is to always plan for scaling, even when the stakeholders don't predict it. If they're even a little bit open to the idea, the chances increase that the product will be made available to more than the predicted number of users sooner rather than later.

Type of Contact Information

The requirements were very specific in the listing of contact. These items were broken down into personal and business contact information. Some items seemed to overlap. I think it's making a severe gamble that, for example, only one e-mail address will be available for personal e-mail. Also, some of the company's clientele may even have things like beach houses as well as personal residences. Just seeing the requirements listed so succinctly makes me wary. I think I'd like to clarify what the real requirements are. It seems to me that in order to demonstrate their need for flexibility (having both personal and business information readily available), they have unfortunately developed requirements that pigeonhole that flexibility into predefined fields.

❏ **Question**: I noticed business and personal address, e-mail, and phone information listed in the requirements. Would you say that you want to restrict that information to only one of each? Or would you rather have the primary options to suggest a business and personal address — while allowing the user to specify more than one of each? Also, I noticed only one listing for things like personal e-mail address or IM client. Would you like to provide the option for more than one of these under each category?

❑ **Answer**: As long as users can set up both personal and business information, do what you think is best. Contacts could have two or three IM clients. You can allow them to add more than one.

By suggesting alternatives in the question, I determined what the actual need is. There is no requirement to limit the interface to only personal and business information. It is just a requirement to make sure that they *can* add that information easily.

The other portion of the answer demonstrates that the stakeholders may not have thought that standard contacts may have more than one of each type of contact information. It appears that they're okay with having more than one of each featured in the interface.

From a design point of view, I've gathered some very important information. I now know that I can develop groups of contact information. The requirements would suggest that groups named "Business" and "Personal" should be suggested first. Also, I'm going to make the assumption that, since they would allow more than one IM client, they really would be fine with allowing more than one of any type of field in the group.

Application Access

As an open source user, you probably join me cringing whenever you see Internet Explorer mentioned in a requirement document. Since that particular browser has such a large market share, it is definitely not a browser that can be ignored. However, in the same way that people tend to use the brand name Kleenex to refer to facial tissue, I want to determine if the requirement is actually Internet Explorer, or if they are trying to say that the most common web browsers should be able to use it.

Another view that was mentioned was the mobile phone. The requirements document talked about using a smart phone to access the application. It is important to determine what type of smart phones they're referring to. The scope could be as grand as any mobile access device or as refined as Internet Explorer on Windows Mobile 6 and above. This is something that I need to clarify.

Both of these clarification steps are particularly delicate to discuss with most ordinary stakeholders. Business requirements should be based on application needs and not technical specifications as much as possible. However, by determining more technical needs up front, I'm hoping to extract some of the other ones that have sneaked their way into the requirements document. The delicateness comes in communicating with the stakeholders in a way that doesn't overly complicate things technically.

Finally, the last thing I want to know about is any additional views. One that I can think of that might be overlooked during this phase is the web service. With the mention of a possibility of selling access, it seems as if a web service view may be an eventuality.

❑ **Question**: Internet Explorer was mentioned as the browser to view the application with. I understand that this may be the most familiar browser to you. Would I be correct in assuming that you'd like to make sure the application could be accessed over the Internet using the most popular browsers — which of course includes Internet Explorer? Also, smart phones were mentioned. Can you point to any specific models of phones that should be supported? Finally, should any bit of the application be available immediately in a Software as a Service method by using web services? Or would you rather have this in a future iteration?

❑ **Answer**: We weren't aware of anyone using other browsers besides Internet Explorer in our organization. Access does not need to be restricted to Internet Explorer, just don't extend the budget to support other browsers. The mobile phones should be our company issued phones. The SaaS application would be nice but is not required.

These weren't exactly the answers I wanted, but they will help me progress through updating the requirements document. I personally was disappointed with the lack of making additional browser support a priority. However, by wording my question the way I did, I think I can help remove some of the specificity in the requirements and move the primary browser support to the constraints section.

The mobile phone answer requires me to find out what the standard issued company phones are. In this case, they are a few different brands — all of which have the Windows Mobile OS installed.

I can tell by the wording of the response that the primary objective of this project is to help facilitate business functionality. The fact that the application will be available outside of the company intranet is just a bonus. It is most important to focus on making sure that the core business deployment hardware and software function with the application flawlessly. Any extra functionality and compatibility is just a surprising bonus.

Contacts Sync

From the wording of the requirements document, the contacts sync process wasn't completely clear to me. Is it two-way sync? Is it ongoing? Should it be automated? Also, there is mention of the company e-mail system. I should get clarification on this as well.

❑ **Question**: One requirement is to have a way to import the contacts from the existing company e-mail system. When you say existing e-mail system, do you mean the instance of Outlook installed on each computer? Also, should this import be ongoing? Should this application support synching in both directions?

❑ **Answer**: The main reason we're building this application is to replace our existing e-mail and contact infrastructure. The licensing costs have become too great. Another team is working on a webmail application. We hope these will be integrated in the future. Right now, we're fine with them being standalone. The import should be a one-time import from the Outlook on the user's computer to the application. After that, we will be asking them to delete their Microsoft Address Book.

Woah! By answering this way, my boss has armed me with a lot more objective than was specified in the original requirements document. Now I have an idea how my application fits in with the grand scheme of development at ACME company.

I've learned that the import will only be one-way, one time, from Outlook. Luckily, I happen to know that Outlook can export contacts in CSV format. (Forgive me for that technical "outburst" during requirements-gathering phase!)

I also learned that the future of my application will be to integrate with a webmail application. This is something that is useful to keep in mind during the design phase.

User Credentials

One of the out-of-scope items was using the same login credentials as the network. I happen to know that the network has an LDAP server. From my experience, I have found that integrating the login with LDAP is not that hard.

This type of clarification can also be particularly difficult. I want to find out more about this out-of-scope requirement. It seems odd to me that it *is* out of scope and not a requirement. From a user's point of view, it seems like it would be a great benefit to keep the credentials the same. Asking the client about this particular requirement may have the potential of being interpreted as snide or even argumentative. I want to make sure that it comes off as a clarification point, not a discussion on the stakeholders' ability to make decisions or as an attempt to increase the budget of the project.

❑   **Question**: One of the out-of-scope items was using the same network credentials to access this application. If it's not synchronizing with the network, can you detail any requirements for the credentials I may need to know?

❑   **Answer**: Right now we haven't determined if we should integrate the login system with the webmail application or if it should be integrated with the network. The webmail team mentioned that they had a few issues with using the network. As of right now, the login system can be standalone.

This answer has given me more fodder for the design portion of the project than the actual requirements document. I know that I have to make sure that the authentication method is very pluggable. It should be able to be swapped out easily. The out-of-scope option seems like a viable option to leave there.

Updated Requirements Document

Now that I've completed analyzing the requirements and receiving answers to my questions, it's time to start putting together my finalized requirement document. I'm going to take their original one and modify it to include the answers to the questions I asked as well as adding additional clarifications.

Let's take a look.

Executive Summary

ACME Company will be shifting all of its employees' contacts to an online web page. This online contact manager will be accessible via most common web browsers as well as the company-issued mobile phones. The contact manager will be a direct replacement for the company's current address book software. The online contact manager will be accessible to any company employee using the Internet by providing their own credentials. The following table shows the in scope and out of scope features.

Scope	Scope Item
In Scope	❏ Creating an online contact system
	❏ Replacing the current Outlook address book functionality with this application
	❏ Separating user accounts with distinct credentials
	❏ Providing an interface for most common web browsers
	❏ Providing an interface for company-issued mobile phone browsers
	❏ Method to execute one-time import of contacts from Outlook's address book
	❏ Allow contact information to be used directly via links
	❏ Flexible authentication system to allow multiple ways to authenticate
Out of Scope	❏ Providing contact information to legacy Outlook system
	❏ Forcing the use of the same credentials as the network
	❏ Web service access to the application at this time

Assumptions/Constraints

The assumptions and constraints that should be made are that the project:

❏ Will not incur any additional licensing costs

❏ Must make use of the existing web server only

❏ Will have an application that focuses on compatibility with Internet Explorer

Detailed Requirements

The following section details the objective specifics for the project.

Website Availability

The website should be available to the entire Internet. It should not be restricted to the company intranet. The website should be able to be viewed using the most common web browsers, specifically Internet Explorer. Employees using company-issued Windows Mobile phones should be able to access the web page via their phone's browser.

Contact Information

A contact should be able to be created, updated, or deleted on the website. The contact should retain a singular First, Middle, and Last name.

Each contact can have unlimited groupings of information. The first group suggested is "Business." Additional group names can be specified by the user.

Each group has at least one label for contact information. Each label can have one or more items associated with it. The specified labels are as follows:

- ❏ E-Mail Address
- ❏ Street Address, including City, State, and Zip
- ❏ Telephone with optional extension
- ❏ Mobile Phone
- ❏ Organization Name
- ❏ Title at Organization
- ❏ Social Network URL
- ❏ Instant Messenger Name
- ❏ Website

For example, John Smith can have a group called Personal, which features two mobile phones, one e-mail address, and three Instant Messenger names.

Contacts should appear on the application with their personal picture, if it exists, followed by a label with their First, Middle, and Last names.

Initial Contact Import

The website should be able to take the existing contact information from Outlook and import it one time.

Updated Requirements Discussion

A few of the changes I've made to the requirements documentation bear the need of some discussion:

- ❏ I refer to the Outlook application directly. I think it's important to detail this throughout the requirements. The executive summary still stays brief, but the scope and specifics mention the application by name. This is important because the executive summary only needs to mention what the objective is. The details should nail down what the company "address book system" really is. It's quite possible that not everyone uses the same address book software. Since the stakeholders have identified the Outlook software as the official address book I should consider, designating this particular software in the requirements protects my interests. I am not expected to develop more than one type of import sequence initially.

- ❏ I removed the mention of Internet Explorer from some of the requirements. Instead, it's a constraint that I should focus on Internet Explorer compatibility first. I did not want to make the requirements falsely state that Internet Explorer was the only browser that could be used to view the application.

- ❏ In regard to the mobile browser, since the only supported mobile phones are those issued by the company, it was important to mention this. With Java-based browsers, Safari-based browsers, and other operating systems hitting phones, it's good to tighten up this requirement. The foremost functionality is business based, so we want to continually urge focusing on business-related applications only.

❑ I changed the wording from "contact sync" to "initial contact import." After I found out that the process was less of a sync and more of an import, I wanted to make sure that there would be no false assumptions about this functionality. It is only one type of import one time per user.

❑ One of the biggest changes I made was in the contact information section. Instead of limiting this to personal and business information, I changed the method to grouping. The Business group will be suggested first. However, users can have unlimited groups. This could allow users to specify multiple business names for contacts who have more than one job.

❑ The subsections of each of these groups were also modified. Instead of focusing on information that seems as if it would be limited to a specific group, I made the information more generic. Also, since a user can have an unlimited number of subtypes, we solve the problem of someone having more than one personal e-mail address or multiple IM names.

❑ I also included a small example detailing this functionality. It has been my experience that when the requirements appear to have changed to the stakeholders, providing an explanation goes a long way to getting them accepted. Another thing I discovered from the response I received from my question about the contact information was the stakeholders' naive interpretation of contact details. It seemed as if they might not have considered a situation where a contact could have more than one of a specific type of detail. Because I was helping them make this jump in this requirements document, I felt a quick demonstration or example added to the document would help. (I know that some pure project manager types may disagree with me on this point — and that's fine. I'm merely giving you the steps I tend to take on my successful projects.)

In this case study, I sent the requirements document back to my boss. And, as if by magic, or because they know I'm writing this book, the stakeholders all agreed 100%. (How lucky!)

Summary

In this chapter, I introduced my version of a case study. I discussed how I plan to cover the business requirements, planning, and actual building of the application throughout the case study. I also detailed my unique way to approaching a case study. Then, I reviewed a sample business requirements document for an online contacts manager for the fictional ACME company. I showed how to pull out questions about the requirements, open a dialog with the stakeholders, and apply that feedback to the requirements. Finally, I created an updated requirements document, which will be the basis of our next few sections. Next up, planning our architecture and choosing some Design Patterns.

21

Choosing Design Patterns and Planning

With a set of requirements that are clearer, it is time to continue with the planning portion of this project. I'm going to step through each section of the application, detailing my thoughts as well as providing UML diagrams. I know it's tempting to just jump in and code right away and hope to sprinkle in some Design Patterns. However, the benefits of preplanning this application will hopefully become very apparent as I analyze each step.

In general, I'm making some assumptions about the sections and pieces of this application. I'm going to draw UML diagrams to keep for the programming portion. Experience has taught me that these blueprints both encourage me to remember to use my collection of Design Patterns and give me a roadmap for development. An added benefit is the chance to provide an updated estimate on the project after the pieces are clearly laid out.

The sections of the application as I see it are:

❑   Main core

❑   User interaction and administration

❑   Contact administration

Let's begin with the core of our application.

Designing the Core

The steps to becoming a great programmer revolve around the core of the application:

1.   You program procedurally using a collection of includes.

2.   Next you build your own framework to use as a base for your next project.

3.   You then abandon your framework and leveraging existing proven frameworks in your project.

Normally, I move forward using what I've learned by getting to step 3 and would recommend one of the frameworks mentioned in Chapter 2. However, because I'm trying to demonstrate the usage of Design Patterns from an initial planning perspective, I am opting to create a very simple framework. While existing frameworks would jumpstart this application, the code is already written by someone else. I can only make guesses as to the thought processes of the original programmers.

A type of architecture I favor is Model-View-Controller, or MVC. To begin the core of the application, I'm going to build three objects, a controller, a module (or model), and a view object.

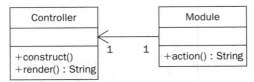

Figure 21-1

The `Controller` object (Figure 21-1) will be responsible for determining what type of action the application is trying to accomplish from the web request. It has two public methods, `__construct()` and `render()`. `__construct()` will be responsible for making sense of the web request. It will also process any posted information. `render()` will be responsible for executing the proper module action and returning the output of that action, if any.

The `Module` object (Figure 21-1) simply is a building block for each of the sections of the website. `Module` contains at least one public method to be executed by the `Controller` object. The `Module` class has been designed using a variation of the Template Design Pattern. Each section of the website will be creating its own type of `Module` similar to the base class.

The last element for our core is the `view` object (Figure 21-2).

view
+start() +end() : String +show(type : String,params : Array) : String +findviewtype()

Figure 21-2

The `view` object will have both a `start()` and `end()` public method. In my own experience, I've developed many different styles of views. I usually settle on using PHP's `ob_start()` method when generating views. It's reasonable to assume that the `start()` method will contain a call to `ob_start()`. The `end()` method should probably return whatever has been captured in the buffer.

The `view` object also has a public static method called `show()`. This accepts a string for the type of view to show. It also accepts a parameter array. The `show()` method needs to find the proper view based on the `type` string. Then, it would pass any of those parameters to the view that it's attempting to show.

My first thought is to have the show() method create view objects based on a Template object. It could then pass in the parameter array to the object or assign it directly as public properties. But after more consideration, I think that would be creating objects just for the sake of creating objects and would introduce too much overhead. Instead, the views will be included files on the file system with the parameter array as local variables.

I added the public static findviewtype() method as well. This will be used to set the current view type so that the show() method can reference it. Remember, the application has to support both conventional browsers and mobile browsers. The thought is to be able to call the show() method from any module without having to worry about what browser is being used. The view object should take care of that transparently for me.

After looking at just the first few objects I've diagramed, I know that I'm going to have a lot of work ahead of me! The programming step should be interesting. Let's continue with the next section of the application.

Designing User Interaction

Now that the core has been designed, the next section can be architected. The user interaction section will be a set of modules to provide an interface to the user. The interactions that are needed are:

- ❑ Authentication/authorization
- ❑ Creating, editing, deleting users
- ❑ Providing admin access to all users

Authentication and Authorization

When users access the first page of the site, there are two possible outcomes (Figure 21-3). If they are authenticated, they will see a listing of their contacts. If they are not authenticated, they will be redirected to a login page.

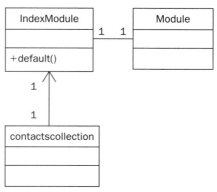

Figure 21-3

The `IndexModule` object will be an instance of the `Module` that I detailed in the core section. It has one public method, called `default()`, which is the action that the `Controller` object would execute during a call to `render()`. This method needs to make a decision whether to show a collection of contacts or to do the redirect.

Logically, I'm going to assume that the next step is to provide the login view for the user. (I'll discuss `contactscollection` later, but suffice it to say it's used if the current user is already authenticated.)

Login functionality will be provided by a module (Figure 21-4).

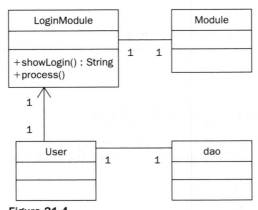

Figure 21-4

`LoginModule` has two public methods. The `showLogin()` method will return a string. This will make use of the `view` object's `show()` method. I'm going to plan that every public method of a module that is tasked with showing something and returning a string will be executing at least one call to the `view` object's `show()` method. Public methods that I name with a prefix of "process" probably won't make use of the `view` object.

Whatever view is displayed by `showLogin()` will accept a username and password. This will be for an employee user to log in to the website. One of the requirements of the application was to have a flexible authentication system. So far, it should still be pretty flexible. If later there is a need to show an e-mail address field, a different view could be shown by this module. Even further down the line, the `process()` public method could be called directly for things like Single Sign-On.

When the login screen is submitted, the `process()` method of the `LoginModule` object will be executed. Since the `Controller` object handles any data that is posted, `LoginModule` will need to interact with the `Controller` object to obtain the data submitted from the last view. It's important to note that I'm expecting to create a `User` object with this data. My thought is to attempt to create a `User` and then authenticate the `User` object with the password. If authentication fails, the `User` object will be discarded. My assumption is that more often than not, the `User` will be authenticated successfully so that it can be passed through to the rest of the system. It would be more wasteful to try to do a query against the user database to first determine if the password matched. If it did, I'd have to make a new `User` object anyway (which probably would execute another query!). It just seems better to create the user right away.

User is an instance of the dao object, which is based on the Data Access Object Design Pattern. Since the process() method of the LoginModule will be creating a new User object, which extends the dao object, the next step is to diagram how I'm going to attempt to implement the Data Access Object Design Pattern (see Figure 21-5).

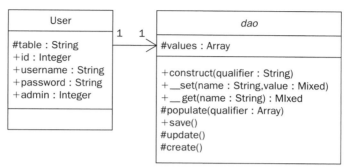

Figure 21-5

The User class extends the dao class. A User is identified by the four public attributes: id, username, password, and admin. The protected property table will be used by the dao class when it tries to access the data source.

The dao object's constructor takes a qualifier. If that qualifier is blank, nothing will happen. This will allow a new blank dao object to be created and later saved. However, to retrieve a dao object, some qualifier would be sent to the constructor of dao. The constructor would then call the protected populate() method with an array of qualifiers. I'm going to predict that I would either send in a username or an ID to retrieve a User. Because of this, I would expect the dao constructor to take the qualifier and determine a mapping based on what the child class's table variable is. The most logical approach is to match the public properties of the class to columns of the table. If all tables are created using a similar pattern, this could be a nearly automatic process. After that mapping is created, that information would be passed to the populate() method so that it can build a query.

The populate() method would be responsible for filling the protected values array with the information for that object. Then, PHP's magic __set() and __get() methods would be used to access that data to mimic properties for the child object's usage. I chose to do it this way, instead of just using properties, because I may, at some point in the future, want to add a few of my own public properties to the dao object. I wouldn't want to overwrite them with a child object's properties.

Looking at the User object UML diagram, I can see where it might be confusing that I've defined the public properties while mentioning above that it won't actually have any. Moving forward, public properties on any object extending the dao should be taken as inferred properties and not defined. This way, the __get() and __set() methods of the dao object will still be executed.

The public save() method of the dao object is called on demand when any change occurs to the child object. It is responsible for knowing if it should be updating an element or creating a new one. It calls either the protected update() or the protected create() method.

145

Both the `update()` and `create()` methods need to communicate with a database. Because the requirements right now include using the existing server, I know that I have access to MySQL. However, I want to make this abstract enough so that I can swap various database systems if need be. At some point, the software may be moving to a different platform, so this flexibility is necessary.

Because of this requirement, the first Design Pattern that pops out is the Factory Design Pattern. Right now, I'll be asking for a MySQL instance of a database connection. However, in the future, I could be asking the factory for a different database connection. Because I want to keep all data connections consistent so that no other modifications need to be made when swapping to a different one, it makes sense to also use the Template Design Pattern. The main `db` class will be a template for any of the specific database objects as well as provide the Factory to build them (Figure 21-6).

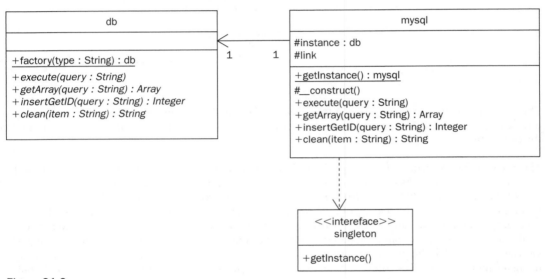

Figure 21-6

The `db` object has a public method called `factory()`. It accepts a string parameter to determine what type of database connection object it should be creating. Then, it will return an instance of that database connection object, which is really an instance of `db` through inheritance.

The remaining four methods are public methods declared abstractly. These are the building blocks of that Template Design Pattern. The `execute()` command will accept a query and run it. The `getArray()` method will accept a query, run it, and return the results as an array. The `insertGetID()` method will accept a query, run it, and return the ID of that insert, which is most likely the primary key. Finally, the `clean()` method will be responsible for filtering the content of a string item to remove any chance of SQL database injection.

The first database connection object I plan to create is the `mysql` object. It will extend the `db` object. The `mysql` object will be based on the Singleton Design Pattern and will implement the singleton interface. The first method of `mysql` is the public static `getInstance()` method required by the singleton interface. This will return an instance of itself that was stored in the protected static instance variable.

Each page on the website should only connect to the data source one time. This seems to suggest designing each database connection object using the Singleton Design Pattern. True to Singleton form, the __construct() method of mysql is protected. This will make it impossible to create a new instance of the class outside of itself — solidifying the need for the getInstance() method. A Singleton interface will force the existence of this needed method. Finally, the mysql object has the four abstract methods that were defined in the db object.

Reviewing my login module, I find that I am nearly there! I can now display a login screen, accept user input, and create a user using a Data Access Object–designed class. The last step is to handle authentication of the user.

During requirements gathering and analysis, I found out that the authentication method was not set in stone (Figure 21-7). Right now the method is unique from anything else in the company. However, I have to plan that it could be Single Sign-On, integrated with the webmail system or make use of the company network authentication system in the future. Because of this, I need that flexibility provided by the Factory method again.

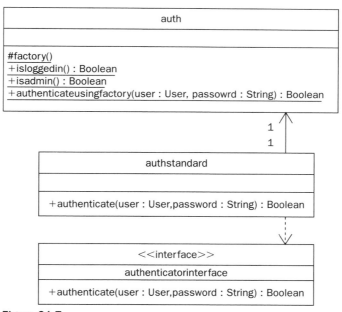

Figure 21-7

Instead of providing a public factory method again, I made it protected instead. My thought is that the auth object really only needs static methods anyway. So, to make it simpler, I'll just call the authenticateusingfactory() method directly. This will accept a User and a string of a password. Internally, the method will be tasked with getting an instance of an authenticator by calling the factory() method.

For lack of a better name, I'm calling the current authentication scheme "standard." The authstandard object is an example of an authenticator that could be used. Every authenticator needs to function the same on the exterior. This will require all to implement the authenticatorinterface. This interface defines only one method, named authenticate(). No matter the internal workings of the authenticator, they will all have the public authenticate() method that the authenticateusingfactory() method expects.

The thought is that a conditional comparison will be done using the static authenticateusingfactory() method. This will get an instance of an authenticator by using the factory() method. Then, without knowing anything else about the authenticator, it will return the output of the authenticate() method of the authenticator. The authenticateusingfactory() method would have to forward the User and password string to the authenticate() method, however.

After all this authentication is done, the user is logged in and forwarded back to the index module. The index module will now show the contactscollection object. I'll discuss this object more in an upcoming section.

Finally, two other things that are needed are accomplished with the remaining two public methods. The index module needs to know if a user is logged in. isloggedin() will determine this and return a Boolean return type. For user administration, the site needs to know if the current user is an admin. The isadmin() method will be used. It will probably return a Boolean type based on the admin property of the current User object.

It's important not to forget the opposite action of everything just planned: the logout. This will also be handled by a simple module (Figure 21-8).

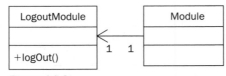

Figure 21-8

The LogoutModule will just have one public method that corresponds to its only action: logout(). This method will log out the current user and then redirect them back to the index module.

The authentication user creation sections overlap a little bit because of the creation of a User object during authentication. However, in this step, I'll define more of the User object interaction.

Creating, Editing, and Deleting Users

Administrators of the site should be able to create, edit, and delete authorized users of the system. This will be handled by the UsersModule (Figure 21-9).

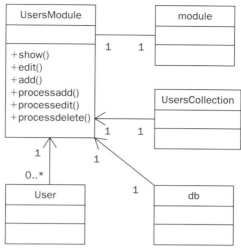

Figure 21-9

This module has six public methods that correspond to the six actions that I've planned for users. The add() and edit() methods will display a view for adding a user and editing a user, respectively. The show() method will display a view of all User objects that the current User has access to by using the UsersCollection object.

The processadd() and processedit() methods will interact with the User object. They will populate the public properties of the User object and then call the save() method on that dao. Because of the design of the dao object's save() method, it will know whether to add the object using the create() method or to invoke the update() method.

The processdelete() method will create a query to delete the user specified. It doesn't make sense to create a User object just to delete it. It seems that this process would probably take two queries instead of just forming one as I planned. I expect to work directly with a query and the db object in this method.

This concludes the methods that would work with an individual User object. The next section involves creating the administration interface to work with User objects. Then, the preceding processes can be executed.

Providing Admin Access to All Users

Since the show() method of the UsersModule works with the UsersCollection to display users that the current User has access to, the next step is to architect the collection class.

Since User is just a specialized instance of the dao object, it makes the most sense for the Users Collection to be a specialized instance of a daocollection. Because I'm creating a collection of objects contained inside of another object, the Iterator Design Pattern is the best choice. Since there will be different specialized collections, the Template Design Pattern will also influence the design of the daocollection object (Figure 21-10).

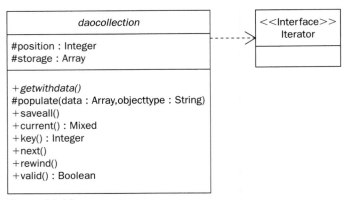

Figure 21-10

The `daocollection` class is an abstract object. It also implements the PHP's SPL Iterator interface named `Iterator`. Because of this, the following five public methods must be present: `current()`, `key()`, `next()`, `rewind()`, and `valid()`. In order to provide the functionality for these methods, two protected properties are added to the class. The first is the storage array, which will hold all of the `dao` objects that are collected. The other property is the position integer, which stores the location inside of the storage array that we're currently keyed into. Each of the previous methods will be tasked with updating or accessing the `position` and `storage` properties.

The protected `populate()` method accepts two parameters: a data array and a `dao` object type string. Basically, I envision it taking an array of data, probably gathered using something like the db object's `getArray()`. Then for each of the elements in the array, it'll create a new `dao` named after the second parameter and assign all values from the first array to that object. Finally, it will add the `dao` to the internal storage array.

The last method is an abstract public method called `getwithdata()`. Each specific type of `daocollection` child will have its own type of query to interact with the data source. Making this an abstract method of the `daocollection` object enforces its existence in accordance with the Template Design Pattern.

After further analysis, I've decided that every collection should have an owner. The collection should be a set of child `dao` objects for that owner. So, each `daocollection` child will need to accept a `dao` object when it's created. I figure that some properties of this owner will be used in order to determine the `dao` objects to populate the collection with.

The `UsersCollection` object (Figure 21-11) is the first collection that I'm planning to make. It extends the `daocollection` object I just described. It will also implement the `daocollection` interface.

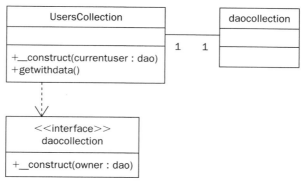

Figure 21-11

The `daocollection` interface specifies that the `daocollection` child should have a constructor that accepts a `dao` owner object.

`UsersCollection` has two public methods. The first, whose existence is enforced by the `daocollection` interface, is the constructor. `__construct()` accepts the current `User` as a parameter. I will probably use the current user instance to determine if the collection should even be made. Only admin type users should be able to see other users on the system. Remember, the `User` object has the public `admin` property.

The second public method is `getwithdata()`, which was defined as abstract in the `daocollection` object. This will get a database connection, build a query to get all of the users on the system, and then call the `populate()` method from the parent `daocollection`, passing in the retrieved results. It should also send in the string "User" to specify that the data should be used to create a collection of `User` `dao` objects.

With the `UsersCollection` object complete, this marks the end of the planning needed for user interaction. However, any user can have contacts in the system. The logical next step in planning is the final section of the application: contact administration.

Designing Contact Administration

Because of the extreme flexibility that the application will demonstrate, this next section works with a more complex set of relationships. In addition to these relationships, interfaces need to be created to add, edit, and delete any of those objects. Another interface needs to be created to adapt a set of contacts from Outlook into new contacts in this system. Finally, users need to be able to view the contacts that they own.

This contact administration is broken up into the following steps:

❑   Working with contacts and information

❑   Contact information relationships

❑   Importing contacts

❑   Viewing contacts

Working with Contacts and Information

The root of the contacts interaction is the ContactsModule. I'm going to start by defining this module (Figure 21-12).

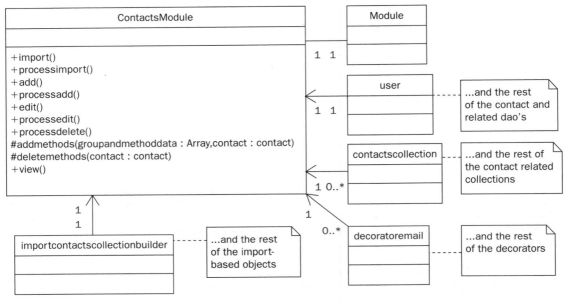

Figure 21-12

Predictably, the ContactsModule is an instance of a Module object. It has eight public methods. Displaying and processing additions, edits, and deletions are represented. Methods for accepting and processing the contacts to be imported are also defined. Finally, the view() method will be used to show an individual contact. There are two protected methods, addmethods() and deletemethods().

addmethods() will accept two parameters. One will be the current Contact that the application is adding methods to. The other will be an array of group and method information. My thought is that the add screen will have a set of boxes that allow the user to specify a group name and at least one method. Because there will be one or more groups, it seems like the best way to handle this would be an array. The name of the HTML input field would be able to use the opening and closing brackets to indicate an array to PHP.

The deletemethods() method takes a Contact object. It will delete all of the contact methods associated with that Contact, which in turn will delete all groups. Initially, I planned to send some sort of indicator or ID with the request to handle deleting only certain methods. But after further analysis, I think that would be too much overhead. During an edit, I'll provide all of the existing information. Then, all existing information will be deleted during the update. Any posted information will take its place.

There are many other classes that will be associated with this module. The User dao will be needed to know who owns the Contact that is being worked with. The contactscollection object will be used to show the entire list of contacts. The importcontactscollectionbuilder object will also be available to handle the Outlook contact imports. Finally, decorators to add functionality to the contact method information will be used in the `view()` method. These decorators will accomplish the requirement to be able to use contact information by clicking links directly inside of the application.

Contact Information Relationships

Earlier, I hinted at the complex relationship of the following items. Let's see this in UML (Figure 21-13).

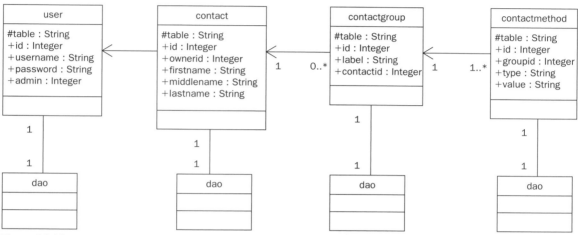

Figure 21-13

As I mentioned, any public attributes of these `dao` children classes should be inferred. They will reference columns in the database and will not be defined in the class itself.

A `User` object can own any number of `Contact` objects. A `Contact` can own any number of `contactgroup` objects as long as the group has at least one `contactmethod`. If no contact methods exist in the group, the `contactgroup` is not created. A `contactgroup` can own one or more `contactmethod` objects.

Importing Contacts

During the creation of this application, no contacts will be available for testing immediately. Because of this, the next logical step in planning is determining how contacts will be created.

A good source of contacts to prepopulate the application for my testing will be my Outlook contacts. This will be handled in the `ContactModule` object's `processimport()` public method.

Since this application works with collections of `dao` child objects, I need an object to convert import of contacts into that collection. Since the import format is complex and very much different from the `dao` collection, I'm going to use an object based on the Builder Design Pattern. My imports-processing method need not be concerned with how it obtains the collection, just that it has one. The builder will take the imported information — in this case a string from the outlook `.csv` file — and assign it to its protected `importedstring` property. The `buildcollection()` public method will return a collection of contact information.

After looking at the data in the .csv file from Outlook, I noticed that the storage mechanism for unique contact information and contact group information is different from our application's methods. The first, middle and last names are just named differently, so a simple object based on the Adapter Design Pattern will work. However, the grouping is a little bit more convoluted. An interpreter will be used to try to determine what groups, if any, exist (Figure 21-14).

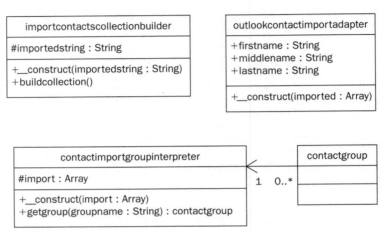

Figure 21-14

My thought is that the outlookcontactimportadapter object will be an adapter over the User dao. Because of this, it will require the firstname, middlename, and lastname public variables. Since this is not a true dao object, these properties will be defined and are not inferred. The constructor of the adapter will take an array representing the imported contact. This will probably be output from the importcontactscollectionbuilder. I think the contacts collection from the importcontactscollectionbuilder may not be a true contact until this adapter is applied to them.

The .csv stores information for groups by prefixing the information column with the group name. So, for phone number, there are a few variations: "Home Phone, "Business Phone," and "Other Phone." The interpreter will take this contact information in array format, similarly to the adapter I just planned, and return a contactgroup based on a name that is supplied to the getgroup() public method.

The interpreter will need to make some decisions based on the contact information and the parameter it receives. First, if it is passed "Home," it would need to look for columns like "Home Phone" to determine if there is a potential "Home" contactgroup. If I always pass in "Home" and "Business" to the interpreter, it would always return two groups because those columns will always exist in the .csv file. However, those columns may not actually have any contact information. The next decision the interpreter needs to make is whether it should actually create the contactgroup. This is based on the requirement that a contactgroup must have at least one contact method. If the "Home" set of columns does not have any information specified, it would not create the "Home" contactgroup.

Since the interpreter is already making sense of groups, it seems that it would be the best place for creating contact methods as well. It will generate import methods from the group it has defined and create them.

Now that the import contacts have been added, the next step is actually showing the contacts to the user.

Viewing Contacts

The `IndexModule` referenced the `contactscollection` class. To display this information (Figure 21-15), I'll use the `contactmodule` object's `view()` method. Since there are possibly a collection of `Contact dao` objects, a corresponding `daocollection` object needs to be created.

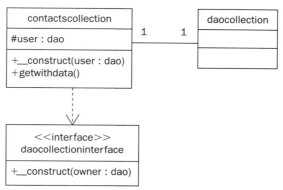

Figure 21-15

The `contactscollection` object is very similar to the `userscollection` object. It extends the `daocollection` object and implements the `daocollecitoninterface`. The one difference here is that the constructor's parameter is a `User dao` object. This `User` is the owner of the collection of `contact` objects. The `getwithdata()` method would use some identifying information from the `User` object to develop a query. From looking at the `Contact dao`, it is most logical to use the `User dao` object's `ID` property to build this relationship.

Now that I can deal with a collection of contacts, I need to focus on the single `Contact` and its collections of groups and methods. As demonstrated earlier, a `Contact` can have any number of `contactgroup` objects associated with it. Because of that, a `contactgroupscollection` object must exist (Figure 21-16).

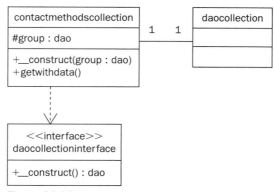

Figure 21-16

This object is similar to every other collection by extending the `daocollection` and implementing the `daocollectioninterface`. The specialty to this collection is the constructor's `dao` object. In this case, it's a `contact dao`, which represents the owner of all of the `contactgroup` objects in the collection. After looking at the relationship in an earlier diagram, I'm planning to include the `getwithdata()` method to make use of the `contact dao` object's public `id` property rather than the `contactgroup dao` object's `contactid` property.

Finally, the last building block of this relationship is the `contactmethod dao`. And, as with every other `dao` I'm dealing with, a corresponding collection object will be created (Figure 21-17).

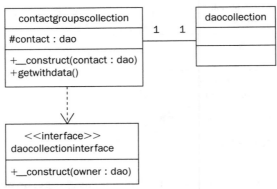

Figure 21-17

The `contactmethodscollection` object extends the `daocollection` and implements the `daocollectioninterface` as expected. The constructor accepts a `contactgroup dao` object. The `getwithdata()` method will use the `contactgroup dao` object's `id` property to compare to the `contactmethod dao` object's `contactgroupid` property.

Stepping back to the section "Working with Contacts and Information," it should be pretty apparent that it will be easy for the `ContactsModule` object's `processadd()`, `processedit()`, and `processdelete()` methods to build the proper relationships. Inserting the data should also be easy because of the features built into each `dao`. Finally, managing the collection should be simple because of the `daocollection` object's implementation of the `Iterator` interface.

Moving back to viewing the contact, I noted in the UML diagram for the `ContactsModule` a reference to an object named after the Decorator Design Pattern. The requirements of the application are to make sure that the information is available for interaction from the web page. This means users would like to click a link to a website instead of having to copy and paste it into an address bar. They should be able to click an e-mail address to send to it and so on.

Because there is information that I want to modify the display of — but not the actual content — the Decorator Design Pattern makes the most sense. These objects will accept the information and add some sort of functionality or markup to them.

Looking back, I notice that this requirement document wasn't entirely clear about what all of the expected functionality should be. I'm going to do some brainstorming and make some assumptions as to what functionality is needed.

This is the interaction list I developed:

- ❑ mailto: link for e-mail
- ❑ Clickable link for website
- ❑ Clickable link for social network
- ❑ Link to map for address
- ❑ Direct dial using mobile phone

The only one that really seems to have any complexity would be the direct dial using the mobile phone. I would have to make sure that that the decorator is familiar with what view the current user is using. All the other decorators are just adding additional information to the data.

To keep all of the objects based on the Decorator Design Pattern the same, I'll create an interface called `decoratorinterface` that will be implemented by each of them. It will be the responsibility of the `ContactsModule` object's `view()` method to apply each of the decorators shown in Figure 21-18 to the `contactmethod` object's output.

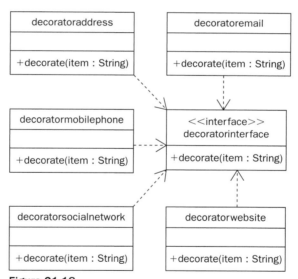

Figure 21-18

With the completion of the decorators, I think I've reached the end of my planning. As I mentioned earlier, I plan to use these UML diagrams as a blueprint and pattern for the actual programming, which will be discussed in the next chapter. Reviewing these UML diagrams, I can tell I have a complex task ahead of me. I would be completely surprised if all of the objects and methods turned out exactly the way I planned. I will make my best attempt to follow what I've planned, however. If things change, I'll make the changes in the programming, and continue on my way. Purists may argue that the UML diagrams should be updated whenever a change in architecture is discovered during the programming phase. While I can see this point, this is not something that I practice.

The next steps are the fun ones: moving from design to the actual application!

Summary

This chapter was an exploration of the planning steps needed to develop a plan for morphing a requirements document into an application. I discussed the three main parts of the application and their use. Starting with the core of the application, I demonstrated with the UML diagrams how I will create the logic and views for the application. As I moved through the user interaction and management section of the application, more objects emerged. Data access objects, collections and database manipulation objects were diagramed. Additionally, the main module pattern was defined for interacting with the web visitor. Finally, the most complex section of the application was addressed. The relationship of users and contacts was described. Additionally, the contact, group, and contact method object relationship was diagramed. The import method from the existing company contact system was also described. Decorators were also defined to provide the required interaction with contact methods. The next chapter will take all of this information and step through the process of coding the application.

22

Programming the Application

This is the chapter that every programmer has been looking forward to — the actual programming used to build this application. The requirements have been gathered and solidified, and the application plan and UML diagrams have been finished.

The first part of this chapter will be a quick reminder on how to prepare any of the information that will be needed for the application. In this particular case, it is only gathering the export from Outlook. Next, I'll pull up the previous chapter's plan and UML diagrams to begin programming each object using the design patterns I've specified. Along with the PHP, programming in JavaScript, HTML, and MySQL will also be detailed. The primary focus will be on PHP, however. This really means that non-PHP programming will be shown and only quickly explained. This supporting code is not the focus of this book.

The analysis of the completed program for any bugs or enhancements will appear in Chapter 23. Let's start with the information preparation.

Information Preparation

The requirements stated that any user of the application would need to import their contacts from the company's existing contact management software, Microsoft Outlook. Early in the plan, I made an assumption that this would be processed as a comma-separated value export.

In this case study, the company is using Outlook 2007 on Microsoft Windows. In order to produce my testing .csv file, I used the following process:

1. Open Microsoft Outlook 2007.
2. Click File ⇨ Import and Export . . .

3. Choose the Export to a file option from the Import and Export Wizard window.

4. Click the Next button.

5. Choose the Comma Separated Values (DOS) option.

6. Click the Next button.

7. Select the Contacts item under the Personal Folders parent item.

8. Click the Next button,

9. Type a location and name in the field labeled with Save exported file as. I used "c:\test.csv."

10. Click the Next button.

11. Click the Finish button to complete the process.

After this process, a new test .csv file should have been made. This is the process the users of the application would need to follow before they could choose to import their contacts.

The actual export file I'm going to use for testing has far too many columns to insert into the body of this book easily. (It can be downloaded with the other program files on this book's companion website.) However, for reference purposes while programming, I'll show a few excerpts from the file as follows (refer to Table 22-1 and 22-2).

Table 22-1: First Record Excerpt

First Name	Last Name	Home Street	Home City	Home State	Home Postal Code
John	Smith	123 Fourth Street	Beverly Hills	CA	90210

Table 22-2: Second Record Excerpt

First Name	Middle Name	Last Name	Company	Job Title	Business Street	Business City	Business State	Business Postal Code
William	Henry	Gates	Bill & Melinda Gates Foundation	Trustee	PO Box 23350	Seattle	WA	98102

There are many more columns in the excerpt. However, these two rows demonstrate that some contacts may have Home information or Business information. Contacts could have all of these fields filled in.

Now that the only external data needed to build the application has been gathered, I can continue on with the application programming.

Application Programming

Just like the planning phase, the programming portion of this chapter will be broken up into steps. These steps will be nearly identical to the steps discussed in the previous chapter. As mentioned before, the UML diagrams make great blueprints to move the programming of the application forward.

Three main sections will focus on:

- ❏ Main Core
- ❏ User Interaction and Administration
- ❏ Contact Administration

The Main Core section will address the UML diagrams of the objects that need to be created. Additionally, the file system layout and any other additional configuration options to make use of the objects will be described. The User Interaction and Administration section will continue on in this fashion. The UML diagrams will be transformed to PHP. Any additional testing processes and configurations will be mentioned. Finally, the Contact Administration process will conclude this chapter's application programming section by following the similar pattern. The Contact Administration section will make use of that `.csv` file that was created earlier.

Programming the Core of the Application

The core of the application is needed to launch any of the functionality in the User and Contacts section. The core is a necessity to having the website function but doesn't heavily showcase any of the design patterns specified in the reference chapters. Patiently follow me through creating the core of the application so that I can get to the sections demonstrating those design patterns in PHP.

The web server that is being used is serving pages using PHP 5.2.5, Apache 2.2.11 and MySQL 5.1.31. The application is designed to work on at least the Major/Minor versions of the previously listed software. The main reason I'm mentioning this is because of the next step regarding an Apache configuration file.

This application expects to be in the Document Root of your Apache instance. If you already have a website running in this instance, create a new Virtual Host and place the code there. The code uses the `$_SERVER['DOCUMENT_ROOT']` value throughout which will not work properly if the application is in a subdirectory.

Generate an .htaccess File for Specialized URLs

In this application, I'm planning on having human readable URLs. This URL scheme will also be used to directly reference specific module function names. As mentioned during planning, the controller object will be responsible for actually making sense and executing these calls.

In the root of the application, I will add the following file named `.htaccess`. Its content is shown here:

```
<IfModule !mod_rewrite.c>
    ErrorDocument 500 "mod_rewrite must be enabled"
</IfModule>
RewriteEngine on
```

```
RewriteCond %{REQUEST_FILENAME} !-f
RewriteCond %{REQUEST_FILENAME} !-d
RewriteRule ^(.*)$ /index.php?u=$1
```

This file does two things. First, it makes sure that the mod_rewrite functionality is active on the server. If not, a suitable error is generated. The other feature of this file is to take any request that is not directly a file or a directory and rewrite the request to call the main index.php file with the request as a Get parameter. The index.php file will have access to the controller and will grab the actions requested from the $_GET['u'] variable. This .htaccess file will go in the root of the application directory.

If you receive a "404 - Not Found" error when attempting to view the application through a browser, there may be an issue parsing the .htaccess file. Make sure that the file exists in the root directory of the application. Additionally, verify that your Apache configuration allows override. See http://httpd .apache.org/docs/2.0/mod/core.html#allowoverride for more information on Apache's .htaccess configuration options.

index.php, Managing Includes, Exceptions, and Controller

From my planning stage, I know that I will need to have included files. For the general functions used to build the core, I'm going to make a subdirectory called "includes." I will also make a subdirectory called "dataobjects" for the dao objects. Finally, I will make one named "modules" for each of the modules.

Next, I will make a file called index.php. This is the file that the .htaccess file will be redirecting all of the requests to. This file will be making use of the controller object. I'm planning on putting this object inside of the "includes" directory. I've decided to use an autoloader scheme to include any of the files from the three subdirectories I've already made. The index.php file will need to only ask for one include — the file where the autoloading logic exists. I also know that I will want to be using the session mechanism in PHP. index.php will take care of that.

This is the contents of index.php so far:

```php
<?php
require 'includes/autoloader.php';
session_start();
```

For the autoloader.php file, I'm using the SPL Autoload functionality. The contents of includes/ autoloader.php are as follows:

```php
<?php
class autoloader
{
    public static function moduleautoloader($class)
    {
        $path = $_SERVER['DOCUMENT_ROOT'] . "/modules/{$class}.php";
        if (is_readable($path)) require $path;
    }

    public static function daoautoloader($class)
    {
        $path = $_SERVER['DOCUMENT_ROOT'] . "/dataobjects/{$class}.php";
        if (is_readable($path)) require $path;
    }
```

```
    public static function includesautoloader($class)
    {
        $path = $_SERVER['DOCUMENT_ROOT'] . "/includes/{$class}.php";
        if (is_readable($path)) require $path;
    }
}
spl_autoload_register('autoloader::includesautoloader');
spl_autoload_register('autoloader::daoautoloader');
spl_autoload_register('autoloader::moduleautoloader');
```

The autoloader class contains three static methods. Each of these methods is responsible for trying to locate a specific type of include file. The one named `moduleautoloader()` tries to load modules. The descriptive names make their functionality self-explanatory.

The method to determine where a class exists is simple. The class exists inside of a PHP file named after the class. Since the SPL Autoload functionality allows multiple autoloader functions to be added to the stack, care is taken in each method to make sure no fatal errors are generated. If the method can find the desired class, whether it be include, module or a data object, it will `require()` it and code execution will go on. Only after all three methods have executed without finding a class named file will a fatal error be generated.

At the end of the file after the class declaration, each of the three autoloader static methods are registered using the `spl_autoload_register()` method.

Moving back to the `index.php` file, my next step would be to create an instance of the `controller` object. However, since I know this object will not only process the requested action but also make available any additional query information from the request, I would like to store this object somewhere where any method can access it.

I'm going to make a generic class called `lib`, which will contain a set of static methods. These will be methods that I may use to set and get information, modify objects or just do an action multiple times agnostic of their context. I'll create the `/includes/lib.php` file with the following contents:

```
class lib
{
    const SETTING_AN_ARRAY = TRUE;

    const NO_PERSISTENT_STORAGE = FALSE;

    public static function getitem($name, $persist = TRUE)
    {
        $return = NULL;

        if (isset($_SESSION[$name])) {
            $return = $_SESSION[$name];
            if (!$persist) unset($_SESSION[$name]);
        }

        return $return;
    }

    public static function setitem($name, $value, $array = false)
```

```
{
    if ($array) {
        if (!isset($_SESSION[$name])) {
            $_SESSION[$name] = array();
            $_SESSION[$name][] = $value;
        }
    }
    else {
        $_SESSION[$name] = $value;
    }
}
}
```

The getitem() and setitem() methods will be working directly with the $_SESSION variable so that I don't have to. The first method to look at is setitem(). It will accept three parameters: $name will signify the key for the information, $value will be the information to store and $array is a Boolean variable dictating if the item is really another value being added on to an array named after $name. By default, this is not something that I'll be doing. However, there are times when I might find it useful. $array, therefore, is set to false in the method declaration. The method simply assigns the value to a named key in the PHP session.

The getitem() method is used to retrieve information possibly set with the setitem() method. It takes two parameters: $name, representing the name of the value to retrieve, and $persist, which is a Boolean variable dictating if the item should continue to exist after being retrieved. The return value is set to NULL initially. Then, if it exists in the PHP session, the return value is set to that value. Finally, if $persist is false, that key in the $_SESSION variable is unset.

Two other things unique to this class are the constant declarations. In an effort to make more readable code, I like to define constants to be used in place of Boolean parameters that are set as default. Imagine implementing a call to setitem() using an array value and retrieving it without persistence. This normally would look like this:

```
lib::setitem('test', 123, TRUE);
$test_once = lib::getitem('test', FALSE);
```

While this does exactly what we want it to do, it's not very readable. Instead, using the constants I defined, my version of this code would look like this:

```
lib::setitem('test', 123, lib::SETTING_AN_ARRAY);
$test_once = lib::getitem('test', lib::NO_PERSISTENT_STORAGE);
```

I find this much easier to read and easier to debug.

Moving on, I'll add the following line to index.php:

```
lib::setitem('controller', new controller($_GET['u']));
```

I use the setitem() method of the lib class to store an instance of a new controller object. The controller object is constructed with access to the $_GET['u'] string that the .htaccess file provided. I'm expecting my includesautoloader() method of the autoloader class to find the file named /includes/controller.php, which will contain the following contents:

```php
<?php
class controller
{
    protected $parts;
    public $params;

    public function __construct($urlString)
    {
        $urlString = strtolower($urlString);

        if (substr($urlString, -1, 1) == '/') {
            $urlString = substr($urlString, 0, strlen($urlString) - 1);
        }

        $parts = explode('/', $urlString);
        if (empty($parts[0])) {
            $parts[0] = 'index';
        }
        if (empty($parts[1])) {
            $parts[1] = 'defaultaction';
        }

        $this->parts = $parts;
        $this->sectionaction = $parts[0] . '/' . $parts[1];
        array_shift($parts);
        array_shift($parts);
        $this->params = $parts;
    }

    public function render()
    {
        if (!class_exists($this->parts[0])) {
            throw new SectionDoesntExistException("{$this->parts[0]} is " .
                "not a valid module.");
        }

        if (!method_exists($this->parts[0], $this->parts[1])) {
            throw new ActionDoesntExistException("{$this->parts[1]} of " .
                "module {$this->parts[0]} is not a valid action.");
        }

        $called = call_user_func_array(array( new $this->parts[0],
                    $this->parts[1]), array($parts));

        if ($called === FALSE) {
        throw new ActionFailedException("{$this->parts[1]} of section " .
            "{$this->parts[0]} failed to execute properly.");
        }
    }
}
```

The controller has two public methods like the UML diagram in Figure 21-1 of Chapter 21 dictated: __construct() and render().

__construct() accepts a single parameter named $urlstring. Since it's responsible for taking this string and executing a module's method, some manipulation needs to be done to this string. First, the string will be converted to lowercase. Next, any ending forward slash will be removed. Finally, the string will be split into an array using the forward slash delimiter. Since its possible to not have any string at all by going to the root of the website, "index" is defined as the default module to process a request if none is given. It's also possible for a user to navigate to a module's URL without specifying an action. If this is the case, the action will be set to "defaultaction." This $parts array will be set to the protected $parts property of the controller object for later use in the render() method. The module and action portions of the $parts array are removed and the remainder of the array is added to the public $params array that any module's method could use. Remember, since this instance of the controller object was assigned to the session using setitem(), any of those methods will have the ability to retrieve it and access the public $params property.

The render() method's job is pretty simple. It first determines if the module exists by calling PHP's class_exist() on the first item in the $parts array. class_exist() will call each of the autoloaders trying to find that class. If it does not exist, a custom exception will be thrown. The same process is performed using method_exists() by accessing both the array element representing the module and the array element representing the action. Remember, every action is directly correlated to a method of the module. If the method is not found, a custom exception is thrown. Finally, this module and method are executed. If they fail to execute, a custom exception is thrown.

Before I go any farther, I want to define each of the custom exceptions that I've used in the controller by creating the file /includes/exceptions.php with the following content:

```php
<?php
class SectionDoesntExistException extends Exception {}
class ActionDoesntExistException extends Exception {}
class ActionFailedException extends Exception {}
class InternalException extends Exception {}
```

I added a fourth exception named InternalException that I plan to use whenever anything unexpected comes up in my programming. I hope to never use it! Finally, since this file doesn't follow the standard includes naming convention (it would be silly to create four nearly empty files for each of these exceptions), I need to add the following line to the index.php file:

```php
require 'includes/exceptions.php';
```

This will make sure that the exceptions are available for the controller and any other class that may make use of InternalException.

Creating the View Object

With the completion of the controller object, the next step is creating the view object. According to the UML diagram in Figure 21-2 of chapter 21, it will have four public methods. The start() method will make use of PHP's ob_start() function and end() will make use of the content-gathering mechanism. In the middle of these two steps, the controller will need to call the module and action specified. With this in mind, I can add the following lines to index.php:

```php
$view = new view();
lib::getitem('controller')->render();
$content = $view->finish();
```

A new instance of the `view` object is created, I access the stored controller object and call `render()`, and finish by capturing the output into the `$content` variable. The `view` object will be loaded by the includes autoloader. The contents of `/includes/view.php` so far are this:

```
class view
{
    public function __construct()
    {
        ob_start();
    }

    public function finish()
    {
        $content = ob_get_clean();
        return $content;
    }
}
```

This is a very simple way to gather the output from the rendered module action.

The next function to add to the view object is the static `setviewtype()` method. I will have the `show()` method accessing a protected static variable named `$viewtype` to find the include files it needs. `setviewtype()` will be executed the first time `show()` is executed. I will add the following method to the view class:

```
protected static function setviewtype()
{
    switch (TRUE) {
        case stripos($_SERVER['HTTP_USER_AGENT'], 'Windows CE')
            ! == FALSE:
            self::$viewtype = 'mobile';
            break;
        default:
            self::$viewtype = 'default';
    }
}
```

This method is built to determine the view based on the HTTP User Agent. Since it's required to support the Windows Mobile platform, I look for that particular identifier. If that's found, I set the view to mobile. Otherwise, it's the default view type. The structure of this method is built to easily allow for more views to be added by adding another case in the switch statement.

In this particular case, the HTTP User Agent header provides the proper information to identify this type of view. This will not always be the case, however. The HTTP User Agent can be modified or misreported by a user's browser. Additionally, future versions of Windows Mobile may not include the string 'Windows CE' in their header. Currently, this method works accurately because of the controlled nature of the browsers accessing the application: business issued standard mobile devices. If this application was distributed to other parties, this would be a portion of code that may need to be revisited.

The `show()` method presented some interesting decisions that I had to make. I finally decided that I'd like to make as few duplicate views as possible. For the most part, if I'm programming proper HTML, the biggest differences in my mobile view verses my browser view should be CSS-based. I also may not allow certain functionality in the mobile version. So, my thought was to build a browser based application. Then, if something besides the default browser view is requested, I'll check for that type of view. If it does not exist, I'll continue with rendering the default view. This way, I reduce the duplicity of views if not needed.

The show() method should also be able to locate the view file on the file system automatically based on the $viewtype variable. Because of this, I decided to make a subdirectory in the application root called "views." It would contain subdirectories for each type of view. In the first iteration of the application, two subdirectories would exist: default and mobile.

Finally, the show() method should be able to allow variables to be passed into the included view file to be evaluated. Since these are being evaluated on the fly, output buffering should be used as well — much like the start() and end() methods of the view object. This is what the static show() method code will be:

```php
public static function show($location, $params = array())
{
    if (empty(self::$viewtype)) {
        self::setviewtype();
    }

    $views = array();

    if (self::$viewtype != 'default') {
        $views[] = $_SERVER['DOCUMENT_ROOT'] . '/views/' .
            self::$viewtype .
                '/' . $location . '.php';
    }
    $views[] = $_SERVER['DOCUMENT_ROOT'] . '/views/default/' .
            $location . '.php';

    $content = '';

    foreach ($views as $viewlocation) {
        if (is_readable($viewlocation)) {
            $view = $params;

            ob_start();
            include $viewlocation;
            $content = ob_get_clean();
            break;
        }
    }

    return $content;
}
```

The show() method accepts two parameters, the location of the view and any parameters to pass to the view. The location variable could just as easily been a name for a view, but I felt that an organizational method of grouping views in folders might work better. This location string will mirror that organization. For example:

```php
echo show('login/form');
// this would reference /views/default/login/form.php
```

The first step in the `show()` method is to check to make sure that the view type is set. If it is not, the `setviewtype()` method created earlier is executed.

Next, an array of view locations is created. This will be looped through to try to find an include file to use. If the current view is not default, a path representing the view type is added to the array. After all this, the default path is also added.

Next, each of the possible views are looped through. The function checks to see if the path is readable. If the path and file is found to be available, output buffering is turned on, the `$params` array is added as a local variable, it's included, and `$content` receives the output. Then, no more instances of the loop happen. This type of loop solves the decision to only create certain views for the mobile view.

It is important to note that this method never generates a fatal error or exception if the view is not found. I debated generating an error because I felt it may be sloppy programming otherwise. In the end, I decided to leave it as it is. This way, I can add extra views that don't exist right now as placeholders to be modified later. If the team grew larger in a real enterprise, the lead architect could generate view locations while assigning other team members the actual creation of said views. Finally, this method returns the `$content` variable.

The final step to be added to `index.php` is a call to show the content of the `controller` object's `render()` method using the `view` objects `show()` method. Since I've incrementally built the `index.php` file, I'll show the final product here:

```php
<?php
require 'includes/autoloader.php';
require 'includes/exceptions.php';
session_start();

lib::setitem('controller', new controller($_GET['u']));

$view = new view();
lib::getitem('controller')->render();
$content = $view->finish();

echo view::show('shell', array('body'=>$content));
```

Creating the Main Views

Now that I'm moving on to making actual output for the screen, I'm adding a new subdirectory called "assets." This will be the location of any CSS and JavaScript files.

The last line of `index.php` references the view location called "shell." This is the main shell of the website. There are two locations for this file: the default location for the browser and a slimmed down version for the mobile view.

The contents of `/views/default/shell.php`:

```
<!DOCTYPE html PUBLIC "-//W3C//DTD XHTML 1.0 Strict//EN"
    "http://www.w3.org/TR/xhtml1/DTD/xhtml1-strict.dtd">
<html xmlns="http://www.w3.org/1999/xhtml">
<head>
    <meta http-equiv="Content-Type" content="text/html; charset=utf-8" />
```

```
        <link rel="stylesheet" type="text/css" href="/assets/main.css" />
        <title>Acme Company Contact Manager</title>
        <script type="text/javascript" src="/assets/jquery-1.3.2.min.js">
            </script>
    </head>
    <body>
        <div id="header"><?php echo view::show('standard/header'); ?></div>
        <div id="body">
            <?php echo $view['body'] ?>
        </div>
        <div id="footer"><?php echo view::show('standard/footer'); ?></div>
    </body>
    </html>
```

The contents of /views/mobile/shell.php:

```
<!DOCTYPE html PUBLIC "-//W3C//DTD XHTML 1.0 Strict//EN"
    "http://www.w3.org/TR/xhtml1/DTD/xhtml1-strict.dtd">
<html xmlns="http://www.w3.org/1999/xhtml">
<head>
    <meta http-equiv="Content-Type" content="text/html; charset=utf-8" />
    <link rel="stylesheet" type="text/css" href="/assets/main.css" />
    <title><?php echo view::show('standard/title')?></title>
</head>
<body>
    <div id="header"><?php echo view::show('standard/header'); ?></div>
    <div id="body">
        <?php echo $view['body'] ?>
    </div>
    <div id="footer"><?php echo view::show('standard/footer'); ?></div>
</body>
</html>
```

In this particular example, the only difference between these two files is the lack of JQuery in the mobile view. Because of this, I'll base my discussion on the default shell.php *file.*

This view builds the standard web page. It includes HTML tags for the title, for including the CSS and the JavaScript. A header block, body, and footer are also included in the content before the HTML file is closed.

The first thing to note is the reference to $view['body']. Since output buffering is being used, these included files can show content that is passed to them by using echo or print. This will be added in the middle of this HTML much like a standard PHP file. The $view variable is the local instance of the parameters that the show() method of the view object made available to the included PHP file.

Notice the other calls to the view object's show() method. I'm including a header and footer view as well. Because of the architecture of the show() method using output buffering, these recursive calls to itself are possible.

The contents of /assets/main.css follow. (It may be useful to bookmark this page of this chapter and flip back now and then to keep these CSS declarations fresh in your memory.)

```css
body {
    font: 14px tahoma, verdana, sans-serif;
    padding: 0;
    margin: 0;
    background-color: #f9f9f9;
}
table {
    border-collapse: collapse;
}
table td {
    border: 1px solid #ccc;
    padding: 3px;
}
hr {
    clear: both;
    margin: 20px 0;
}
fieldset, legend {
    padding: 3px;
    border: 1px solid #aaa;
}
legend {
    font-weight: bold;
    background-color: #ddd;
    margin-bottom: 6px;
}
fieldset {
    margin-bottom: 10px;
}
form div.row {
    clear: left;
    display: block;
    margin: 5px 0 0;
    padding: 1px 3px;
}
label {
    display: block;
    float: left;
    width: 150px;
    font-weight: bold;
    text-align: right;
    margin: 0 0 5px;
    padding: 3px 5px;
}
input {
    border: 1px solid #ccc;
    padding: 1px 3px;
    width: 200px;
    float: left;
}
```

```css
select {
    float: left;
    margin-right: 2px;
}
input:focus, select:focus {
    background-color: #f9f9f9;
}
input.submitbutton {
    border: 2px solid #333;
    background-color: #369;
    color: #fff;
    cursor: pointer;
    font-weight: bold;
    width: auto;
}
input.radio {
    width: auto;
    border: none;
    float: none;
}
.radiooption {
    margin-right: 10px;
}
.error {
    color: #f00;
}
#header {
    border-bottom: 1px solid #ccc;
}
#footer {
    text-align: center;
    clear: both;
}
#header, #footer {
    background-color: #333;
    padding: 5px;
}
#header ul {
    list-style: none;
    margin: 0px;
    padding: 0px;
}
#header li {
    display: inline;
    margin-right: 10px;
}
#header a, #header a:visited, #footer a, #footer a:visited {
    color: #eee;
}
#body {
    width: 990px;
    margin: 0px auto;
    border: solid #ccc;
```

```css
    border-width: 0 1px;
    padding: 5px;
    background-color: #fff;
    min-height: 500px;
}
.sidebar {
    padding: 5px;
    float: right;
}
a.featured {
    padding: 10px;
    color: #000;
    font-weight: bold;
    background-color: #6f6;
    margin: 5px;
}
a.featured:hover {
    background-color: #292;
    color: #fff;
}
.sidebar a.removal {
    background-color: #f66;
}
.contactgrouping {
    border: 1px solid #ccc;
    background-color: #f9f9ff;
    margin-bottom: 10px;
}
.contactgrouping a, .contactgrouping a:visited {
    display: block;
    font-size: 10px;
    color: #00f;
}
.contactgrouping a.addcontactgrouping,
    .contactgrouping a.deletecontactgrouping {
    padding-top: 20px;
    clear: both;
}
.methodboxvaluebox {
    display: none;
}
#contactgroupingcontainer {
    display: none;
}
.hasvalue {
    display: block;
}
#browsecontacts a {
    padding: 5px;
    border: 1px solid #f4f4f4;
    display: block;
    font-weight: bold;
    color: #000;
}
```

```
#browsecontacts a:hover {
    border-color: #69f;
    background-color: #def;
}
#loginbox {
    margin: 0 auto;
    width: 500px;
}
```

Since I've already planned out the `auth` object in the UML diagram in Figure 21-7 of Chapter 21, I can write the header view from start to finish. Granted, if I ran it right now, there would a fatal error. However, I can make a pretty good assumption on how to use the methods I've already diagramed.

The contents of `/views/default/standard/header.php`:

```php
<?php
if (auth::isloggedin()) {
    $links = array('/'=>'Home',
                    '/contacts/add'=>'Add Contact',
                    '/contacts/import'=>'Import Contacts');

    if (auth::isadmin()) {
        $links['/users'] = 'User Admin';
    }
    $links['/logout'] = 'Log Out';

    echo '<ul>';
    foreach ($links as $link=>$title) {
        echo '<li><a href="' . $link . '">' . $title . '</a></li>';
    }
    echo '</ul>';
}
```

This view basically checks to see if the user is logged in. If they are not, nothing happens. However, if they are logged in, a menu is built and displayed as an unordered list. If the user is an admin, an additional link is added to the menu.

The browser version of this is stripped down. (I promise there won't be this many duplicate views going forward!) The contents of `/views/mobile/standard/header.php`:

```php
<?php
if (auth::isloggedin()) {
    $links = array('/'=>'Home', '/logout'=>'Log Out');

    echo '<ul>';
    foreach ($links as $link=>$title) {
        echo '<li><a href="' . $link . '">' . $title . '</a></li>';
    }
    echo '</ul>';
}
```

The mobile view simply doesn't give options for the User or Contact administration. The rest is the same.

The footer view, located only at `/views/default/standard/footer.php`, has the following contents:

```
<a href="http://www.acmecompany.com">Corporate Site</a>
| <a href="mailto:helpdesk@acmecompany.com">Contact Helpdesk</a>
```

While the application still can't load a single page, you've made progress! The core is built and some views are generated. The next section will focus on the modules and their actions. That is where you'll start to see the fruits of this hard work.

Programming User Interaction and Administration

The core is in place. The next step in our UML diagrams is to build the `index` module. Although the UML diagrams in Chapter 21 shows that each of the modules extend a `Module` class, I haven't really found a good use for that. So far, I haven't been able to determine a set of shared methods or properties that would require this. Because of this, I'm just going to create each module independently.

Index and Login Modules

The modules subdirectory was created to hold any of the modules. The content of `/modules/index.php` is:

```php
class index
{
    public function defaultaction()
    {
        if (!auth::isloggedin()) {
            lib::sendto('/login');
        }
        else {
            $contacts = new contactscollection(lib::getitem('user'));
            $contacts->getwithdata();

            echo view::show('contacts/browse', array('contacts'=>
                                                      $contacts));
        }
    }
}
```

Remember, the controller object assigns the "index" module as the section if none is specified. And, if no action is specified, the action is defined as `defaultaction`. Because of this, and the fact that the index view is a simple forward slash on the URI, the only method needed in the index module is `defaultaction()`.

The `defaultaction()` method makes the decision to show the `contactscollection` object or to redirect the user to the login screen. Once again, I am referencing the `auth` object's static `isloggedin()` method. According to my planning, that will return a Boolean. I will work with this after the login process is programmed. The reason I'm putting this off is because I want to figure out how to actually log in a user first. This will be decided when programming the `login` module. After that, I'll have my template for dealing with authenticated users, so the `isloggedin()` method will be an easy addition.

I've created another static method in the `lib` class to handle any of my redirects called `sendto()`:

```php
public static function sendto($url = '')
{
    if (empty($url)) {
        $url = '/';
    }

    die(header('Location: ' . $url));
}
```

This method simply accepts an URL to redirect the user to using an HTTP header. If no URL is specified, the user is redirected to the index page.

Since the URL that is being sent to `sendto()` contains the word "login," the next module to program is the login module. The contents of `/modules/login.php` so far is:

```php
class login
{
    public function defaultaction()
    {
        echo view::show('login/form');
    }
}
```

Remember, since the request URI only contains "/login," the `defaultaction()` public method is implied and will be executed. The default action of the login module is to show the login form. The following content makes up the `/views/default/login/form.php` file:

```php
<div id="loginbox">
    <h1>Login</h1>
    <?php
        echo view::show('standard/errors');
    ?>
    <form action="/login/process" method="post">
        <div class="row">
            <label for="username">Username:</label>
            <input type="text" name="username" id="username"
                value="<?php echo lib::getitem('username')?>" />
        </div>
        <div class="row">
            <label for="password">Password:</label>
            <input type="password" name="password" id="password" />
        </div>
        <div class="row">
            <label for="submit"> </label>
            <input id="submit" type="submit" value="login"
                class="submitbutton" />
        </div>
    </form>
</div>
```

This view simply displays a login form. The login form will submit to the URL /login/process which will be the process() method of the login module. Another view is inserted at the top that will be used to show any errors. I can imagine that users may accidentally type their password wrong, so they need to be notified of this. Finally, the only other notable item is the value of the username HTML Input item. The getitem() method of the lib class is executed here. If the user has not previously submitted a username, NULL will be returned and nothing will be printed. I need to make sure to set the username using lib::setitem() in the process() method, however.

The view that was inserted is located at /views/default/standard/errors.php:

```php
<?php
    $errors = lib::getitem('error', lib::NO_PERSISTENT_STORAGE);
    if (is_array($errors)) {
        print '<ul class="error"><li>' .
            implode('</li><li>', $errors) . '</li></ul>';
    }
```

This view will try to retrieve the error key from the session. Note, it will only allow the error key to exist once. Then, after retrieving it, the extra parameter passed to lib::getitem() will make sure it's unset. If the result is an array, it's looped through and displayed.

After this is complete, you should be able to see a screen very similar to the one in Figure 22-1.

Login

Username:
Password:

login

Corporate Site | Contact Helpdesk

Figure 22-1

The next method is the `process()` method of the login module. Without planning, this would be a pretty hit and miss programming excursion. However, I've planned out enough about my `User` and `Auth` objects that I can write this method start to finish pretty simply. Here is the content of `process()` — a public method of the login module:

```
public function process()
{
    $username = $_POST['username'];
    $password = $_POST['password'];

    if (empty($username)) {
        lib::seterror('Please enter a username.');
        lib::sendto('/login');
    }

    if (empty($password)) {
        lib::setitem('username', $username);
        lib::seterror('Please enter a password.');
        lib::sendto('/login');
    }

    $user = new user(array('username'=>$username));

    if (auth::authenticate($user, $password)) {
        lib::setitem('user', $user);
        lib::sendto();
    }
    else {
        lib::setitem('username', $username);
        lib::seterror('Invalid username or password.');
        lib::sendto('/login');
    }
}
```

This method is also pretty simple. It retrieves the username and password from the posted content. If either of them is empty, an error is set and the user is redirected back to the login page. Don't forget to set the username if the password was empty. The newest edition here is a static method called `seterror()` to the `lib` class. I wanted to save some time by creating a method to easily set errors that my errors view would parse through. The content of the `lib::seterror()` method is:

```
public static function seterror($error)
{
    self::setitem('error', $error, self::SETTING_AN_ARRAY);
}
```

This method is just a quick call to the existing `setitem()` static method using its array feature.

The last few steps of the `process()` method were earlier notes of discussion. I tried to determine which would be better: creating a `user` and then authenticating it or authenticating the credentials and then creating a `user`. Because of my decision, the next step is to make a new `user` object. The planning of my project told me that the `dao` object that `user` is based on can accept a qualifier that maps to the user table. In this case, I'm sending the `$username` variable in to be used to locate a `user` by the username column.

Next, the `authenticate()` public method of the `auth` object is executed. My `auth` UML diagram in Figure 21-7 in chapter 21 shows this to be the only method that I need to call. Choosing the proper authentication scheme will all be handled by the factory call inside of this method. If `authenticate()` returns false, I'll store the username and redirect the user back to the login page. If it returns a success, I'll store the current `user` object to the session. This way, I'll know about the current user when it comes to building the `contactscollection` object. This also gives me a hint on how to build my `auth::isloggedin()` and `auth::isadmin()` methods: they need to access the stored `user` object by executing `lib::getitem()`. Seems pretty simple! The next step is to figure out exactly how that `dao user` object was created.

Data Access Object and User Object

Since a necessity of the `Login` module was creating a new `User` object, I need to reference that set of UML diagrams in Figure 21-5 of Chapter 21. The first class I'm going to build is the abstract `dao` class. Since this is not an actual data object but an included class to build from, it will be located at /includes/dao.php with the following content:

```
class dao
{
    protected $values = array();

    public function __construct($qualifier = NULL)
    {
        if (!is_null($qualifier)) {

            $conditional = array();

            if (is_numeric($qualifier)) {
                $conditional = array('id'=>$qualifier);
            }
            else if (is_array($qualifier)) {
                $conditional = $qualifier;
            }
            else {
                throw new Exception('Invalid type of qualifier given');
            }

            $this->populate($conditional);
        }
    }

    public function __set($name, $value)
    {
        $this->values[$name] = $value;
    }

    public function __get($name)
    {
        if (isset($this->values[$name])) {
            return $this->values[$name];
        }
        else {
            return null;
        }
    }
```

```php
    }

    protected function populate($conditional)
    {
        $connection = db::factory('mysql');

        $sql = "select * from {$this->table} where ";
        $qualifier = '';

        foreach ($conditional as $column=>$value) {
            if (!empty($qualifier)) {
                $qualifier .= ' and ';
            }
            $qualifier .= "`{$column}`='" . $connection->clean(
                $value) . "' ";
        }

        $sql .= $qualifier;
        $valuearray = $connection->getArray($sql);
        if (!isset($valuearray[0])) {
            $valuearray[0] = array();
        }

        foreach ($valuearray[0] as $name=>$value) {
            $this->$name = $value;
        }
    }

    public function save()
    {
        if (!$this->id) {
            $this->create();
        }
        else {
            $this->update();
        }
    }

    protected function create()
    {
        $connection = db::factory('mysql');

        $sql = "insert into {$this->table} (`";
        $sql .= implode('`, `', array_keys($this->values));
        $sql .= "`) values ('";

        $clean = array();
        foreach ($this->values as $value) {
            $clean[] = $connection->clean($value);
        }

        $sql .= implode("', '", $clean);
        $sql .= "')";

        $this->id = $connection->insertGetID($sql);
```

```
    }

    protected function update()
    {
        $connection = db::factory('mysql');

        $sql = "update {$this->table} set ";

        $updates = array();
        foreach ($this->values as $key=>$value) {
            $updates[] = "`{$key}`='" . $connection->clean($value) . "'";
        }

        $sql .= implode(',', $updates);
        $sql .= "where id={$this->id}";

        $connection->execute($sql);
    }
}
```

The UML diagram showed that the dao object would have a lot of methods, so don't be surprised by the length of this code snippet. It breaks down pretty easily — especially if you remember the decisions and planning that I mentioned in the previous chapter.

The first method is the constructor. This accepts an optional qualifier. If it is NULL, nothing besides the initial creation of the object will happen. However, if it is sent, a conditional is built. If a single numeric variable is sent, it's assumed that that will be the primary key of the table labeled "id." Otherwise, the array of the qualifier is sent through as is. This allows the creation of a new dao object — such as user — in multiple ways:

```
$u = new user(12); //by primary ID = 12
$u = new user(array('username'=>'ted')); //username column = ted
$u = new user(array('username'=>'ty', 'admin'=>1));
    //username column=aaron,admin=1
```

Then, the qualifier/conditional information is sent to the protected populate() method to fill the properties of the dao object.

The protected method property() of the dao class deals directly with the data source. In this case, I'm using the factory method of the db object to retrieve a connection to the MySQL database. Then, the SQL statement is built.

Three important things should be noted about the creation of the query. First, it references the table property of the class. Any of the children of the dao object must define this property in order for the query to be created successfully. The next thing to notice is the way the conditional is applied to the statement. Because the class accepts or converts the qualifier into an array, the SQL statement can anonymously build this query. The final thing to notice is the call to the clean() method of the db object. I will leave it up to the database object to determine how to sanitize the user input.

The last step of the populate() method is executing the query. If a result is attained, each of the values of that array are assigned to public properties of the dao object. During the planning phase of the dao object and children classes, I decided that the class should take advantage of the PHP magic methods of __get() and __set(). Each just executes operations against the protected $values array of the object.

The public save() method determines if the object is new or needs to be updated. Then, it calls either create() or save() as I planned. Both share similarities with the populate() method by their acquisition of the database object and the automation of the query building. The only thing that should be noted is the assignment of the primary key "id" to the object after it is created for the first time.

With the creation of the parent dao class, I can now shift to creating the User dao object located at / dataobjects/user.php:

```php
<?php
class user extends dao
{
    protected $table = __CLASS__;
}
```

Right now, the only thing this object needs to do is define the protected $table property that the populate(), update(), and create() methods need. I've decided to name the table for the User dao object "user" in the MySQL database. The following statement is used to create the database:

```
CREATE TABLE `contacts`.`user` (
  `id` int(10) unsigned NOT NULL AUTO_INCREMENT,
  `username` varchar(64) NOT NULL,
  `password` varchar(40) NOT NULL,
  `admin` tinyint(3) unsigned NOT NULL DEFAULT '0',
  PRIMARY KEY (`id`)
) ENGINE=InnoDB;
```

Database Connection Objects

Obviously, the dao object relies heavily on the database. Moving along to the next UML diagram in Chapter 21, Figure 21-6, I can see my plans for the db, mysql, and singleton objects.

The first thing I want to create is the db object. Most of this class is abstract, so the definition should be quite short. It is located in the /includes/db.php file:

```php
abstract class db
{
    public static function factory($type)
    {
        return call_user_func(array($type, 'getInstance'));
    }

    abstract public function execute($query);
    abstract public function getArray($query);
    abstract public function insertGetID($query);
    abstract public function clean($string);
}
```

Just like the UML diagram specified, the db class is abstract and so are the four public methods named execute(), getArray(), insertGetID(), and clean(). The only method defined in this class is named factory() because it is based on the Factory Design Pattern. It simply returns the results of calling the getInstance() method of a class named after the $type parameter.

For more on the Factory Design Pattern, see Chapter 9.

In the dao object, I asked for an instance of the mysql database connection object. This is located at / includes/mysql.php and has the following contents:

```php
<?php
class mysql extends db implements singletoninterface
{
    protected static $instance = null;
    protected $link;

    public static function getInstance()
    {
        if (is_null(self::$instance)) {
            self::$instance = new self;
        }

        return self::$instance;
    }

    protected function __construct()
    {
        $user = 'user';
        $pass = 'pass';
        $host = 'localhost';
        $db = 'contacts';

        $this->link = mysql_connect($host, $user, $pass);
        mysql_select_db($db, $this->link);
    }

    public function clean($string)
    {
        return mysql_real_escape_string($string, $this->link);
    }

    public function getArray($query)
    {
        $result = mysql_query($query, $this->link);

        $return = array();

        if ($result) {
            while ($row = mysql_fetch_array($result, MYSQL_ASSOC)) {
                $return[] = $row;
            }
        }

        return $return;
```

```
    }

    public function execute($query)
    {
        mysql_query($query, $this->link);
    }

    public function insertGetID($query)
    {
        $this->execute($query);
        return mysql_insert_id($this->link);
    }
}
```

The first method defined is the public static getInstance(). The UML diagram defines it, the db object's factory() method will call it and the singleton interface (which I'll discuss next) requires it. This method simply checks to see if the protected static property of $instance is holding an instance of the mysql object. If not, it creates an instance and assigns it to $instance. Then, the method ends by returning the reference to that mysql object by using $instance as its return property.

The constructor of the mysql object simply creates a connection to the database. It then stores the link to the database in the protected $link property. Finally, it selects the proper database. The link property will be used whenever queries are executed or strings are cleaned.

> *When working with possibly multiple data sources, it's good to explicitly reference the link you'd like to work with. Otherwise, the query could execute using a different connection, possibly destroying a buffered request. Additionally, if character encoding types are different on the databases, cleaning of the string based on one encoding may still leave troublesome characters in the string for the other connection's encoding.*

The other four public methods are required to be defined by their definition as abstract in the db object. I'll thank the Template Design Pattern for that helpful bit. The first is the clean() method. It accepts the "dirty" string, executes the MySQL string sanitization function, and returns the "clean" string. The next is the execute() method. It simply runs the query passed in via the $query parameter. The insertGetID() method is also very short. It calls the execute() method, followed by returning the ID retrieved by calling mysql_insert_id() on the MySQL connection link that execute() used.

> *For more on the Template Design Pattern, see Chapter 18.*

The final method is getArray(). It executes the MySQL query and holds on to the result pointer. Then, it loops through all of the results and builds a numeric keyed array of associative keyed arrays from the results. Finally, it sends this out by returning the $return array.

The last piece of the UML diagram was the singleton interface. This simple interface is located at /includes/singletoninterface.php:

```php
<?php
interface singletoninterface
{
    public static function getInstance();
}
```

This interface just forces the db child objects to have that getInstance() method that db::factory() is expecting.

Authentication Objects

It seems like ages ago when I last touched the Login module. However, I'm still in the middle of this module's process() method. The last undefined portions are the auth object's methods.

The three public methods of the UML diagram's representation of the auth object have already been used in the code base (see Chapter 21, Figure 21-7 for the diagram). I'm going to create /includes/ auth.php with the following contents:

```php
<?php
class auth
{
    public static function isloggedin()
    {
        return !is_null(lib::getitem('user'));
    }

    public static function isadmin()
    {
        return self::isloggedin() && (1 == lib::getitem('user')->admin);
    }

    public static function authenticate(user $user, $password)
    {
        $authenticator = self::factory('standard');
        return $authenticator->authenticate($user, $password);
    }

    protected static function factory($type)
    {
        $class = "auth{$type}";
        if (class_exists($class)) {
            return new $class;
        }
        else {
            throw new InternalException($type . ' is not a defined
                                        auth module.');
        }
    }
}
```

The first public static method is named isloggedin(). This was both used in the header view as well as the Login Module. Since I already created the successful version of authentication, which is storing the current User object into the session, this method is simple. It simply checks to see if there is a user object in the session. If there is, the user had logged in successfully.

The next public static method is named isadmin(). You may remember this being used earlier in the header view to add additional menu options to the header. After making sure the user is logged in, this method checks the current user object's admin property. If it is set to 1, it is assumed the user is an admin.

185

I mentioned earlier that sometimes programming changes slightly after the planning steps. In the UML diagram, I identified the next method to be named `authenticateusingfactory()`. However, when coding this object, I decided that calling it `authenticate()` would make more sense and be easier to read. This method executes the `factory()` method of the `auth` object to obtain an instance of a standard authenticator. In the future, if more authenticators are added, this statement may become more dynamic. Then, the `authenticate()` method's parameters are forwarded to the new authenticator's `authenticate()` method. The result of this process is sent as the return property.

The last method is the protected `factory()` method. It builds the name of the authenticator class. If it exists, it returns a new instance of it. Otherwise, an exception is thrown. By the format defined here, I can tell that my class for the standard authentication will be called `authstandard`. If I created one using LDAP, it might be named `authLDAP`. The `factory()` method would be called using a parameter of "LDAP."

Since I know that every authenticator will have to have an `authenticate()` method and that the `auth` objects `authenticate()` method will call it regardless, I am going to enforce this method with an interface. The `authenticatorinterface` interface is located in the `/includes/authenticatorinterface.php` file with this content:

```php
<?php
interface authenticatorinterface
{
    public function authenticate(user $user, $password);
}
```

It simply forces that each authenticator will work with a `User dao` object and a password.

Finally, I can take a look at the `authstandard` class requested by the `factory()` method in the `auth` object. This is located at `/includes/authstandard.php` with the following contents:

```php
<?php
class authstandard implements authenticatorinterface
{
    public function authenticate(user $user, $password)
    {
        if ($user->password == lib::makehashedpassword($user,
                                                       $password)) {
            return true;
        }
        else {
            return false;
        }
    }
}
```

When the `User dao` object is created, it obtains the password column from the table regardless if it's authenticated or not. This method makes a hashed version of the submitted password and compares it to the one owned by the `user` object. If they match, the user is authenticated.

I added one more method to the `lib` class named `makehashedpassword()`. At first I thought that I might add it to this authenticator as a protected method. But, the User administration sections may also need access to it. The best solution right now seems to put the following mechanism in the `lib` class:

```
public static function makehashedpassword(user $user, $password)
{
    return sha1($user->username . $password);
}
```

The mechanism I'm choosing to hash passwords with is SHA-1. I combine the user object's username property and the password string and return the SHA-1 hashed version of this.

To test the application, it is necessary to insert the first user by hand. Use the following MySQL statement:

```
insert into `contacts`.`user` (`username`, `password`, `admin`)
values ('admin', 'efacc4001e857f7eba4ae781c2932dedf843865e', 1);
```

This will allow you to login with the username of 'admin' with the password of 'password'.

With these steps complete, I can now log in as a `User dao` object. The `Index` Module would now be able to execute the code to create the `contactscollection` object and show the user's contacts. However, I think I want to follow my plan and start working on the `LogOut` module next. I'm going to comment out the code inside of the else portion of the conditional of the `Index` Module object's `defaultaction()` method. I may just have it print out "You are Here." By doing so, I'll be able to test my login process and access the menu options without executing code that is not yet completed. I'm going to continue on with creating the logout functionality next.

The LogOut Module

If users can log in, they may want to log out at some point. Because of this, the header view contains a link to the log out URL: /logout. From the module pattern that I've developed combined with my UML planning in Figure 21-8 of Chapter 21, I can create a `LogOut` module. This module is located at /modules/logout.php with the following contents:

```
<?php
class logout
{
    public function defaultaction()
    {
        lib::setitem('user', NULL);
        lib::sendto();
    }
}
```

This is by far the simplest module I've yet created. When this module is accessed, it basically undoes storing the current `user` object in the session. Then, it redirects the user to the index page, completing the loop.

Administration with UserModule and Userscollection

I've already created a User dao object for the login process. This becomes more useful now because I've planned that certain User dao objects can have access to other users. This is determined by the property of $admin of the User object. The header view checks if the current user has access by calling the isadmin() method. If the user is an admin, they have the ability to go to the User administration sections.

The link added to the header references the Users module. According to the UML diagram in Figure 21-9 of Chapter 21, the UsersModule object will have six public methods: three to show views and three to process action on a User. The first of these methods is the show() method. Similarly, to how I've planned the ContactsModule, the default action of UsersModule should be to show a collection of User dao objects that the current User has access to. This will reference a collection object.

Since I know that the Contacts Module will be dealing with a UsersCollection object, I'm going to program that first. The UML diagrams in Figure 21-10 and 21-11 of Chapter 21 show that an abstract daocollection object needs to be created. The UsersCollection will extend this class. The daocollection class can be found at /includes/daocollection.php with the following contents:

```php
<?php
abstract class daocollection implements Iterator
{
    protected $position = 0;
    protected $storage = array();

    abstract public function getwithdata();

    protected function populate($array, $dataobject)
    {
        foreach ($array as $item) {    •
            $object = new $dataobject;
            foreach ($item as $key=>$val) {
                $object->$key = $val;
            }
            $this->storage[] = $object;
        }
    }

    public function saveall()
    {
        foreach ($this as $item) {
            $item->save();
        }
    }

    public function current()
    {
        return $this->storage[$this->position];
    }

    public function key()
    {
        return $this->position;
```

```
    }

    public function next()
    {
        $this->position++;
    }

    public function rewind()
    {
        $this->position = 0;
    }

    public function valid()
    {
        return isset($this->storage[$this->position]);
    }
}
```

According to the Template Design Pattern, in addition to declaring the whole class abstract, the public getwithdata() method is defined as abstract.

The Template Design Pattern was discussed in Chapter 18.

The populate() public method is interesting. It takes an array of information and a string that represents a data access object class. Because this daocollection is really a collection of dao objects, this makes sense. Next, it loops through each element of the data array. It then creates a new data access object based on the name that was passed in. It, then, assigns the public values to the dao object. This is one of the reasons why I defined the dao abstract class to accept the qualifier optionally and not to force it to exist. In this particular case, I have all of the information I need to create the dao — so no additional calls to the database are required. Finally, each element is stored to the class.

The five public methods named current(), key(), next(), rewind(), and valid() are required by PHP's Iterator interface, which the daocollection implements. As I determined during planning, I have stored the array of information in the protected $storage array.

The final method created in this class is the saveall() public method. It simply loops through each of $this and executes the save() method on that object. Since $this is a PHP iterator, the previous mentioned methods will take care of returning the proper dao object when treating $this as an array. Since each data object must have a save() method, this can be called worry free. This particular method could be used later during an implementation of the Mediator Design Pattern. I may run across a scenario where I need to make some modifications to the whole collection. Then, each would need to be saved.

For more on using the Mediator Design Pattern, see Chapter 12.

Just a few more steps and I can revisit the Users module object. First, however, review the UML diagram in Figure 21-11 of Chapter 21. This one shows the UsersCollection extending the daocollection object that was just created. Additionally, it implements a daocollection interface to make sure that each daocollection child class accepts an owner dao object.

The contents of the `daocollectioninterface` can be located in the file at `/includes/daocollectioninterface.php`:

```php
<?php
interface daocollectioninterface
{
    public function __construct(dao $item);
}
```

The last step is creating the `userscollection` class, located at `/includes/userscollection.php`, with the following content:

```php
<?php
class userscollection extends daocollection implements
    daocollectioninterface
{
    public function __construct(dao $currentuser)
    {
        $this->currentuser = $currentuser;
    }

    public function getwithdata()
    {
        $connection = db::factory('mysql');

        $sql = "select * from user order by username";
        $results = $connection->getArray($sql);

        $this->populate($results, 'user');
    }
}
```

The constructor simply sets the owner `dao` to a public property of the collection object. Initially, I don't have any restrictions to apply. If the accessing user is an admin, they will retrieve all user `dao` objects. In the future, additional requirements or restrictions may be introduced. Then, I'll be happy to have this current user object stored and available to access.

The only abstract method in the `daocollection`, `getwithdata()`, is defined in this class. The `daocollection` object's child class populates itself with data similarly to the way that the `dao` does. This particular one generates a query to retrieve all user objects from the system from the user table. Then, that information, which is retrieved in the array format, is passed into the `populate()` method of the `daocollection` class. The last parameter sent in is the string `'user'` because I'm expecting a collection of `User` dao objects.

With the collection object build, I can revisit the `Users` module. The following content is located at `/modules/users.php`:

```php
<?php
class users
{
    public function defaultaction()
    {
```

```
        $users = new userscollection(lib::getitem('user'));
        $users->getwithdata();

        echo view::show('users/show', array('users'=>$users));
    }

    public function add()
    {
        echo view::show('users/add');
    }

    public function edit()
    {
        $controller = lib::getitem('controller');

        if (empty($controller->params[0])) {
            lib::sendto();
        }
        else {
            $user = new user((int) $controller->params[0]);
            echo view::show('users/edit', array('user'=>$user));
        }
    }
}
```

Since the header view supplies a URI that contains only the module name, the `defaultaction()` method will take the place of `show()` in the UML diagram in Figure 21-9 of Chapter 21. This method will create a new instance of the `userscollection` module. I can retrieve the current `user` dao object using the same method that I used to check to see if the user was logged in or an admin. Then, the `userscollection` object is populated by calling the `getwithdata()` method. Finally, a view is shown. The call to the `show()` static method sends an array to be forwarded as parameters to the view. This parameter array contains the `userscollection` object I just created.

The contents of `/views/default/users/show.php` is:

```
<div class="sidebar"><br />
<a class="featured" href="/users/add">Add User</a>
</div>

<h1>User Admin</h1>
<p>
    Create, Edit or Delete users of the Contact System here.
</p>
<table>
<tr>
<th>Username</th>
<th>Admin?</th>
<th></th>
<th></th>
</tr>
<?php
```

```
foreach ($view['users'] as $user) {
    echo view::show('users/row', array('user'=>$user));
}
?>
</table>
<script type="text/javascript" src="/assets/removal.js"></script>
```

This view provides the option to add a new user. Then, it generates a table to view the existing users on the system. The userscollection object is iterated through using another view to show each user in a row. Note how the current user dao object from the collection is passed into the next view in the parameters array.

The file /views/default/users/row.php has the following content:

```php
<?php
echo '<tr>';
echo "<td>{$view['user']->username}</td><td>";
echo $view['user']->admin == 1 ? 'Yes' : 'No';
echo "</td><td><a href='/users/edit/{$view['user']->id}'>Edit</a></td>";
echo "<td><a class='removal' href='/users/processdelete/
      {$view['user']->id}'>";
echo "Delete</a></td>";
echo '</tr>';
```

This view simply takes the current user dao object and displays the username and admin status. It also adds links to access different methods of the Users module for editing and deleting the current user.

The last line of the users/show view was a link to include the following JavaScript content:

```javascript
if (typeof jQuery != 'undefined') {
    $(function() {
        $(".removal").click(function(){
            if (!confirm('You really want to delete this?')) {
                return false;
            }
        });
    });
}
```

This simply prompts the user to agree to continue if they click any link that has the class of 'removal' — like the Delete User link does. I wanted to add a safeguard for the administrators of the site. This was the easiest way to do it.

With this step completed, I can now log in and click the User administration link. It shows the collection of Users on the system in a table. My view looks like Figure 22-2.

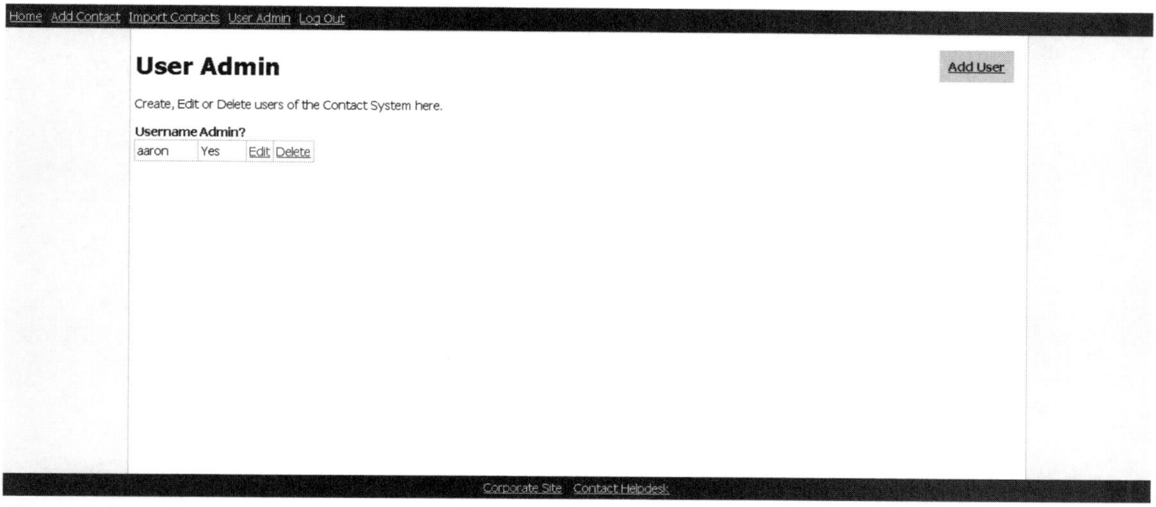

Figure 22-2

The next step is to create the user addition view which is referenced by the add() public method of the Users module.

I think that the addition of a user and the editing of a user will be very similar. Because of this, I think I can create one interface and just customize it for the add or edit functionality. The contents of the /views/default/users/add.php file are:

```php
<?php
    echo view::show('users/manage',
                    array('title'=>'Add User',
                          'action'=>'/users/processadd'));
```

The shared interface I'm referring to will be the users/manage view. The two things that I need to customize are the heading and the action of the form. As is probably obvious, the user addition version of this will want to reference the processadd() method, so the form action reflects this. The contents of /views/default/users/manage.php is a bit more complex:

```php
<?php
    echo '<h1>' . $view['title'] . '</h1>';

    echo view::show('standard/errors');

    echo '<form method="post" action="' . $view['action'] . '">';

    if (!is_null($view['user'])) {
        echo '<input type="hidden" name="id" value="' .
            $view['user']->id . '" />';
    }

    echo '<div class="row"><label for="username">Username:</label>';
    $value = $view['user']->username;
```

```
echo '<input type="text" name="username" id="username" value="' .
    $value . '" /></div>';

echo '<div class="row"><label for="password">Password:</label>';
echo '<input type="password" name="password" id="password" /></div>';

echo '<div class="row"><label>Is Admin?</label>';

$options = array('No', 'Yes');
$value = (int) $view['user']->admin;

foreach ($options as $key=>$option) {
    echo '<input class="radio" type="radio" name="admin" value="'
        . $key . '" ';
    if ($value == $key) echo 'checked="checked"';
    echo ' /><span class="radiooption">' . $option . '</span>';
}

echo '</div>';

echo '<div class="row"><label for="submit"> </label>
        <input id="submit" type="submit" class="submitbutton" value="'
        . $view['title'] . '" /></div>';

echo '</form>';
```

The first step is printing that header that was passed in with the parameter array. Next, the familiar standard/errors view is added. Remember, this will show any errors that the processadd() or processedit() decide to generate. The last predictable thing is the creation of the HTML form tag. This accepts the action parameter from the call to this view.

If I'm using this in an edit user capacity, I will pass in a user dao object in the parameters as well. So, the view checks to see if this exists. If the user dao object parameter does exist, the view generates a hidden input to track the user object's id property. The primary key ID will be needed when the update is processed.

A username and password field are generated. If a user dao object was passed in, this username value is populated. It is good security policy to *never* pre-populate a password field, so this field is left blank whether I'm adding or editing a user.

Finally, the admin option is presented using a HTML radio input. If there is no user object, the admin property will evaluate as zero. Otherwise, the user object's public admin property is evaluated — and it still may end up being zero. This is used to automatically check the proper radio button. Then the form is completed. See Figure 22-3 to review how this form should look.

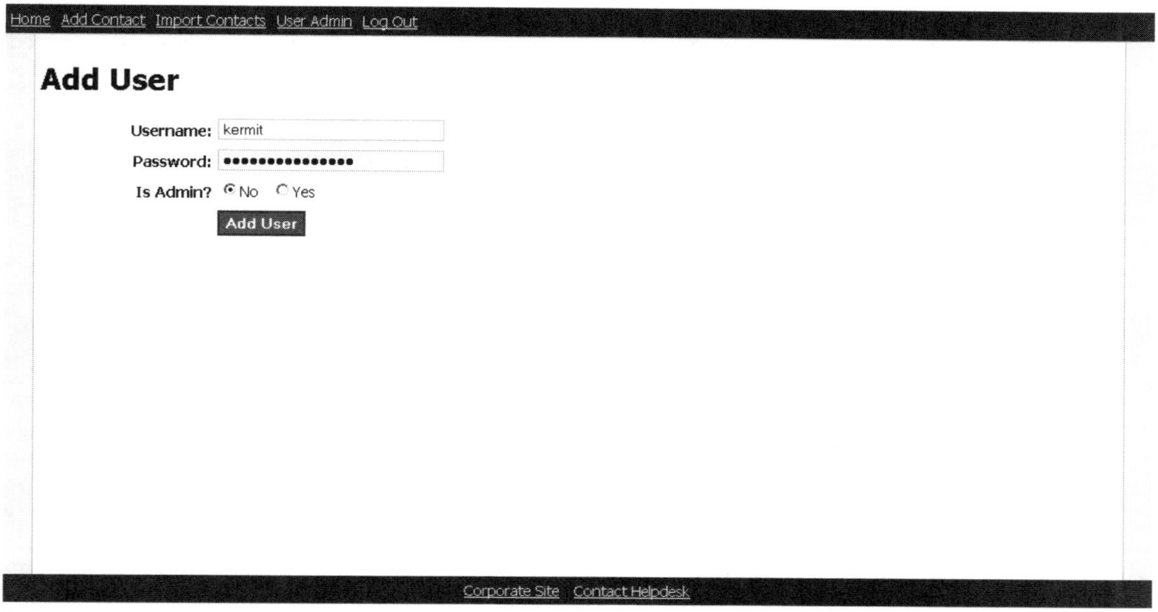

Home Add Contact Import Contacts User Admin Log Out

Add User

Username: kermit

Password: ●●●●●●●●●●●●●●

Is Admin? ⦿ No ○ Yes

Add User

Corporate Site   Contact Helpdesk

Figure 22-3

Now that the building blocks to create a new user are in place, it's time to add the public `processadd()` method to the `users` module:

```php
public function processadd()
{
    $username = $_POST['username'];
    $password = $_POST['password'];
    $admin = $_POST['admin'];

    $user = new user(array('username'=>$username));

    if (!is_null($user->id)) {
        lib::seterror($username . ' is already in use');
        lib::sendto('/users/add');
    }

    $user->username = $username;
    $user->password = lib::makehashedpassword($user, $password);
    $user->admin = $admin;
    $user->save();

    lib::sendto('/users');
}
```

This method accepts the three posted items. It then tries to create a new user object using the $username variable. If the user gets populated successfully, the user already exists. An error is generated and the user is sent back to the add screen. Otherwise, the username and admin are added to the user dao object. A hashed password is also added to the object. Finally, the user object is saved and created using the dao parent object's save() method. The user is then sent back to the display of the userscollection to view the fruits of their labor.

Next I'll move on to editing a user object. The edit() method of the users module above should be pretty easy to follow. Each row showing a user dao object had an edit link that featured the user object's ID property in the URL. This would translate into the first parameter stored by the controller. The edit() method retrieves the controller object and checks for this parameter. If it doesn't exist, the user is just sent out of the process. Hopefully, there should never be a time that this code is executed, so I'm fine with not presenting an error message. Once this parameter is retrieved, a new user dao object is created using this ID. Then, the users/edit view accepts the user and is shown.

The contents of this view are similar to the users/add view with only a few exceptions. This view is found at /views/users/edit.php:

```php
<?php
    echo view::show('users/manage',
                    array('title'=>'Edit User',
                          'action'=>'/users/processedit',
                          'user'=>$view['user']));
```

This time, the title and the action of the form are different. Additionally, the users/manage view now gets the instance of a user dao object that it was looking for.

In order to handle the edit, the processedit() method is added to the users module:

```php
public function processedit()
{
    $id = $_POST['id'];
    $username = $_POST['username'];
    $password = $_POST['password'];
    $admin = $_POST['admin'];

    $user = new user($id);
    $user->username = $username;
    if (!empty($password)) {
        $user->password = lib::makehashedpassword($user, $password);
    }
    $user->admin = $admin;
    $user->save();

    lib::sendto('/users');
}
```

Just as with the processadd() method, the username, password, and admin status are retrieved. Additionally, the unique ID element is also retrieved. A new instance of the user dao object is created using this ID. Then the username and admin status are updated. If a password was sent from the previous screen, a new hashed password is assigned to the user. Otherwise, the password property is not modified. Finally, the `user` object's parent `dao` object `save()` method is executed, which invokes the `update()` protected method. The user is then redirected back to the `userscollection` view to see their updated user in the list.

The last thing to do is make the ability to delete users. You may have noticed that there was not a method called `delete()`. I decided that the JavaScript prompt would be enough of a confirmation. I did not need to generate a new view for this action. Each row displaying a user has a delete URL that points to the users module's `processdelete()` method. The URL ends with the ID property of the `user dao` object just like the edit link does. The `processdelete()` method should be added onto the `users` module with the following content:

```
public function processdelete()
{
    $controller = lib::getitem('controller');

    if (empty($controller->params[0])) {
        lib::sendto();
    }
    else {
        $userid = (int) $controller->params[0];

        $connection = db::factory('mysql');

        $sql = "delete u.* from user u
                where u.id = {$userid}";

        $connection->execute($sql);

        lib::sendto('/users');
    }
}
```

Just like `processedit()`, the same method is used to retrieve the id of the `user` that will be modified. However, the next statements is where `processdelete()` differs from the other two similar methods. Instead of creating that `user dao` object and then deleting it, a query is generated to directly work in the database. I felt like this was the most efficient way of handling this process. The query is created and executed using the connection object from the `db` object's `factory()` method. Finally, the user is redirected to the view of the `userscollection` to verify that the user is no longer available.

This marks the end of the User administration section of the application. While the actual process of administrating a `User` compared to a `Contact` is far simpler, a lot of the required building blocks for the entire application were created in this section. Because of this, I can expect the next section to continue smoothly.

Programming Contact Administration

Users can now successfully use the application. However, the application isn't very exciting yet — it's just a shell. The next step is to start programming the Contact Administration portions. This will allow the user to actually import contacts, manage, and view them. They'll have a reason to actually log in!

Generating Relationships, Creating Data Access Objects

My UML diagram and planning show that the `ContactsModule` needs to be created next. However, I'm going to skip ahead and create all the other data access objects and their associated MySQL tables. Sometimes it makes more sense to create things in a different order than they were planned in.

I've already created my `User` dao object. I've determined that a user can have zero or more `contact` dao objects associated with them. The `contact` dao object is located at `/dataobjects/contact.php` with the following content:

```php
<?php
class contact extends dao
{
    protected $table = __CLASS__;
}
```

The `contact` data access object is created in identical fashion to the `User` dao object. In fact, the rest of the data access objects in the relationship will also be created this way. The following statement is used to create the MySQL table that matches with the UML diagram in Figure 21-13 in Chapter 21 for this object:

```
CREATE TABLE  `contacts`.`contact` (
  `id` int(10) unsigned NOT NULL AUTO_INCREMENT,
  `ownerid` int(10) unsigned NOT NULL,
  `firstname` tinytext NOT NULL,
  `middlename` tinytext NOT NULL,
  `lastname` tinytext NOT NULL,
  PRIMARY KEY (`id`)
) ENGINE=InnoDB;
```

A `contact` can have zero or more groups of contact information referred to as a `contactgroup` object. The following content is located in `/dataobjects/contactgroup.php` file:

```php
<?php
class contactgroup extends dao
{
    protected $table = __CLASS__;
}
```

The following MySQL statement is used to create the table according to the properties from the UML diagram:

```
CREATE TABLE  `contacts`.`contactgroup` (
  `id` int(10) unsigned NOT NULL AUTO_INCREMENT,
  `contactid` int(10) unsigned NOT NULL,
  `label` text NOT NULL,
  PRIMARY KEY (`id`)
) ENGINE=InnoDB;
```

In order to exist, however, the `contactgroup` must have at least one `contactmethod` object assigned to it. This integrity is enforced in the application and not in the database, however. The content of `/dataobjects/contactmethod.php` is as follows:

```php
<?php
class contactmethod extends dao
{
    protected $table = __CLASS__;
}
```

The following MySQL statement is used to create the table according to the properties from the UML diagram:

```sql
CREATE TABLE `contacts`.`contactmethod` (
  `id` int(10) unsigned NOT NULL AUTO_INCREMENT,
  `contactgroupid` int(10) unsigned NOT NULL,
  `type` tinytext NOT NULL,
  `value` text NOT NULL,
  PRIMARY KEY (`id`)
) ENGINE=InnoDB;
```

Now that I have the remaining data access objects created, I can start working with viewing and managing them.

Programming Contacts Collection

Earlier in this chapter, I commented the code inside of the `defaultaction()` method of the `index` module. It referenced the `contactscollection` object that I had not created.

After creating the parent abstract `daocollection` object and the `userscollection` object, the `contactscollection` object should be easier. Most of the building blocks are already created. The `contactscollection` class is located in the `/includes/contactscollection.php` file with the following content:

```php
<?php
class contactscollection extends daocollection implements
    daocollectioninterface
{
    protected $user;

    public function __construct(dao $user)
    {
        $this->user = $user;
    }

    public function getwithdata()
    {
        $connection = db::factory('mysql');

        $sql = "select * from contact where ownerid=" . $this->user->id
             . ' order by firstname';
        $results = $connection->getArray($sql);

        $this->populate($results, 'contact');
    }
}
```

199

Similarly to the `userscollection`, the `contactscollection` object extends the functionality of the `daocollection`. The Template Design Pattern nature of the `daocollection` requires the public `getwithdata()` method to be defined. The `daocollectioninterface` is also implemented forcing the constructor to accept a dao object.

For more on the Template Design Pattern, see Chapter 18.

The `contactscollection` object `__construct()` method assigns the user that it was passed to a protected property. This will be used in the `getwithdata()` method.

The `getwithdata()` method gets the connection to the database. Then, a query is built to collect all of the rows from the contact table in MySQL that belong to the protected `$user` object. Finally, the parent `populate()` method is executed using the contact object as the target dao object for the collection. It's good to see that all of the hard work and planning around the `userscollection` object makes making new collections very easy!

Viewing the Contacts Collection

Now that the `contactscollection` object is complete, I am going to restore the index module's `defaultaction()` method to the following code:

```php
public function defaultaction()
{
    if (!auth::isloggedin()) {
        lib::sendto('/login');
    }
    else {
        $contacts = new contactscollection(lib::getitem('user'));
        $contacts->getwithdata();

        echo view::show('contacts/browse',
                        array('contacts'=>$contacts));
    }
}
```

If the user is logged in, a new instance of the `contactscollection` object is created. The current logged-in user's `user` dao is sent to the collection object. The `getwithdata()` method makes use of that by gathering the requested collection of contact objects. Finally, that collection is passed to a new view called `contacts/browse`.

The `contacts/browse` view is located at `/views/default/contacts/browse.php` with the following contents:

```php
<h1>Your Contacts</h1>
<div id="browsecontacts">
<?php
    foreach ($view['contacts'] as $contact) {
        echo view::show('contacts/small', array('contact'=>$contact));
    }
```

```
echo '</div>';

if (!isset($contact)) {
    echo view::show('index/welcome');
}
```

This view creates the heading called Your Contacts. Then, it loops through the contactscollection that was passed into it. Just as when viewing the users on the site, each contact has its own view as well. This is called contacts/small and accepts a contact dao as a parameter. This view, located at /views/default/contacts/small.php, has the following content:

```php
<?php
echo '<a href="/contacts/view/' . $view['contact']->id . '">';
echo "{$view['contact']->firstname} ";
echo "{$view['contact']->middlename} {$view['contact']->lastname}";
echo '</a>';
```

All this smaller view does is generate a link to the contacts module's view() action using the contact dao object's id property as a parameter. It labels the link with the contact's first, middle and last name.

The last portion of the contacts/browse view checks to see if any contacts were actually retrieved. If none were, a friendly welcome message in the /views/default/index/welcome.php file is displayed:

```
<div class="sidebar">
    <br />
    <a class="featured" href="/contacts/add">Add Contact</a>
    <a class="featured" href="/contacts/import">Import Contacts</a>
</div>
<h2>Welcome To Acme Company Contact Manager</h2>
<p>
    Welcome to the replacement system for the Outlook Address book.
</p>
<p>
    Cool things to know:
</p>
<ul>
    <li>You can easily <a href="/contacts/add">add contacts</a></li>
    <li>
        You can <a href="/contacts/import">import your address book</a>
        from Outlook
    </li>
    <li>You can view this using your mobile phone</li>
    <li>
        You can send email directly to a contact by clicking their
        email address.
    </li>
</ul>
<p>
    If you have any questions, please contact the help desk.
</p>
```

This just informs the user who probably has not used the system before what options that they have available.

Now, I can successfully log in and view all of my contacts, however, I'm being presented with the welcome message because I have none. Figure 22-4 shows this.

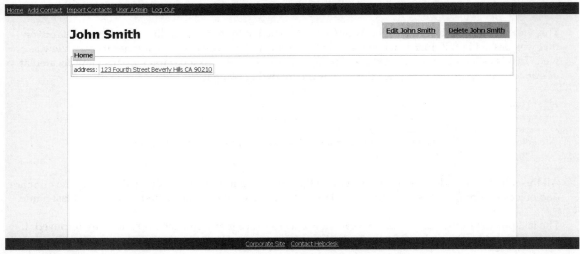

Figure 22-4

Programming Contacts Module and Import Functionality

The contacts module is one of the most important parts of the application. Because of this, it is also the largest module in the application. I'm going to split it up into steps so as not to get overwhelmed.

The first thing I know I want to do is create the import functionality. The fastest way for me to get a large amount of testing data will be to import my own Outlook .csv file. Besides, the welcome message is encouraging me to do so with the /contacts/import link.

The contacts module is located at /modules/contacts.php. I'm going to start it out with just the import() and processimport() methods:

```php
<?php
class contacts
{
    public function import()
    {
        echo view::show('contacts/import');
    }

    public function processimport()
    {
        if (is_uploaded_file($_FILES['csv']['tmp_name'])) {
            $contents = file_get_contents($_FILES['csv']['tmp_name']);
            unlink ($_FILES['csv']['tmp_name']);

            $builder = new importcontactsarraybuilder($contents);
```

202

```php
            $imports = $builder->buildarray();

            $currentuser = lib::getitem('user');

            foreach ($imports as $import) {
                $contact = new contact();
                $adaptor = new outlookcontactimportadapter($import);

                $contact->firstname = $adaptor->firstname;
                $contact->middlename = $adaptor->middlename;
                $contact->lastname = $adaptor->lastname;
                $contact->ownerid = $currentuser->id;
                $contact->save();
                $possiblegroups = array('Business', 'Home');

                foreach ($possiblegroups as $groupname) {
                    $groupfinder =
                     new contactimportgroupinterpreter($import);
                    $group = $groupfinder->getgroup($groupname);
                    if ($group instanceof contactgroup) {
                        $group->contactid = $contact->id;
                        $group->save();

                        $methods = new contactmethodscollection($group);
                        $methods->generateimportmethods($import);
                        $methods->saveall();
                    }
                }
            }

            lib::sendto();
        }
        else {
            lib::seterror(array('Please upload a file.'));
            lib::sendto('/contacts/import');
        }
    }
}
```

The public `add()` method simply shows a new view. This view should contain an HTML element to upload a file. This view is located at `/views/default/contacts/import.php` with the following content:

```html
<h1>Import Your Contacts</h1>
<p>
    Upload a .csv file from Outlook. Contact helpdesk for assistance.
</p>
<?php
    echo view::show('standard/errors');
?>
<form action="/contacts/processimport" method="post"
    enctype="multipart/form-data">
    <div class="row">
        <label for="csv">CSV File:</label><input type="file"
```

```
            id="csv" name="csv" />
    </div>
    <div class="row">
        <label for="submit"> </label>
        <input id="submit" type="submit" class="submitbutton"
            value="Upload" />
    </div>
</form>
```

The view tells the user to upload their `.csv` file. In the future, I can imagine the help desk asking to have instructions on this page. However, it wasn't in the requirements, so I'm just putting a helpful reminder to contact them for assistance. Next, the standard errors view is added to display any errors that happen during the file upload. These errors could be that no file was uploaded or the file isn't the right format.

The last step in this view is generating a form with the proper encoding type to accept file uploads. The important thing to note is the name of the input element whose type is "file." It is named "csv." I use this name in the `processimport()` method, which I'll take a look at next.

The first thing that the public method `processingimport()` does is make sure that the file did successfully upload. If the result from PHP's `is_uploaded_file()` function is false, an appropriate error will be set and the user will be redirected back to the previous view. The errors view will display the message that the file did not successfully upload.

Next, the contents of the file are retrieved and the file itself is deleted. This is followed by a new instance of the `importcontactsarraybuilder` class. As I defined in the UML Diagram in Figure 21-14 of chapter 21, this class is based on the Builder Design Pattern. The instance is created with the full contents of the uploaded file. Finally, the class' `buildcollection()` public method is called and its results are stored in the `$imports` variable.

For more on the Builder Design Pattern, see Chapter 4.

The `importcontactsarraybuilder` class is located at `/includes/importcontactsarraybuilder.php` with the following contents:

```php
<?php
class importcontactsarraybuilder
{
    protected $importedstring;

    public function __construct($importedstring)
    {
        $this->importedstring = $importedstring;
    }

    public function buildarray()
    {
        $lines = explode("\n", $this->importedstring);
        $keys = explode(',', array_shift($lines));

        $array = array();

        foreach ($lines as $line) {
```

```
                 if (!empty($line)) {
                     $keyed = array_combine($keys, explode(',', $line));
                     $array[] = $keyed;
                 }
             }

             return $array;
         }
    }
```

Initially, in this UML diagram, this class had the term "collection" in its name and method names. In other parts of the application, the term collection was used synonymously to an instance of a daocollection object. I felt that this could be confusing considering this class is actually building an array and not a collection of dao objects.

The constructor of the class assigns its parameter to the protected property $imported string. The public method named buildarray() is where the actual manipulation happens. First, new lines are used to separate the string (which is the contents of the .csv file) into lines. The first line should be the headings of the document and is removed and stored in its own array named $keys. Then, the rest of the document is iterated through. The $keys array is combined with the current line to make a new associative array. Once this is complete, it is added to the return parameter $array. The end process of this method is an associative keyed array whose keys are the first line of the file and content is the rest of the file.

Continuing on with the processimport() method of the contacts module, the current user is retrieved. Then, the $imports array, which contains the contents of the buildarray() method's return parameter, is looped through.

For each instance of the import array, a new contact dao is created. Next, a new instance of outlookcontactimportadapter is created. During planning, I recognized that the imported array would not be in a format the contact dao could understand and use. The content of the /includes/ outlookcontactimportadapter.php file is:

```php
<?php
class outlookcontactimportadapter
{
    public function __construct($import)
    {
        $this->firstname = $import['First Name'];
        $this->middlename = $import['Middle Name'];
        $this->lastname = $import['Last Name'];
    }
}
```

This adapter is simply using what it knows about the import array and assigning public properties identical to those that a user dao would have. This is useful in the next step of the processimport() method, where the contact dao object's properties are assigned from this instance of this adapter object.

Finally, the contact gets its owner ID property from the current user. The contact dao object's save() method completes the creation of the object.

The next step in the process is determining if this `contact` has a need for any `contactgroup` objects to be created. The two groups I know about in the Outlook `.csv` file are prefixed with "Business" and "Home." For each of those group names, the next process is executed.

An instance of `contactimportgroupinterpreter` is created. The intent is that the import array will have a certain set of keys that can be interpreted as the building blocks of a group. This object was based on the Interpreter Design Pattern during planning to resolve this issue. After a new instance is passed the import array, the `$group` variable receives the return parameter from a call to the `contactimportgroupinterpreter` object's public `getgroup()` method. Note how the current group name in the loop is being sent into this method.

For more on the Interpreter Design Pattern, see Chapter 10.

The `contactimportgroupinterpreter` class exists in the `/includes/contactimportgroupinterpreter.php` file:

```php
<?php
class contactimportgroupinterpreter
{
    protected $import;

    public function __construct($import)
    {
        $this->import = $import;
    }

    public function getgroup($groupname)
    {
        $contactgroup = NULL;

        if (!empty($this->import["{$groupname} Street"])) {
            $contactgroup = new contactgroup();
            $contactgroup->label = $groupname;
        }

        return $contactgroup;
    }
}
```

Similar to the adapter class I created earlier, the constructor of this method just has to assign it received to a protected property of the class. The `getgroup()` public method is where the interpretation starts.

To determine that a contact group should exist, I'm checking for content in the array for the group name's street. The two columns that I know about in the `.csv` file are "Business Street" and "Home Street." My assumption is that if a value is in this field, the whole address probably exists. That will make a `contactmethod dao` possible later on. This means that this `contactgroup` object can be created. So, if that field is found to have content, a new `contactgroup` object, whose label is assigned from the `$groupname` variable, is created and returned. If the field is empty, NULL is returned.

Since it's possible that NULL will be returned, the next line of the processimport() method checks to see if the $group variable is really a contactgroup object. If it is not, nothing else happens and the next group name is tried.

If a valid contactgroup object was found, it is updated with the contact object's id property as its owner ID. Then, the dao parent class's save() method is called to finish the creation of this contactgroup object.

The last step is adding the contact methods to the group. An instance of the contactsmethodscollection daocollection is created. The owner element, the contactgroup, is passed into the constructor. The import array is then sent as a parameter to a call to the public generateimportmethods(). Finally, the first use of the saveall() public method of the daocollection object is executed. The plan is to create a normal collection object just like the userscollection object. The extra method named generateimportmethods() should be able to generate a collection of contactmethod dao objects, similar to the way that a call to getwithdata() would, but the objects would have their content based on the import array instead of an array generated by a MySQL query.

The content of the /includes/contactmethodscollection.php file is:

```php
<?php
class contactmethodscollection extends daocollection
implements daocollectioninterface
{
    protected $group;

    public function __construct(dao $group)
    {
        $this->group = $group;
    }

    public function getwithdata()
    {
        $connection = db::factory('mysql');

        $sql = "select * from contactmethod where contactgroupid="
            . $this->group->id . ' order by type';
        $results = $connection->getArray($sql);

        $this->populate($results, 'contactmethod');
    }

    public function generateimportmethods($import)
    {
        $results = array();

        $addressline =  $import["{$this->group->label} Street"] . ' ' .
                        $import["{$this->group->label} Street 2"] . ' ' .
                        $import["{$this->group->label} Street 3"] . ' ' .
                        $import["{$this->group->label} City"] . ' ' .
                        $import["{$this->group->label} State"] . ' ' .
                        $import["{$this->group->label} Postal Code"];
```

```
$results[] = array('type'=>'address', 'value'=>$addressline,
                   'contactgroupid'=>$this->group->id);

$this->populate($results, 'contactmethod');
        }
    }
```

The constructor of this `daocollection` acts as expected. It assigns the owner `dao` object to a protected property. The next public method, named `getwithdata()`, is also built in a familiar way. It generates a query that retrieves the rows from the MySQL table that the group `dao` object owns. The call to the `daocollection` object's `populate()` method is used to make new `contactmethod` dao objects.

The `generateimportmethods()` public method is very similar to the `getwithdata()` method. But instead of retrieving results from the MySQL connection, this method builds a result type using what I know about the import array's keys. Then, this is morphed into an array identically to the way that the `db` objects `getArray()` method would return SQL result sets. Then, the `populate()` method is called. The `populate()` method processes this information identically to the way that it's executed in the `getwithdata()` method.

After each group and contact method is added to the `contact`, the `contacts` module redirects the user to the home page. Here, they will be able to see all of the newly imported contacts.

With the contact import functionality completed, I now have a good base of contacts to continue my testing with. Figure 22-5 shows my test group so far.

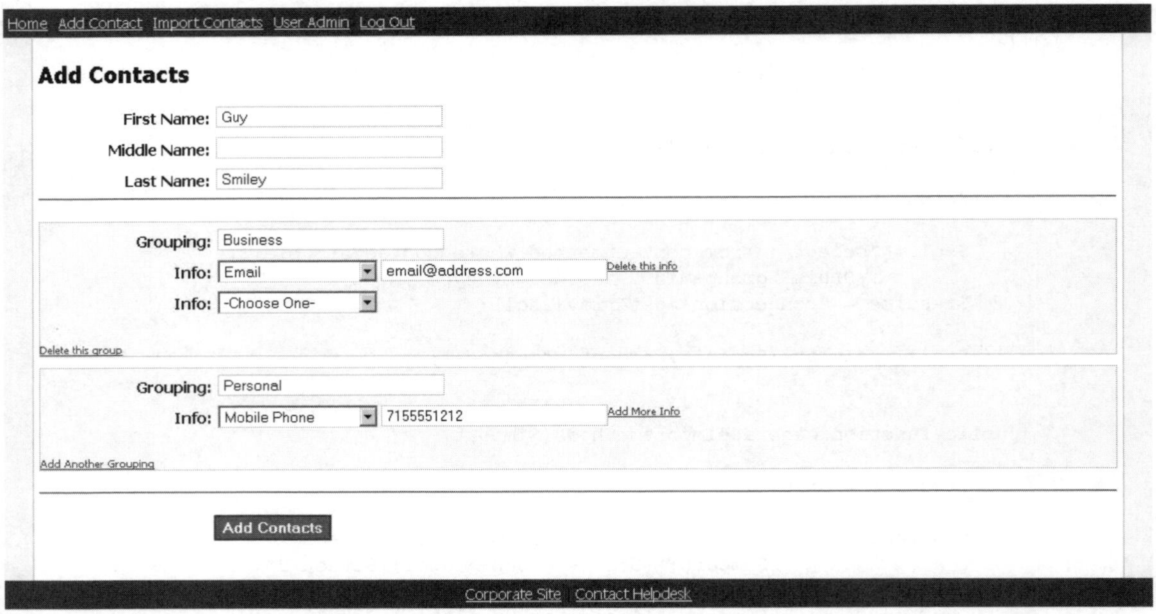

Figure 22-5

The next steps will be finishing up the rest of the `contacts` module. I will be able to add and edit contacts, and their groups and methods, or delete a whole contact. Since I want to continue my testing and verify my results, I think the next thing to create is the single `contact` view. I'll continue with this programming in the next section.

Moving from the Contacts List to a Single Contact View

The `index` module does a great job of iterating through a `contactscollection` object and showing links to access each contact. The link to view the individual contact begins with `/contacts/view`. This means that the `view()` public method of the contacts module is being called. I already created the `import()` and `processimport()` methods. I'll add the `view()` method:

```php
public function view()
{
    $controller = lib::getitem('controller');

    if (empty($controller->params[0])) {
        lib::sendto();
    }
    else {
        $contact = new contact((int) $controller->params[0]);
        $groups = new contactgroupscollection($contact);
        $groups->getwithdata();

        echo view::show('contacts/view',
                        array('contact'=>$contact,
                              'groups'=>$groups));
    }
}
```

Since the `contact` ID property is passed as a parameter on the URL, the same process used to edit and delete `user dao` objects is used in this method. After that parameter is retrieved, a new instance of a `contact dao` object is created passing in that ID. This should populate the `$contact` variable with the `contact` object. Next, a new instance of the `contactgroupscollection` object is created. Since this is a `daocollection` object, the next step is calling its `getwithdata()` public method. Finally, a view is shown with the `contact` object and its `contactgroups` collection.

The `contactgroupscollection` object is going to be very similar to the other `daocollection` child classes I've created. It is located in the `/includes/contactgroupscollection.php` file with this content:

```php
<?php
class contactgroupscollection extends daocollection
implements daocollectioninterface
{
    protected $contact;

    public function __construct(dao $contact)
    {
        $this->contact = $contact;
    }

    public function getwithdata()
```

```
    {
        $connection = db::factory('mysql');

        $sql = "select * from contactgroup where contactid="
               . $this->contact->id . ' order by label';
        $results = $connection->getArray($sql);

        $this->populate($results, 'contactgroup');
    }
}
```

The `contact dao` owner object is assigned to the protected `$contact` property by the constructor. Then, all rows from the `contactgroup` MySQL table are retrieved whose `contactid` column match the owner `contact` objects ID property. The `populate()` method creates a collection of `contactgroup` objects out of this data.

Both the `contact` object and the `contactgroups daocollection` object were passed to the contacts/ view view. This view located at `/views/default/contacts/view.php` has the following contents:

```php
<?php
    $contactname = "{$view['contact']->firstname}
                    {$view['contact']->middlename}
                    {$view['contact']->lastname}";

    echo view::show('contacts/viewsidebar',
                    array('contactname'=>$contactname,
                          'id'=>$view['contact']->id));

    print "<h1>{$contactname}</h1>";

    foreach ($view['groups'] as $group) {
        print "<fieldset><legend>{$group->label}</legend>";

        $methods = new contactmethodscollection($group);
        $methods->getwithdata();

        print '<table>';
        foreach ($methods as $method) {
            $decoratorclass = "decorator{$method->type}";

            if (class_exists($decoratorclass)) {
                $decorator = new $decoratorclass;
                $method->value = $decorator->decorate($method->value);
            }

            print "<tr><td>{$method->type}:</td><td>
                    {$method->value}</td></tr>";
        }
        print '</table>';

        print "</fieldset>";
    }
?>
<script type="text/javascript" src="/assets/removal.js"></script>
```

This is probably the most involved view created so far. First, a nicely formatted contact name was created. Then, another view is displayed, called `contacts/viewsidebar`. This view will have links to edit and delete this particular contact. I'll look at this later.

The next step is to loop through each of the contact groups that the contact has. The `$view['groups']` variable is a reference to the `contactgroups` object that was created outside this view. Each group follows this same next process.

First, the label property of the `group dao` is displayed. So far, I have the possibility of using "Business" or "Home" here. However, when I create the interface to add contact information by hand, I could see duplicate "Business" labels or even more exotic descriptions. The next step is to get a collection of contact methods from this current group. I created this class earlier with the import functionality. This should populate the `$methods` variable with a `daocollection` object full of `contactmethod dao` objects.

For each of the methods retrieved, a row is added to the table. Before the value is displayed, however, I will look for the existence of a decorator class. In my planning process, I had brainstormed a bunch of decorators that I could apply to the contact method information. The UML diagrams in Figure 21-18 of chapter 21 show some what I'll have to create next. Given the way this is created, however, if I never created a single decorator, the method would still execute fine. It's not a requirement to have a decorator. Moving on, if the decorator exists, its instantiated and the method's value is decorated using the decorator's `decorate()` method. The last step of this loop is printing the row with the type of method and the possibly decorated value.

At the very bottom of the view, the `removal.js` script is added again. This is because the `contacts/viewsidebar` will have a delete link for the current contact.

The missing piece of the view puzzle is the `contacts/viewsidebar` view. This is located at `/views/default/contacts/viewsidebar.php` with the following content:

```php
<?php
    print '<div class="sidebar"><br /><a class="featured"
        href="/contacts/edit/';
    print $view['id'] . '">Edit ' . $view['contactname'] . '</a>';
    print '<a class="featured removal" href="/contacts/processdelete/';
    print $view['id'] . '">Delete ' . $view['contactname'] . '</a>';
    print '</div>';
```

It simply generates an edit and delete link for the current contact. In a few more sections, I'll be creating the methods to deal with each of these links.

Because of the extensive JavaScript that I plan to have on the Add and Edit Contact pages, I've opted to not provide these options to the mobile browsers. In order to provide an alternate view for the mobile browser, I've created a view at `/views/mobile/contacts/viewsidebar.php` with the following content:

```
<div class="sidebar"><br />Editing is restricted to the browser only</div>
```

With these views complete, I can now see that my import process worked successfully. I can see the contact, its groups, and the methods associated with it. The methods are looking kind of bland, however. This will be solved in the next section.

Programming the Decorators

The UML diagram in Figure 21-18 of Chapter 21 shows that I have five decorators to create as well as a decorator interface. The decorator interface is the first element I want to create. It will simply enforce the existence of the `decorate()` method that the `contacts` module's `view()` method expects to call. This interface is located at `/includes/decoratorinterface.php`:

```php
<?php
interface decoratorinterface
{
    public function decorate($item);
}
```

The next step is to create each of the decorators themselves. The first one is for addresses. I wanted to make the address a link to Google Maps with that location featured. I did a bit of research on the Maps link and was able to figure out how the URL worked. The `decoratoraddress` class exists at `/includes/decoratoraddress.php` with just one method:

```php
<?php
class decoratoraddress implements decoratorinterface
{
    public function decorate($item)
    {
        $return = '<a href="http://maps.google.com/maps?q=' .
                    urlencode($item)
                    . '">' . $item . '</a>';
        return $return;
    }
}
```

All of these decorators will be very similar. Each will implement the decorator interface. They will accept the item to decorate and modify it somehow. The final step is sending the modified item as a return parameter. This decorator creates the properly encoded URL for the Google Maps link and gives it the address label.

The next decorator is the `decoratoremail` class. It will modify the email address to be a "mailto" link. This class is located at `/includes/decoratoremail.php` with this content:

```php
<?php
class decoratoremail implements decoratorinterface
{
    public function decorate($item)
    {
        $return = '<a href="mailto:' . $item . '">' . $item . '</a>';
        return $return;
    }
}
```

Some mobile phones support the Wireless Telephone Applications Interface. The company-issued Windows Mobile phones support the WTAI protocol, so I've created a decorator to make use of this when a mobile phone number is the contact method. It will generate a link that the mobile browser will be able to use to dial a call. This decorator will make sure that the current view is actually a mobile view. If it isn't being accessed by a mobile browser, the WTAI protocol would have no effect, so it's not executed. The content of /includes/decoratormobilephone.php is:

```php
<?php
class decoratormobilephone implements decoratorinterface
{
    public function decorate($item)
    {
        $return = $item;

        if (view::$viewtype == 'mobile') {
            $return = '<a href="wtai://wp/mc;' . $item . '">' .
                        $item . '</a>';
        }

        return $return;
    }
}
```

The next decorator is for the social network URL. Since this is just expected to be a simple hyperlink, it will be created to a HTML Anchor element. The decoratorsocialnetwork class is located at /includes/decoratorsocialnetwork.php with the following code:

```php
<?php
class decoratorsocialnetwork implements decoratorinterface
{
    public function decorate($item)
    {
        $return = '<a href="' . $item . '">' . $item . '</a>';
        return $return;
    }
}
```

The final decorator is for the website contact method. This currently is identical to the social network decorator. It is located at /includes/decoratorwebsite.php:

```php
<?php
class decoratorwebsite implements decoratorinterface
{
    public function decorate($item)
    {
        $return = '<a href="' . $item . '">' . $item . '</a>';
        return $return;
    }
}
```

This completes my collection of decorators that I had brainstormed during planning. This also gives me a robust view of a contact. In Figure 22-6, I'm viewing one of the imported contacts.

Figure 22-6

I still have to develop the method to add a contact, edit them, and delete them. This will be covered in the next sections.

Adding a Contact

I liked the way that I was able to make use of the same users/manage view for the User management section. I'm going to try to use the same sort of mechanism with the Contact management. The first step in this process is to show the view for the link `/contacts/add` that is featured in the header. To do this, I'm going to add the following method to the `contacts` module:

```php
public function add()
{
    echo view::show('contacts/add');
}
```

This simply loads the content of the file located at `/views/default/contacts/add.php`, which is:

```php
<?php
echo view::show('contacts/manage', array('title'=>'Add Contacts',
                                          'action'=>'/contacts/processadd',
                                          'formid'=>'addform',
                                          'type'=>'add'));
```

Similar to the add user view, this view is building parameters for a shared view called `contacts/manage`. The title is defined and a form action is specified. Two additional parameters, called `formid` and `type`, are also sent forward to that view. Next, I'll create the contents of the `/views/default/contacts/manage.php` file:

```php
<h2><?php echo $view['title']?></h2>
<form action="<?php echo $view['action']?>" method="post"
    id="<?php echo $view['formid']?>">
```

```php
<?php
    echo '<input type="hidden" name="id" value="' .
        $view['contact']->id;
    echo '" />';

    $vals = array('firstname'=>'First Name',
                  'middlename'=>'Middle Name',
                  'lastname'=>'Last Name');

    foreach ($vals as $name=>$label) {
        echo '<div class="row"><label for="' . $name . '">'
            . $label . ':</label>';
        echo '<input name="' . $name . '" id="' . $name .
            '"value="';
        echo $view['contact']->$name;
        echo '" /></div>';
    }
?>
<hr />

<?php
    if (isset($view['groups'])) {
        foreach ($view['groups'] as $counter=>$group) {
            echo view::show('contacts/group',
                            array('group'=>$group,
                                  'counter'=>$counter,
                                  'type'=>$view['type']));
        }
        $counter++;
        $group = null;
    }
    else {
        $counter = 0;
        $group = new stdClass;
        $group->label = 'Business';
    }
    echo view::show('contacts/group',
                    array('group'=>$group, 'counter'=>$counter,
                          'type'=>'add'));
?>

<hr id="lastclone" />
<div><label for="submit"> </label>
    <input id="submit" type="submit" value="<?php echo
        $view['title']?>"
        class="submitbutton" />
</div>
</form>
<div id="contactgroupingcontainer">
    <?php echo view::show('contacts/group',
                    array('label'=>'Business', 'counter'=>0))?>
</div>
<script type="text/javascript" src="/assets/managecontact.js"></script>
<script type="text/javascript">
var groupcount = <?php echo $counter?>;
</script>
```

Before I go through this step by step, let me talk about the basic idea. The idea is to have first name, middle name, and last name fields. Then, a box for each contact group will be featured. If no contact groups exist, which would be the case when creating a new contact, one is created and named "Business" per the requirements. Each group has the link to create a new group box. This process will basically duplicate the blank hidden group box.

Now, each group box has one contact method specified. The value is blank, however. If the user chooses not to add a contact method, the processing method will make sure not to include this group. Each contact method also has a link to create another contact method. This is done with a similar duplication method to the groups. Now, let's step through the lines of this complicated view.

The first few lines are pretty simple. The title is retrieved and displayed. In the case of the add() method, the title will reflect that the user is adding a contact. Then, the form is built with the action and id parameters.

When editing a contact, I'm planning to pass in a contact dao with the parameters. The next line attempts to retrieve the id property of that contact and store it as a hidden HTML Input element. When adding a contact, this field will be blank.

Next, the First Name, Last Name, and Middle Name elements are added to the form. In each case, the contact dao public properties are retrieved to fill in the default values for each of these fields.

The next section of the form supports the contactgroup architecture. When editing a contact, a contactgroups daocollection will be passed into this view. The next step is to check to see if this exists. If it does exist, each of the collection's dao objects are accessed and passed to a new view called contacts/group. This view expects to receive a contactgroup, a counter variable, and a type of view this is.

In the case that there are no groups sent and the contact is being added for the first time, a standard class is created. This is designed to mock the public properties of a contactgroup. Notice how the label is set to "Business" to fit the requirement of the first group being named "Business" This will be used outside of the conditional statement.

Before I create the contacts/group view, I want to examine the last line of this section. The last line generates another call to the contacts/group view. In the case where the user is creating a new contact, the group object whose label is "Business" is sent into the view. There are obviously no other attributes to this object, so this will create the default blank "Business" group. If the user is editing a contact, multiple calls to the view may have already occurred. The last step of that loop was to increase the counter and set the group variable to NULL. Then, when this last view is executed, a new contact group box is created, but its label is blank because the $group it is passed does not have any public properties.

Before I create the contacts/group view, I'm going to finish stepping through this view. After the group boxes are created, another horizontal rule is added, this time with an id attribute. This will be used by the JavaScript when generating clones. A submit button completes the form.

Below the form, I generate a new HTML Div with the id attribute set to contactgroupingcontainer. This will be used as a key for the JavaScript to find an instance of a contact group box to duplicate and put before the "lastclone" horizontal rule. Inside of this div, one more call to the contacts/group view is executed. This will be the contact group box that is actually cloned.

Finally, two JavaScript snippets are added. The variable `groupcount` will be used by the JavaScript located in `/assets/managecontacts.js`. I'll look at this JavaScript quickly after I've completed all of the views in PHP.

Because of the unique relationship that I've developed with the `contact`, `contactgroup` and `contactmethod` objects, the views are understandably nested. So far, I've created the `contact` view. Next, I need to focus on the `group` view which is located at `/views/default/contacts/group.php`:

```php
<div class="contactgrouping">
    <div class="row"><label>Grouping:</label>
    <input name="type[<?php echo $view['counter']?>][label]"
        value="<?php echo $view['group']->label?>" /></div>
    <div>
        <?php
            if ($view['group'] instanceof contactgroup) {
                $methods =
                 new contactmethodscollection($view['group']);
                $methods->getwithdata();
                foreach ($methods as $method) {
                    echo view::show('contacts/method',
                                    array('method'=>$method,
                                        'counter'=>$view['counter']));
                }
            }
            echo view::show('contacts/method',
                            array('method'=>null,
                                'counter'=>$view['counter']));
        ?>
    </div>

    <?php
        if ($view['type'] == 'edit') {
            echo '<a href="#" class="deletecontactgrouping">
                    Delete this group</a>';
        }
        else {
            echo '<a href="#" class="addcontactgrouping">
                    Add Another Grouping</a>';
        }
    ?>
</div>
```

Each contact group is enclosed in a div with the `"contactgrouping"` class. The first step is defining the label of the `group`. When editing a `contact`, I had passed in a full `contactgroup` object, which has a public property of label. When creating a new one, the default "Business" label was sent in on a standard class. This is where I make use of it.

Recognizing that the group parameter might not be a `contactgroup` dao, a quick conditional checks this. The architecture of this duplicate box for methods is very similar to that of the groups' boxes. On the parent view, I looped through any groups, and then displayed a blank group box. Here, if the group is a `contactgroup`, I know that there must be at least one `contactmethod`. I loop through each of those and display them with the proper method. Then, no matter what, a blank method box is generated.

Inside of the conditional to determine if the group parameter is a `contactgroup`, a new `contactmethodscollection` object is created. As required, the owner `contactgroup` is sent into the constructor and the data is retrieved using `getwithdata()`. Then, for each of the `contactmethod dao` in the collection, the `contacts/method` view is shown.

Before I look at that last nested method, I will finish this one. If the user is editing a `contact`, the option to delete the group box is displayed. Otherwise, the option to add a new group is shown. The JavaScript will have to make sense of these links to provide the proper action.

The last nested view is located at `/views/default/contacts/method.php` with the following content:

```php
<?php
    echo '<div class="row"><label>Info:</label>
        <select name="type[' . $view['counter'] . '][methodtype][]">';

    $options = array(
                    '' => '-Choose One-',
                    'organization' => 'Organization',
                    'title' => 'Title',
                    'email' => 'Email',
                    'website' => 'Website',
                    'address' => 'Complete Address',
                    'telephone' => 'Telephone',
                    'mobilephone' => 'Mobile Phone',
                    'socialnetwork' => 'Social Network URL',
                    'im' => 'IM Name'
                );
    foreach ($options as $value=>$description) {
        echo '<option value="' . $value . '" ';
        if ($view['method']->type == $value) echo 'selected="selected"';
        echo '>' . $description . '</option>';
    }

    echo '</select>';

    echo '<span class="methodboxvaluebox ';
    if ($view['method']->value) {
        echo 'hasvalue';
    }

    echo '"><input name="type[' . $view['counter'] .
        '][methodvalue][]" value="' . $view['method']->value .
        '" />';

    if ($view['method']->value) {
        echo '<a href="#" class="deletecontactmethod">Delete this
            Info</a>';
    }
    else {
        echo '<a href="#" class="addcontactmethod">Add More Info</a>';
    }


    echo '</span></div>';
```

The counter variable is used to keep track of which contact method goes with which group. The select box is generated next using a list of predefined contact methods. Since I'm adding these all in a select box, building the HTML Input element's name with brackets (which will be translated into an array when posted to PHP), I am meeting the requirement to allow more than one of each type of contact method per group.

Just as with the group view, I share this view between the adding and editing methods. When the select box is being generated, it keeps checking the contactmethod parameter's type property. If a user is editing a method, the contactmethod object is passed in using this parameter. If it's a new method, nothing exists and this match is never successful.

When the method type is blank, I don't want to feature the HTML Input element. Because of this, I'm enclosing it in the span with the class of methodboxvaluebox. This has particular styling including some making it invisible. However, if the method parameter has a value, the 'hasvalue' class is added on. This class supersedes the previous class with a request to have the box displayed.

The HTML Input element is created with a name similar to the HTML Select elements. This will help them stay in sync. The contactmethod object's value is inserted into the element, if it exists. Finally, similar to the group box, one of two links is shown. If the method exists, an option to delete it will be shown. Otherwise, a link to add another method will be shown. JavaScript will need to make sense of these links and execute the proper functionality.

Finally, the method box is completed with the closing HTML Span and Div tags. This completes the design of the three nested views needed to add or edit a contact. The last step is to create the JavaScript to execute the cloning and change of visibility features. This is located at /assets/managecontact.js and was included in the contacts/manage view. Its content is:

```
if (typeof jQuery != 'undefined') {
    $(function() {
        $("select").change(function(){
            if (this.value) {
                $(this).next().show().children('input').focus();
            }
            else {
                $(this).next().hide().children('input').val('');
            }
        });

        $(".addcontactgrouping").click(function(){
            groupcount++;
            var cloning =
             $("#contactgroupingcontainer").children('div');
            var myclone = cloning.clone(true);

            myclone.find('input,select').each(function() {
                this.value = '';
                this.name = this.name.replace(/\[\d*\]/, '
                            [' +groupcount + ']');
            });

            myclone.insertBefore($("#lastclone"));

            $(this).html('Delete this group').unbind('click').blur();
```

```
            $(this).click(function(){
                $(this).parent('div').remove();
            });

            return false;
        });

        $(".deletecontactgrouping").click(function(){
            $(this).parent('div').remove();
            return false;
        });

        $(".addcontactmethod").click(function() {
            var cloning = $(this).parent().parent();
            var myclone = cloning.clone(true);

            myclone.children('select').val('').trigger('change');
            myclone.children('span').children('input').val('');

            myclone.insertAfter(cloning);

            $(this).html('Delete this info').unbind('click').blur();
            $(this).click(function(){
                $(this).parent().parent().remove();
            });

            return false;
        });
        $(".deletecontactmethod").click(function(){
            $(this).parent().parent().remove();

            return false;
        });

    });
}
```

I'll just quickly go through this functionality to give an idea of what is happening. First, the HTML Select element is watched. Whenever it changes, it looks to see if it's set to a value. If there is no value, the next sibling, which is the HTML Span element that contains the Input element, is hidden. That Input element's content is also removed. Conversely, if a value exists, the Span element is shown and the Input element is focused.

The next function watches for the links to add a contact group based on a class. It increases the groupcount variable, which is used to associate each of the child methods to the group. It then clones the contact group box that is a child of the HTML Div element that was set up as a container. It then changes the names of each of the HTML Input and Select elements in that clone to reflect the new group counter. Finally, it inserts the clone right before the horizontal rule with the ID of 'lastclone.' To the user this looks like a new box was added below the one that hosts the link that they just clicked. The last step of this function is to change the text of this link to "Delete this group" and unset this action, which was just executed. It changes the functionality of that link to now remove this group if the user requests it.

When editing groups, the link generated was labeled "Delete this group" with the class of `"deletecontactgrouping"`. The next function looks for this link and removes the contact group that holds the link that was clicked.

The next method does a similar process but on a smaller level. It duplicates the method box. It is executed by the link to the right of the contact method HTML `Input` element. It basically makes a clone of the HTML `Div` element that holds it and inserts it after that same `Div`. It also makes sure to unset the values of the cloned element by changing the HTML `Select` element to no value and triggering the change event. Finally, it modifies the link that was just clicked to have the reverse behavior and matching text.

The last method is executed when the "Delete this info" link appears when editing existing methods. It simply removes the parent HTML `Div` element successfully removing that contact method from the HTML form.

In Figure 22-7, I'm demonstrating some of the interactive features of adding a contact.

Figure 22-7

With all of the interfaces complete, the next step is the processing method. The form is submitted to /contacts/processadd, which means that the contacts module must have a public processadd() method. I'm going to add the following method to the contacts module:

```
public function processadd()
{
    $firstname = $_POST['firstname'];
    $middlename = $_POST['middlename'];
    $lastname = $_POST['lastname'];
```

```
$contact = new contact();
$contact->firstname = $firstname;
$contact->lastname = $lastname;
$contact->middlename = $middlename;

$currentuser = lib::getitem('user');

$contact->ownerid = $currentuser->id;
$contact->save();

$this->addMethods($_POST['type'], $contact);

lib::sendto("/contacts/view/{$contact->id}");
    }
```

For the most part, this method is pretty simple. The real magic happens in the call to the addMethods() protected method. However, I don't mean to neglect the important steps that this method accomplishes.

The First, Middle, and Last names are retrieved from the post. A new contact dao is created and the names are assigned to it. The last step in creating this contact dao from this posted data is assigning the ownerid property. The current user is retrieved and that user object's id property is assigned to this contact. Finally, the dao object's save() method is called. This will populate the id property of the contact object. The user is then sent to an URL built to view the contact that they just created.

Before the user is forwarded to the final product, however, the addMethods() method is called. It is passed two parameters, the posted 'type' array and the contact object. I'm going to add the addMethods() method to the contacts module:

```
protected function addMethods($types, contact $contact)
{
    foreach ($types as $groupid=>$type) {
        if (!empty($type['label'])) {
            $group = new contactgroup();
            $group->contactid = $contact->id;
            $group->label = $type['label'];

            foreach ($type['methodtype'] as $methodtypekey=>$methodtype) {
                if (!empty($methodtype)
                    && !empty($type['methodvalue'][$methodtypekey])){
                    if (is_null($group->id)) $group->save();
                    $method = new contactmethod();
                    $method->contactgroupid = $group->id;
                    $method->type = $methodtype;
                    $method->value = $type['methodvalue'][$methodtypekey];
                    $method->save();
                }
            }
        }
    }
}
```

Because of the way the names of the HTML Input and Select elements were created, a nice multidimensional array named 'types' was built. This method loops through each of the elements that exist in the $types parameter. First, if the label is blank, it is skipped. The label key is the first HTML Input in the contact group box. Because I allow for them to be generated without requiring any content, this step needs to be here.

Next, a new contactgroup is created. The owner contact id property is retrieved from the contact dao that was the second parameter of this method. The label is also added. A very important thing to note is that the contactgroup object is not saved yet! Because I should never have a contactgroup if it doesn't have at least one contactmethod child, I can't write it to the database. And since I don't know if there are any contact methods yet, it will have to remain unsaved.

The next step is to loop through each of the method type keys. For each of these, a conditional is created to make sure that the type is set and that there is actually some value being assigned to that type. If that conditional passes, only then will I consider making a new contactmethod object.

The next step inside of that conditional is to check on the contactgroup object. If it does not have a public id property, I know this must be the first contact method that passed the test and it needs to be saved. Note that this calculation is done based on the existence of the id property and not the $methodtypekey variable. It is possible to have a set of blank methods ahead of a valid method. Or it could be a set of all blank methods. Because of this, I can never take the $methodtypekey value to actually mean this is a legitimate first method.

A new contactmethod object is created. It receives its required values of the contactgroup owner ID, the type, and the value assigned with that type. Finally, that contactmethod is saved.

This completes the whole process of creating a new contact. With this solidified, the editing of a contact will be much easier. I'll look at that next.

Editing a Contact

Each row of contacts has an edit link. This link references the public edit() method of the contacts module. The last part of the link contains the id property of the user dao that is meant to be manipulated. I'm going to add the following code to the contacts module:

```
public function edit()
{
    $controller = lib::getitem('controller');

    if (empty($controller->params[0])) {
        lib::sendto();
    }
    else {
        $contact = new contact((int) $controller->params[0]);
        $contactgroups = new contactgroupscollection($contact);
        $contactgroups->getwithdata();
        echo view::show('contacts/edit',
                        array('contact'=>$contact,
                              'groups'=>$contactgroups));
    }
}
```

The same method as in the process to edit a `user` is used to retrieve the `id` property from the URL, using the stored `controller` object. If it's empty, the user is simply sent to their index page. Otherwise, a new instance of a `contact dao` is created, using the retrieved `id` property. Then, an instance of `contactgroupscollection` is created, using that `contact` as the owner object. This is followed by the call to the method to populate the object. Finally, view named `contacts/edit` is displayed. The `contact dao` and the `contactgroupscollection` object are passed in as parameters. Since I've developed the system to share the manage view, you may already be able to predict the contents of the `/views/default/contacts/edit.php` file:

```php
<?php
echo view::show('contacts/manage',
                array('title'=>'Edit Contact',
                      'action'=>'/contacts/processedit',
                      'formid'=>'editform',
                      'type'=>'edit',
                      'contact'=>$view['contact'],
                      'groups'=>$view['groups']));
```

The call to the `contacts/manage` view is heavily populated with additional parameters. The first four are similar to the `contact` addition process. The title and form action are set. The HTML Form `id` attribute is also specified. Finally, the type is set to "edit."

The big difference with this view is the `contact dao` and groups `daocollection` being passed through to the view. Now, the manage view has objects to use when trying to pre-populate itself.

The action of the form refers to the `processedit()` public method of the `contacts` module. I'll add the following code to create this method:

```php
public function processedit()
{
    $firstname = $_POST['firstname'];
    $middlename = $_POST['middlename'];
    $lastname = $_POST['lastname'];
    $id = $_POST['id'];

    $contact = new contact($id);
    $contact->firstname = $firstname;
    $contact->lastname = $lastname;
    $contact->middlename = $middlename;
    $contact->save();

    $this->deleteMethods($contact);

    $this->addMethods($_POST['type'], $contact);

    lib::sendto("/contacts/view/{$contact->id}");
}
```

This method is very similar to the `processadd()` method that I created earlier. The First, Middle, and Last names are retrieved from the post. Additionally, the `id` of the current `contact` object is also retrieved and used to create a new instance of that object. Then, the names are overwritten and the object is saved.

I decided that it would be easier to just delete all of the contact methods from the user. This would be easier than trying to parse through each of the ones that currently exist and update them. Besides, any contact method that the user wants this contact to have should have been displayed on the previous form. A call to the `deleteMethods()` protected method is called passing the current `contact dao` to it. Then, the `addMethods()` protected method is called and the user is forwarded to the single contact view page to view their changes.

The content of the `deleteMethods()` protected method is just a quick MySQL operation. I'll add the following content to the `contacts` module:

```
protected function deleteMethods(contact $contact)
{
    $connection = db::factory('mysql');

    $sql = "delete g.*, m.* from contactgroup g
            left join contactmethod m on g.id=m.contactgroupid
            where contactid={$contact->id}";

    $results = $connection->execute($sql);
}
```

A new instance of the `mysql` database connection object is retrieved. Then, a MySQL query using the owner `contact dao` object's public `id` property is created. This query takes into account the relationship between the groups and methods. The last step is executing this delete statement.

With this method complete, the whole Contact Administration portion of the application is complete! The use of various different Design Patterns made this a breeze. I noticed that throughout the entire programming process, when I knew what Design Pattern I had planned to use, the creation of the object itself was almost instinctual. I didn't have to put in a lot of extra thought.

This was a long process. I can see many places where I can make improvements. I see a few places where I could have added some extra security and error checking. I need to make one immediate change, however, before calling this first iteration of this project complete.

Data Integrity in the User Administration

Because of the set of relationships I've developed in the Contact Administration section, I see one miss that I had in the User administration section. When deleting a user, only the `user dao` object's table row was removed. It's quite possible that this `user` has some of these `contact`, `contactgroup`, and `contactmethod dao` objects in the system. I should remove those as well.

In the previous section, I worked with the `users` module. I created a public method called `processdelete()`, which would handle deleting the user objects. However, I find that I need to replace the MySQL statement with a more robust version. The final step in creating this application is making this change to the `processdelete()` method of the `users` module:

```
$sql = "
        delete u.*, c.*, g.*, m.* from user u
        left join contact c on c.ownerid = u.id
        left join contactgroup g on g.contactid=c.id
        left join contactmethod m on g.id=m.contactgroupid
        where u.id = {$userid}
        ";
```

This will not only delete the `user` object but will also follow the relationship through to the other objects and delete them as well. This final step was needed to make sure that no orphan `dao` objects were left in the system. I don't think I could have done this properly without finishing the whole Contact Administration section first.

Summary

Congratulations on completing this case study! The goal of this case study was to show how a PHP application could be created using Design Patterns. The use of Design Patterns not only made the process quicker but also helped develop the application so that it is more structurally sound.

The application made use of a slew of PHP Design Patterns. The Data Access Object Design Pattern was used in the `contact`, `contactgroup`, `contactmethod` and user classes. The Iterator Design Pattern was used in the `userscollection`, `contactscollection`, `contactgroupscollection`, and `contactmethodscollection` classes. The Factory Design Pattern was used in the `auth` and `db` classes. The Singleton Design Pattern was used in the `mysql` class. The Decorator Design Pattern was used in the `decoratoraddress`, `decoratoremail`, `decoratormobilephone`, `decoratorsocialnetwork`, and `decoratorwebsite` classes. A form of the Builder Design Pattern was used in the `importcontactsarraybuilder` class. An Adapter Design Pattern was used to create the `outlookcontactimportadapter` class.

Now, a complete iteration of the ACME Company Contact Manager application has been programmed. As with most programming, however, the first version is not perfect. The next chapter will diagnose any bugs, fix security issues, and identify any areas where the Design Pattern–based programming could be improved. Because I already have a solid code base based on PHP Design Patterns, I predict the hardest part of the next step will be finding the issues, not fixing them!

23

Improving with More Design Patterns

The first iteration of the application is complete. A fully functioning prototype has been created and is theoretically ready for bug testing. However, there are still things that I can change using the help of some more Design Patterns.

The first thing I want to look at is the Contact Import functionality. I made this particular portion of the application very coupled to the requirements. While this may seem acceptable in theory, requirements don't always stay as solid as we'd like them to be. It's possible to have the requirements change along the way to allow more types of contact imports. If the requirements don't change, it may be one of the soonest requested feature updates. Couple this with the foresight that I have that access to this application may be sold to different parties; I should have created this section of the application more abstract. I'm going to look through some Design Patterns that can assist me with this task.

The second area I'm going to look at is the view system. There should be a clear separation between the creation of objects and the displaying of the user interface. The contents for one particular view of the contract were difficult to create. I mistakenly allowed some object creation and data retrieval method calls to enter this view. I'll use a pattern from my arsenal to fix this issue as well.

Let's tackle the Contact Import functionality first.

Working with Contacts Import

Even though the specifications said that only one type of import would be specified, I've decided to be more safe than sorry. Currently, the requirement is to accept contact imports from the official company address book in the Microsoft Outlook program. However, after some of the employees see the ease with which this tool can be used, I am predicting that a need for other unofficial address book migrations will arise. As much as the company has tried to make a piece of software the official supported tool, there will always be users using other pieces of software (especially us in IT).

There are two parts to this process that remain tightly coupled. The first is the `Adapter` object that manipulates the Contact name information. The other is the object that builds an array of items to traverse from the file's contents. I'll look at each of these individually next.

Outlook Contact Adapter

Right now, the import is being accepted as a `.csv` file that was exported from Outlook. I don't want to confuse the users of the software by giving them too many options that aren't available, however. I am going to modify the processing portions of the code to be more flexible, using some Design Patterns. The view for the import will look relatively the same.

I've created the following UML diagram (Figure 23-1):

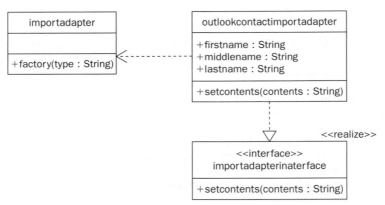

Figure 23-1

The `importadapter` class will have a method called `factory()` which is an implementation of the Factory Design Pattern. This will accept a string parameter named `type`. This will be used to create the new instance of the adapter object.

The `outlookcontactimportadapter` class will be modified to have a `setcontents()` method instead of doing all of the logic in the constructor.

Finally, the `outlookcontactimportadapter` class will implement the `importadapterinterface` interface. This will keep consistency among any future adapter objects.

The first thing I am going to do is specify the `'type'` of import the user is doing. I'll accomplish this by adding a hidden field to the form. Additionally, I'm going to name the HTML File `Input` element a little bit more vague. It's definitely possible that future uploads won't be `.csv`-based files.

The changes I've made are in the `/views/default/contacts/import.php` file:

```
<h1>Import Your Contacts</h1>
<p>
    Upload a .csv file from Outlook. Contact helpdesk for assistance.
</p>
<?php
    echo view::show('standard/errors');
?>
<form action="/contacts/processimport" method="post" enctype="multipart/form-data">
    <input type="hidden" name="importtype" value="outlook" />
    <div class="row">
        <label for="contactsfile">Contacts File:</label>
        <input type="file" id="contactsfile" name="contactsfile" />
    </div>
    <div class="row">
        <label for="submit"> </label>
        <input id="submit" type="submit" class="submitbutton" value="Upload" />
    </div>
</form>
```

The addition of the hidden HTML Input element named 'importtype' is the first change. This will contain a value of 'outlook' to specify the type of import that is being created.

The next changes are the name and id attributes of the HTML File Input element. There values are now 'contactsfile' to be more abstract.

Now that the view has been modified, the next step is the contacts module's processimport() method. Instead of creating a new instance of the outlookcontactimportadapter class, I'm going to create a new class that features an implementation of the Factory Design Pattern. First, here are the relevant changes to the processimport() method:

```
if (is_uploaded_file($_FILES['contactsfile']['tmp_name'])) {
    $contents = file_get_contents($_FILES['contactsfile']['tmp_name']);
    unlink ($_FILES['contactsfile']['tmp_name']);

    $builder = new importcontactsarraybuilder($contents);
    $imports = $builder->buildarray();

    $currentuser = lib::getitem('user');

    foreach ($imports as $import) {
        $contact = new contact();
        $adaptor = importadapter::factory($_POST['type']);
        $adaptor->setcontents($import);

        $contact->firstname = $adaptor->firstname;
        $contact->middlename = $adaptor->middlename;
```

For more on the Factory Design Pattern, see Chapter 9.

The conditional to check for the uploaded file has a small change. It is now checking for a file named "contactsfile" instead of "csv." This matches the changes to the view I applied.

Moving down a few lines, the first line of the import loop is still the same. Now, instead of creating the new instance of `outlookcontactimportadapter`, the public static method `factory()` of the `importadapter` class is called. It is passed the posted `'type'` value. This should contain the string `'outlook'`, which was specified in the view I modified earlier. Next, the `setcontents()` method of that particular adapter is executed with the contents of the import. Then, the method continues as in the previous iteration of the code.

The next step I'm going to perform is to create the `importadapter` class. This is located at `/includes/importadapter.php` with the following content:

```php
<?php
class importadapter
{
    public static function factory($type)
    {
        $classname = "{$type}contactimportadapter";
        return new $classname;
    }
}
```

The `importadapter` class has one public static function, called `factory()`. This accepts a single parameter, which is used to build the name of the contact import adapter class. Then, this class is created and returned to the caller function.

Finally, in order for it to function correctly with the changes, I had to modify the `outlookcontactimportadapter` class. The file at `/includes/outlookcontactimportadapter.php` now contains:

```php
<?php
class outlookcontactimportadapter implements importadapterinterface
{
    public function setcontents($import)
    {
        $this->firstname = $import['First Name'];
        $this->middlename = $import['Middle Name'];
        $this->lastname = $import['Last Name'];
    }
}
```

There were only two simple changes to this class necessary to make it function with the `importadapter` Factory Design Pattern addition. First, the constructor was renamed `setcontents()`. There was no other change to that function. The other change was the implementation of the `importadapterinterface`. Since I'm predicting that more of these will be created in the future, and I don't want to change the contacts module, I wanted to enforce the existence of the `setcontents()` method.

The content of `/includes/importadapterinterface.php` is:

```php
<?php
interface importadapterinterface
{
    public function setcontents($contents);
}
```

With these changes complete, the adapter is far more flexible, while still providing the Outlook-based functionality in the requirements.

Building the Contacts Array

Continuing with the same vein of making the contact import more abstract, I noticed another area where I can put my collection of Design Patterns to use. When the initial file is uploaded, a PHP array is built from the contents of the file. This logic is executed in a method that is specific to the Outlook .csv file. I like the way this array is built, but think this logic shouldn't be in this class. This is the perfect time to use the Delegate Design Pattern. I'm going to have the array-building class delegate the actual responsibility of parsing the string to an array to a different class.

For more on the Delegate Design Pattern, see Chapter 7.

During my analysis, I made the following UML diagram (Figure 23-2):

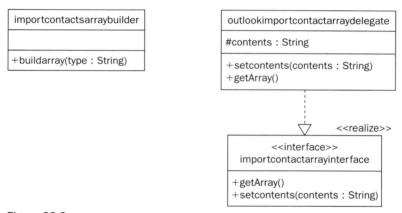

Figure 23-2

The importcontactsarraybuilder class will be created to build the array from the input string. It has a method called buildarray() which will accept a type string to generate the proper calls to build the array.

The outlookimportcontactarraydelegate class is used to process the Outlook form of the contact import. It stores the contacts in its protected property named contents. It has two public methods. The first is setcontents() which is responsible for taking the contact import string and assigning it to the object. The second is getArray() which will be responsible for processing the contents of the protected contents property and returning an array.

Finally, the importcontactarrayinterface is needed to force consistency in all delegate objects.

The first change will be applied to the processimport() method of the contacts module again:

```
unlink ($_FILES['contactsfile']['tmp_name']);

$builder = new importcontactsarraybuilder($contents);
$imports = $builder->buildarray($_POST['type']);

$currentuser = lib::getitem('user');
```

The first two lines are the same and given for context. The change is the way the buildarray() public method of the importcontactsarraybuilder class is called. Now, I am sending in the posted "type" of the import. This will be set to 'outlook' from the changes in the last section to the view.

Next, a few changes have been made to the /includes/importcontactsarraybuilder.php file. The buildcollection() method now has this content:

```
public function buildcollection($type)
{
    $classname = "{$type}importcontactsarraydelegate";

    $delegate = new $classname;
    $delegate->setcontents($this->importedstring);
    $array = $delegate->getArray();

    return $array;
}
```

The method is now accepting a single parameter named $type. Then, a new class name is built using this parameter. A new instance of this class is assigned to the $delegate variable. The imported content is then passed into the class based on the Delegate Design Pattern by calling its setcontents() public method with the content as a parameter. Finally, the object's getArray() method is called to retrieve the $array variable. The last line of this method is familiar: it sends the $array variable as a return parameter.

Looking at the construction of the $classname variable and knowing that the only value I can receive will be "outlook," I will create a new class named outlookimportcontactarraydelegate. I've removed the logic from the buildcollection() method and will be inserting it into the new class. This class can be found at /includes/outlookimportcontactsarraydelegate.php with the following content:

```
<?php
class outlookimportcontactarraydelegate implements importcontactarrayinterface
{
    protected $contents;

    public function setcontents($contents)
    {
        $this->contents = $contents;
    }

    public function getArray()
    {
```

```
        $lines = explode("\n", $this->contents);
        $keys = explode(',', array_shift($lines));

        $array = array();

        foreach ($lines as $line) {
            if (!empty($line)) {
                $keyed = array_combine($keys, explode(',', $line));
                $array[] = $keyed;
            }
        }

        return $array;
    }
}
```

The class contains only two methods, both public methods that the importcontactarraybuilder class had called. The first, setcontents(), accepts a parameter named $contents. This is assigned to the protected $contents variable in this class.

The getArray() method should look very familiar. It is a direct copy of the previous content of the buildcollection() method. I've only changed the first line to reference $this->contents instead of $this->importedstring.

Finally, since more than one Delegate object may be created, the exterior interface should be the same. The file /includes/importcontactarrayinterface.php contains the following interface to enforce the public methods:

```
<?php
interface importcontactarrayinterface
{
    public function getArray();
    public function setcontents($contents);
}
```

Using the Delegate Design Pattern inside of the array building class is a great idea. The Outlook .csv file is pretty easy to parse. However, if other types get added, they may not be as easy. Delegating this logic to exterior objects is the best practice for a scenario like this.

Removing Logic from Views

I strive to keep my logic outside of the view of the application. However, whether because of an oversight or programmer laziness, a few lines sometimes sneak in. This is very bad: the view should never have to perform any data or object manipulation duties. Instead, the entire set of information should be provided to the view. The view can make decisions on which bits of that information to display.

In this application, the requirement to have more than one view right away makes this doubly important. If the default view contains some logic to build an object, the mobile view must contain this exact same logic. If a third view is added, this logic must also be copied to that view as well. This creates code duplication and is not best practice.

In this application, I made the mistake of allowing the complexity of the `contact dao` relationship retrieval process to deter me from what I knew was best practice. This next section describes where this problem happened and how to fix it.

Modifying the Single View of a Contact

When building the view for looking at a single contact, gathering the information together ahead of time outside of the view became very complex. This should have been a dead give away to use one of the Design Patterns to deal with this complexity. Instead, I created a `contact dao` and a `contactgroupscollection` object. Inside of the view, I created individual `contactmethodcollection` objects. The way I look at this, I was executing logic inside of the views. Instead, all of this information should have been passed to the view so that it could display it. It shouldn't be responsible for having to acquire new objects to do its job.

Since gathering together all of the contact information is a complex process, I decided to use the Façade Design Pattern. Instead of creating a bunch of logic before the single contact view is executed, I will create a new `Façade` object to do all of this for me. Then, I'll pass in the required information to the view.

For more on the Façade Design Pattern, see Chapter 8.

The following UML Diagram details my vision for the changes (Figure 23-3):

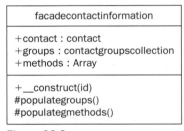

Figure 23-3

The `facadecontactinformation` class has the potential to be pretty complex. However, the instantiation of the object will be relatively simple, and such is the beauty of the Façade design pattern. The public function `__construct()` will take one parameter. This will be the integer ID of the `contact dao` that is requested. It will assign the `contact dao` to the public `contact` property. Then, it will call the two protected methods.

The protected method `populategroups()` will be responsible for creating an instance of the `contactgroupscollection` object for the `contact dao` belonging to this object. It will assign that `contactgroupscollection` object to the public `groups` property.

Finally, the protected method populatemethods() will be called. This will be responsible for creating all the necessary instances of the contactmethodscollection objects for each group dao in the contactgroupscollection object stored in this class. Each of the contactmethodscollection objects will be added to the public methods array property.

The first area to change is the contacts module. The view() method has the logic to display a single contact. I've changed it to the following content:

```php
public function view()
{
    $controller = lib::getitem('controller');

    if (empty($controller->params[0])) {
        lib::sendto();
    }
    else {
        $params = new facadecontactinformation((int) $controller->params[0]);
        echo view::show('contacts/view',
                        array('contact'=>$params->contact,
                              'groups'=>$params->groups,
                              'methods'=>$params->methods));
    }
}
```

The method is still the same through the first portion of the conditional. However, now instead of creating a new contact dao and a new contactgroupscollection object, a new instance of the facadecontactinformation class is created. This is passed the identifier from the controller like the previous contact dao had accepted.

The line that shows the view has changed as well. Instead of pointing to local variables, the parameters are now public properties of the facadecontactinformation object. In addition to the 'contact' and 'groups' keys, the 'methods' key is defined with the associated public attribute.

The next step is to take a look at the Façade object located at /includes/ facadecontactinformation.php:

```php
<?php
class facadecontactinformation
{
    public $contact;
    public $groups;
    public $methods = array();

    public function __construct($id)
    {
        $this->contact = new contact($id);
        $this->populategroups();
        $this->populatemethods();
    }

    protected function populategroups()
    {
        $this->groups = new contactgroupscollection($this->contact);
```

```
            $this->groups->getwithdata();
    }

    protected function populatemethods()
    {
        foreach ($this->groups as $group) {
            $this->methods[$group->id] = new contactmethodscollection($group);
            $this->methods[$group->id]->getwithdata();
        }
    }
}
```

This class starts out by defining the three public properties that will be retrieved to display the view. Next, the constructor is defined to accept a single parameter named `$id`. This is used to assign a new instance of the `contact dao` to the public `$contact` property. Then, in true Façade form, the next bit of logic is sheltered by calling two additional protected methods.

The `populategroups()` protected method probably looks similar. It is a near complete copy of the logic from the `contacts` module. Instead of using the local `$contact` variable, however, it is using the `$contact` property from the current instance. The `contactgroupscollection` object is assigned to the public `$groups` property.

To replace the logic in the view, the `populatemethods()` protected method is created. A loop similar to the one located in the view is created. Then, for reach group that is part of this instance's `$group` property, an entry is made to the `$methods` property. The array is keyed by the current group object's id property. Then, the value is set to an instance of the `contactmethodscollection` object built from the current group. Finally, the `getwithdata()` method of the `contactmethodscollection` object is called. This generates a fully populated `$methods` property associated with each contact group this contact has.

The final change that is required to make use of this new `Façade` object is to modify the contacts/view view. I've modified the following lines of the `/views/default/contacts/view.php` file:

```
        print "<fieldset><legend>{$group->label}</legend>";

        print '<table>';
        foreach ($view['methods'][$group->id] as $method) {
```

I've removed the two lines after the label of the group. It is no longer necessary to create a new instance of the `contactmethodscollection` object. Then, I've modified the next `foreach` loop to refer to the proper key of the `'methods'` parameter that was sent into the view.

With these changes in place, this view is no longer working directly with object creation. This is now a good example of keeping logic separate from the view.

Try Implementing Design Patterns

While I'm not a fan of "homework," I am a fan of hands-on learning. You've seen me take this application through a portion of a second iteration by applying more Design Patterns to the code. The work is not done, however. I encourage you to take a look at the following areas that can be based on some Design Patterns. Try your hand at implementing your own version of the Design Pattern against this working code base.

Design Patterns and Error Checking

A good portion of the application is void of error checking. The only real error checking put in place is in user creation. The process simply makes sure that the user does not exist. What other ways could you implement error checking using PHP Design Patterns?

You may investigate into using the Strategy Design Pattern to check various types of strings for a valid type. For example, knowing that a username or a password should not be a blank string, a `Strategy` class validating that the string contains at least one character could be created.

For more on the Strategy Design Pattern, see Chapter 17.

Another route to take would be to have a `Visitor` object visit the instance of the `dao` before the `save()` method is called. The visitor could validate the required fields and flag the `dao` as valid or not. This could happen during both the creation and modification processes.

You might also create a method named `isvalid()`, which makes use of some `Delegate` objects to check various properties of the object. Then, the Boolean response to this could be used to determine if the `dao` should call its `save()` method.

Design Patterns and Contact Administration

In the second section of this chapter, I talked about the best practice of removing logic from the views in the application. Unfortunately, this application still has one particular view with object logic in it: the contacts/manage view. How would you remove the logic from this view?

Creating an instance of a `Façade` object similar to that in the single view of a contact is an acceptable solution. Once this `Façade` is built in the `edit()` method of the contacts module, the logic could be removed from the contacts/manage view.

Design Patterns and View Types

The view class has a static method named `setviewtype()`. This particular method is pretty simple right now. However, as time goes on and more view types are requested, this particular method will become more complex. What Design Patterns could you use to handle this complexity?

The Delegate Design Pattern could be used to create an object to try to deduce the view type. This object could be called within the `setviewtype()` method.

If a common method of identifying the view type is requested, such as analyzing the HTTP User Agent for an identifier, the Interpreter Design Pattern could also be used. This class would be used to interpret the view type based on the information it was passed.

For more on the Delegate Design Pattern, see Chapter 7. For more on the Interpreter Design Pattern, see Chapter 10.

Design Patterns and Deleting Objects

The current process to delete an object from the data source is to create a complex MySQL statement. If the application had to be migrated to a different data source, these statements might need to be modified. What other types of Design Pattern–based objects could be used to provide this flexibility?

The Mediator Design Pattern would be a great choice. When deleting a user, it would also notify each `contact dao` that it should also be deleted. In a similar case, the deletion of a `contact dao` would trickle down with the mediators' help to the `contactgroup` and `contactmethod` objects that the contact owned.

For more on the Mediator Design Pattern, see Chapter 12.

Share Your Design Pattern Work

Try your best to come up with some Design Pattern–based solutions for the areas of the application I've mentioned above. This practice will help train you to use these Design Patterns the next time you are programming your own application.

When you come up with new ways to solve existing problems using PHP Design Patterns, tell everyone! Share them with your colleagues or post them on your blog. When you do this, you are killing two birds with one stone. You are contributing to the open source community as well as encouraging your fellow developers to practice better coding practices.

After you've looked through this code, created your own versions of the solutions, or just modified this application, tell me about it! Come out and comment on my blog at http://aaronsaray.com/blog. Tell me what you've learned, share with everyone your newest creations, or even show me how you've modified my Design Pattern–based code to fit into best practices.

Summary

In this chapter, I focused on continuing to strengthen the architecture of the application. Existing code was updated to use new objects based on some of the PHP Design Patterns I covered in the reference chapters.

The import contacts functionality was the first area to modify. I aimed to uncouple the Outlook requirements from the actual contact import logic. An object based on the Factory Design Pattern was created to generate the `Adapter` object instead of forcing an instance of the one designed around Outlook. Next, a `Delegate` object was introduced to construct an array of information from the contact file import. Similar to the `Factory` object, this moved code from a tightly coupled object into a more specific `Delegate`–based object. These few changes allow for enormous flexibility.

The other area I focused on was the view system. In one specific view, I allowed object creation to happen. A Façade object was created to accomplish some of the existing logic in a more encapsulated way. Then, I was able to migrate the code from the view into that Façade. This generated a simple way to gather the Contact information, while solidifying the barriers between the views and the logic.

The last section of this chapter directed your attention to other areas of the application that could benefit from some Design Pattern–based objects. Various opportunities were presented with possible solutions. I encourage you to continue updating this application with those suggestions to attain some of that hands-on learning.

Congratulations on completing this book. It is both an honor and a privilege to share this knowledge with you. I hope you join me in the excitement I feel to see PHP continuing to move forward and mature. Please continue to create open source software applications using PHP Design Patterns so that proper design and architecture can flourish in the PHP community!

Index

A

H

I

N